HOW TO DO GROUPS

COMMENTARY

This book was written for mental health professionals who are about to begin leading groups. It addresses the concerns and questions which the student is likely to have at the outset and to the second or third group session. This is, then, a clinical manual. The bibliography and references are expressly suited to its purpose as a brief introduction for the clinical student who is harried and hurried. Its practical guidelines and illustrations are based on the author's experiences as cotherapist and supervisor over a period of years.

Dr. Friedman provides a digression into theory—its role from the standpoint of the procedural problems to faced—as an initial orientation for the novice group therapist especially. He explores the interaction between theory and observed events, and the role of supervision; a complete chapter covers the application of Freud's *Theory of Group Psychology* as a theoretical framework to facilitate the development of a point of view from which technical interventions can be formulated.

Of special interest is the book's focus on a description of the problems the clinician might reasonably expect to encounter during the process of learning how to do groups, and how to resolve these problems.

HOW TO DO GROUPS

A Brief Introduction to
Group Psychotherapy

WILLIAM H. FRIEDMAN

New York • Jason Aronson • London

Contents

Preface

This book is intended for students in the mental health professions who are just about to begin leading groups. My original intent was to provide a quite slim volume, to be read in the hour or so before the first group session was to begin. However, it seemed prudent to begin this introductory text at an earlier point, namely, the point at which the student decides to lead a group. For the most part, the book addresses the concerns and questions which the student is likely to have at that point and up to the second or third group session. By the time a group has met two or three times, most of what is learned about groups should be coming from supervisory sessions, not from textbooks.

The book is intended for practicing clinicians at the graduate or postgraduate level. Thus, graduate students in psychology, education, social work, and nursing who are on internship or field placement, as well as psychiatric residents, should find the present work useful. Except for the last two chapters, which discuss group therapy in mental hospitals, the issues raised here are applicable to groups in a range of nonmedical settings. I have used the terms *group therapist* and *group leader* interchangeably; the terms *group member* and *patient* are similarly interchangeable.

This is, then, a clinical manual. It is not intended as a scholarly work. The bibliography and the references cited are adequate for the limited purpose and emphasis of this work: a *brief* introduction for the clinical student who is harried and hurried. For the preclinical student who is seeking an entry into the literature on groups and who has the time to follow up references, the following bibliographical resources are available: Yalom's *The Theory and Practice of Group Psychotherapy,* 2nd edition (1975); Bednar and Lawlis' chapter on empirical research in group psychotherapy, in Bergin and Garfield's *Handbook of Psychotherapy and Behavior Change* (1971); the annual reviews of the group psychotherapy literature which appear in the *International Journal of Group Psychotherapy;* and Zimpfer's exhaustive *Group Work in the Healing Professions: A Bibliography* (1976).

Much of what is written here is based on my experiences as cotherapist and supervisor over a period of years. I do not think that any student has been without influence on me. I would like to express thanks in particular to Donna Avery, Rich Leventhal, Rich Hanish, Donna Frick, Jim Thompson, and Becca Osborn. Alan Bell provided me the opportunity of supervising his students in group counseling, and that experience was especially fruitful, both in terms of what I learned and the people I met.

Ruth Klein read much of the manuscript, and provided a detailed, line-by-line critique which was funny and enormously helpful; I made virtually all of the changes she suggested, and am grateful to her for the signal improvements she made possible.

Except for one month in the summer of 1976 and one week that fall, the book was written during evenings, weekends, and whatever time I could find during the day. That kind of schedule can put considerable strain on family life, but it didn't. My wife Liz was encouraging throughout the years I worked to complete this task. Sometimes her encouragement was gentle, sometimes vigorous; it was unflagging. She drew on her own background in journalism and her own talent as a writer to provide editorial critique of the manuscript. I sought to write with clarity and simplicity. Where I have achieved that, it has been with her help and because I heeded her advice. The responsibilty for turgidity in the prose is mine alone. Liz's help and encouragement has been an act of love carried out with intelligence and skill.

I would also like to thank Patti Fisher, who typed and retyped the manuscript, uncomplainingly, unfailingly cheerful. It was Patti who helped me to find those daytime hours which I devoted to this work. Without her secretarial efficiency the work would not yet be complete.

HOW TO DO GROUPS

Chapter 1

The First Steps

In the beginning, the novice therapist who wants to do a group will have to find a cotherapist, a supervisor, space, time, and patients. Accordingly, the first thing the novice discovers is that it is considerably more difficult and time-consuming to put a group together than he might have anticipated. How much longer it will take, and how much harder it is than expected, will depend in part upon the strength of the group program in the particular setting, the time of year, the rate of referral, and other factors. In the absence of systematized group referral procedures, eight to ten weeks from conception to first meeting is neither unusual nor a pessimistic estimate.

Finding a Cotherapist

Picking a cotherapist may be somewhat less important than selecting a spouse, but it is certainly no less an art. The therapist-to-be is looking for someone with whom he will share many hours of heightened emotional experience, hard work, and indeed stress. How can you tell who will work most effectively with you?

There are no hard and fast rules, and you may not have much choice anyway, depending upon the exigencies of your particular clinical setting. The following are some rather general guidelines, which assume that the cotherapists are of approximately equal status and experience. The supervisor as cotherapist is discussed later.

1. If possible don't ask strangers to lead groups with you—even if they're attractive. The better you know someone, the easier time you're likely to have communicating with that person during and about group. Working with a friend, or a colleague whom you know and like, is generally going to be easiest.

2. Personalities, and the therapeutic styles of communication manifested through them, are probably more important than agreement about theory, goals, or technique. In order to avoid or minimize problems in the cotherapy relationship, there needs to be a good deal of commonality in the emotional language you and your cotherapist speak. Similarity in the handling of emotions, not complementarity, will help things go more smoothly. Someone who handles anger and affection in the same general way you do, who is either as open or as closed as you, will make a better *first* cotherapist than someone who is different from you, someone who may have qualities which you lack but admire (such as high verbal facility, or a greater cognitive grasp of technique and how to apply it, etc.). There will be enough differences even between cotherapists whose styles are similar; complementarity or noncongruence can't really be avoided. Similarity does not mean identity.

3. Following the general principle of similarity rather than complementarity, a cotherapist whose theoretical orientation is similar to yours will probably be easier to work with. Paulson,

Burroughs, and Gelb (1976) found that cotherapists of different theoretical beliefs chose not to work together again significantly more frequently than cotherapists of similar beliefs. Other factors which contribute to the willingness of cotherapists to work together again include agreement on how active each should be and on whether or not a given interaction in group is a problem.

4. It is not necessary to seek a cotherapist of opposite sex, though there are some potential advantages in such a pairing. Most pertinent at this point is that opposite-sex cotherapists can serve as role models, and their relationship as a model of opposite sex social relations. However, if you choose a cotherapist of the same sex, you will find that in the group one of you will assume roles which could be called feminine, and the other, roles which could be called masculine. Such sex-role labeling may be incorrect and may, as Hilberman (1973) suggests, result from a confounding of biological and cultural traits. Behavior which is comforting is more likely to be perceived, and perhaps experienced, as feminine rather than masculine. Confrontation is perhaps more likely to be perceived as masculine. The role divergence occurs even with cotherapists of the same sex, because people (including therapists) differ in the amount of nurturance (warmth, empathy, and the like) they are willing to offer. One of the cotherapists will offer more than the other, and it may therefore seem that he (or she) will come to assume a "feminine" role in the group. It is not unusual for this role to devolve upon a highly nurturant male, with a female cotherapist gradually assuming what some might consider the paternal role model in group.

The cotherapy relationship is discussed further in chapters 7 and 8.

Supervisory Models

Supervision is an integral part of learning to do groups. The novice therapist should be aware of the various supervisory models, and, if possible, should choose a model within which he is most likely to learn effectively. Choice of supervisory model is as necessary, and as difficult, a part of doing groups as is the selection of cotherapist and group members.

Supervisory models are important because they are the context in which learning to do groups occurs. Doing a group is, of course, itself a learning experience for the therapist. However, experiential learning cannot, in this context, be more than rudimentary, and supervision is required to help the therapist (a) become aware of the relevant sensory input and (b) interpret and generalize from the experience of doing a particular group. Training and competence may not be isomorphically related, but they are related. Doing a group does not of itself constitute training. Supervision is training.

Groups are usually supervised in one of four ways. These are: (1) the supervisor as cotherapist; (2) the supervisor observing, through a two-way mirror; (3) remote observation, by means of audio or video tape; and (4) in a group consisting of several cotherapist pairs, the supervisor acting as group leader.

The Supervisor as Cotherapist

The great advantage of supervisor as cotherapist is that the student has an opportunity to watch, literally at first hand, how an experienced group leader does things. The shared immediacy of the group experience probably makes the postgroup supervisory sessions more meaningful. The supervisor, having been in the room, knows damn well what was going on. Because he has shared the experience, he can make better sense of it to the cotherapist than if he had observed it from behind a two-way mirror or via videotape.

One of the disadvantages of having a supervisor as cotherapist is that the student is not a coleader but an assistant leader, especially during the early meetings of a group. The assistant leader's task can be construed as knowing or figuring out what the group leader is doing and maintaining readiness to help him do it. Thus an assistant's status would seldom involve initiating group interaction or trying to formulate where the group should go next. The feeling of being in there with a bunch of people, not knowing what to say, but having to say *something,* is not likely to be particularly intense if you're an assistant leader. This is because you know (a) that it isn't really your group anyway but your supervisor's, and (b) that if you do say something, on cue from your supervisor or as response in an interaction initiated by someone else, you know that your supervisor will come to your rescue if you get stuck. Consequently, when you're doing your second group, and the supervisor *isn't* there, and that feeling occurs of having to say something and not knowing what to say, it may be more intense—after all, you should know what to say since you've already done a group.

It could be said that one disadvantage of the supervisor as cotherapist is that being in there with you he lacks objectivity. This is a nominal disadvantage. In our society, objectivity usually means *without emotion,* and emotion is the stuff of experience, especially in psychotherapy. So a supervisor sitting behind a mirror making cool, detached, objective judgments (which aren't objective anyway, but may be somewhat less emotional than those of participant leaders) is one step removed from the data of the group. That may be a very big step indeed. Passionate subjectivity which the supervisor can articulate without being defensive can lead to a learning experience at least as meaningful as an objective critique of the application of the technique of group psychotherapy.

A more serious disadvantage of the supervisor as cotherapist stems from the difference in power or status which may obtain between teacher and student, and which is manifested in the leader–assistant leader structure. It is highly likely that at some point disagreement or other passions will arise in the relationship between the two. Because of the power differential, the experience differential, and perhaps other factors, the junior cotherapist is likely to feel considerable pressure to defer. If the match between cotherapists is poor, the position of the student may be precarious indeed. The supervisor, coming out of the same experience as the student but holding very different views or interpretations of it, may feel that the reasons for the differences in perception or interpretation of that experience lies in the pathology rather than the inexperience of the cotherapist. The latter, in turn, may come to feel that group therapy, or perhaps psychotherapy in general, is a poor professional choice. Problems in supervision are discussed more fully in chapter 8. When strong feelings, either positive or negative, arise between cotherapists of equal status, these issues can be dealt with more readily than when the supervisor is directly involved in the therapy itself, for he can then function as a mediator.

The Supervisor Observing through a Two-Way Mirror

Whenever there is observation of a group, the possibility exists that the awareness, on the part of one or more group members, of observation by unknown others constitutes an intrusion into the group room and influences the interaction. The question of whether observation influences a group is susceptible of empirical resolution, and need not be dealt with further.

If a group is to be observed, whether by a supervisor or others, the informed consent of the group members must be obtained. This is not usually difficult. The supervisor might sit in on the pregroup screening interviews, introduce himself to the group at its first meeting, or remain anonymous—but the group *must* be made aware of the fact that he or she is there.

The effect the supervisor will have on the group leaders' behavior is also researchable, but some comments are nevertheless in order. For one thing, if you know that your supervisor is behind the mirror, you also know that he's evaluating you, and that you're going to have to be able to justify whatever intervention you make or fail to make, and to go through all the other unpleasant aspects of supervision which characterize learning to do individual therapy. Thus, the supervisor's presence behind the mirror is likely to increase the anxiety or other discomfort of the novice therapist. To what extent that anxiety is increased depends on a variety of factors, for example, the magnitude of the therapist's approval-dependency.

One disadvantage of this supervisory model is that it may make novice therapists more nervous, and their nervousness is likely to be transmitted to the group members during the initial meetings, making the work of therapy more difficult. However, as the relationship between therapists and supervisor becomes more comfortable (assuming that it does), this particular problem is likely to diminish.

A more serious shortcoming, as noted in the previous section, is that the supervisor is once-removed from the immediacy of the interaction. Yet at the same time this can be the strongest advantage of this supervisory model, provided allowances are made, during the supervisory session, for the loss of this immediacy. The less involved supervisor frequently is able to perceive things about group which are difficult for coleaders to see because of their participation in the process.

What the supervisor *does* with what he perceives—how he interprets and talks about his view of group—is in part a function of the theory he espouses, and we will discuss that in chapter 3. The data which the supervisor can gather in this supervisory model include some sense of the flow or sequence of events, and the manner in which the cotherapists respond to the influence exerted by the group. The supervisor can also attend to cues neither cotherapist can see, especially if their attention must be focused on the speaker (or, during an exercise, upon the doing).

With this model, the meeting between supervisor and cotherapists is probably best held immediately after the group meeting, while events are still relatively fresh in everyone's minds. If there is audio- or videotape, the timing of the supervisory meeting becomes less important.

Supervision with Audio- or Videotape

When audiotape is used, the supervisor is blind, and usually hard of hearing. His comments will therefore be less helpful than if he were able to pick up the visual cues and to hear the people mumbling in the background while someone else is talking. However, sometimes this is the only way you can get supervision.

By comparison videotape is infinitely better. However, it has some problems. Primary among these is the question of who runs the equipment. Whether the camera should be in the same room, have an operator, etc., can also be major problems. Some of these questions may be answered by the availability of resources in your clinic. A suggestion: if videotape is *not* routinely used in your setting, don't pioneer. The time and energy you'll be devoting to electronics aren't worth it.

Group Supervision

The advantages of this model are:

1. It is most economical of the supervisor's time, and is an efficient way to utilize his expertise if he is a consultant or part-time employee of the clinic.
2. There is a sharing of problems and a pooling of experiences which can, in sum, broaden the student therapist's acquaintance with or exposure to doing groups. There is probably no better way to experience both the commonalities and the idiosyncrasies of groups than this.
3. In the process of dealing with particular problems in the student's group, the supervisory group can provide the opportunity for role-playing. The therapist who comes to the supervisory session with the question, How is this patient's behavior to be understood? or How might I have handled this situation differently? can play the role of his own patient. The supervisor, and other members of the supervisory group, can take the role of group leader. Thus the therapist may gain not only greater understanding of what it must have been like for that patient in his group, but may also experience the effect of different leadership styles upon what the patient is doing and upon the interaction between patient and group.

The material brought by the cotherapists to the supervisory group session is grist for the supervisory mill. As such, it is necessarily secondhand, and lacks the immediacy of direct experience. Role playing is the mill itself, and although it may start off with the therapist trying to remember what the patient said, he will quickly have to go beyond that into what the patient would have or might have said. At some point the experience stops being secondhand. As the episode is played out to a resolution different from what happened in the therapy group, the members of the supervisory group may gain not only understanding of what has already happened but also, ideally, some notion of how it might happen again in other groups and how it might be dealt with. The ability to generalize from supervisory session to group is as important for the therapist as the ability to generalize from therapy session to "real life" is for the patient.

The problems of this supervisory model are magnifications of those stemming from the supervisor's distance from the group experience. Here the supervisor has no direct access, either in person or via tape, to the data of the group. It is therefore not possible to do the detailed, meticulous examination of what happened, a molecular analysis of events or episodes or sequences of episodes, which is the best learning experience in both individual and group therapy.[1] During the supervisory group it may be possible to play out one or two such episodes at the molecular level. However, they are likely to be from different groups, and the sequence of episodes is lost. Just as in the therapy group itself, in a supervisory group not every cotherapist pair may be in the spotlight at every meeting. You may come to the supervisory group meeting with some questions of (in your judgment) fair-to-middling importance, and one of your colleagues may present a problem the supervisory group spends half an hour on, never getting to you at all.

Supervision cannot be as close as in the supervisor-cotherapist pair situation. At the same time, it is possible to learn more about how others do groups and about group problems, but rather less about *you* and groups. This model is, therefore, not recommended for people who are doing their

1. Molecular analysis involves discussion of several cue dimensions or communication modalities which comprise a single comment or a brief series of comments. Tone of voice, facial expression, and posture, as well as what preceded and followed the comment(s), are explored and perhaps interpreted. Thus, molecular analysis consists of attention to the minutiae of interpersonal interactions.

first groups, unless it is in addition to individual supervision. It is better for people doing their fourth or fifth groups, who are therefore less in need of the kind of detailed examination of events which individual supervision can afford.

It should be acknowledged that there is another supervisory model, which involves the reliance by the supervisor upon the verbal report of the cotherapists as to what happened in group. At times, when the supervisor can't be there (as participant or observer) or when the recording equipment breaks down, this kind of supervisory session becomes unavoidable. It is probably the least helpful of the supervisory models, and should be avoided wherever possible. Supervisors, not cotherapists, should determine what to attend to in the complex group interaction and cannot do so without some kind of firsthand data. This is because the novice may not yet know what is of critical importance and thus may fail to present it.

Supervisory Models: Concluding Comment

Having discussed the various supervisory models, we come to the question of which is best for the novice therapist. The exigencies of any particular clinical setting will probably lead toward answering that question one way or another: you have to start with what's available. But let us assume, for a moment, that the opportunities are there, and that you have a genuine choice. Ideally, in other words: do a short group with an experienced leader first, and then a longer one with a colleague, with the supervisor observing. Group therapy is an art, and modelling is frequently a highly effective teaching device which can help the student recognize his own potential for artistry.

The Selection of Group Members

The selection of group members is a highly complex process because of the large number of issues and people involved.

These include: (a) the referring therapist and those reasons for referral which stem from individual patient-therapist interaction; (b) the interest or need, on the part of the training clinic, to provide group therapy as a training experience for its students; (c) the purpose of group in terms of potential benefits to patients (that is, service functions as somewhat distinct from training functions); and (4) other factors.[2]

A number of authors have described attributes or characteristics of patients which render the patient more or less suitable for therapy. (See, e.g., Bach 1954, Mullan and Rosenbaum 1963, Johnson 1963, Yalom 1975.) Our focus here is not upon these intraindividual attributes, but upon the selection process and what constitutes a good group referral from the standpoint of group.

Reasons for Referral

There is only one legitimate reason for referral of a patient for group therapy. That is the expectation, on the part of both patient and therapist, that the patient will benefit from the experience, and the judgment on the part of the therapist that group therapy is the treatment of choice, the best possible therapy for this patient.

There are a number of reasons for referral which might be classified nonlegitimate, and a few which are illegitimate. *Nonlegitimate referrals* are those made primarily for the benefit of someone other than the patient, but from which the patient can reasonably be expected to benefit. One type of nonlegitimate referral is that made because of the lack of availability of individual therapy for patients for whom this technique would be the treatment of choice. Individual therapy may not be available because the demand exceeds the supply of

2. Portions of this section appeared in somewhat different form in *Hospital and Community Psychiatry,* Volume 27, Number 2, February, 1976.

therapists and there is a waiting list; because no extended individual therapy is offered in the clinic (e.g., most student mental health services); or because the patient is for whatever reason ineligible for individual therapy in the clinic and cannot (or will not) afford individual therapy on a private basis. In these instances, group therapy might be offered to the patient by his therapist primarily for reasons of convenience and cost, even though as a treatment modality it is second best. Patients referred in these circumstances are understandably enough going to be difficult to work with during the initial group sessions.

A second nonlegitimate reason for referral involves the clinic's need to provide a group therapy experience as part of its training function. The individual therapist's knowledge that group referrals are needed may influence his clinical judgment as to disposition in some cases, and perhaps more so if he knows that it is a friend of his who is trying to get a group going. The situation is no different in purely service-oriented clinical facilities which offer groups; informal peer pressure exists for the individual therapist to make group referrals. It should be emphasized that we are discussing here a situation which is reasonably expected to benefit the patient. It is listed as nonlegitimate because it is of primary benefit to the clinic rather than to the patient.

Illegitimate referrals involve phenomenological rejection of the patient by his individual therapist. Such a rejection may occur for a wide variety of reasons, and indeed usually for a multiplicity of reasons. The therapist may abandon hope, lose interest, or feel that the patient is getting too involved (transference), or that he himself is getting too involved (countertransference), or that he cannot meet the various demands the patient makes on him and may therefore hope to dilute those demands by sharing the patient with a group. A successful illegitimate referral involves (a) a change of attitude on the part of the therapist such that he desires to abrogate the original contract he made with the patient; (b) his decision not to inform the patient of his change in attitude (this is what makes the referral illegitimate); and (c) convincing the patient (and perhaps himself) that such a referral for group therapy is appropriate.

Neither the nonlegitimate nor the illegitimate reasons for referral necessarily preclude admitting a patient into group. However, the group therapists will probably find it quite helpful to be cognizant of the factors involved in the primary therapist's decision to refer his patient. Unless you know the referring therapist quite well, some direct contact prior to the screening interview with the patient may save both of you, and the patient, some difficulties later on.

Criteria for Selection of Group Members

Trying to define criteria for the "good" group member is rather like trying to define mental health. It is easier to say what it isn't, and to describe exclusive rather than inclusive criteria for group membership. But even guidelines for exclusion are hard to determine.

Some therapists will accept into group patients who are actively hallucinating and delusional (e.g., in inpatient groups). Extremely withdrawn or reticent individuals can, if they themselves are willing, be taken into a group, and may have as much chance as anyone to benefit from the experience—provided one does not assemble an homogeneous group of such folk. Group therapy has been offered to patients exhibiting a wide range of psychopathological behaviors (see, e.g., Yalom 1975, Feinstein and Cavanaugh 1974, Gootnick 1973, Rogers, Roback, McKee, and Calhoun 1976, Kaplan and Sadock 1971), and growth groups to a similarly broad spectrum of people who did not define themselves as patients (e.g., Lakin 1972, Samuels 1971, Wechsler, Messarik, and Tannenbaum 1962). In such a situation, perhaps the surest guidelines may involve personal predilections.

Novice therapists should, then, for the most part select patients with whom the therapists feel it would be easy to work. There will be time and opportunity enough later on to work with more difficult patients. Allowing for personal predilections, a good group member (that is, one who is generally easy to work with) is one who: (1) defines his problem as interpersonal, or emphasizes the interpersonal aspects of his problem; (2) is committed to change in interpersonal behavior; (3) is willing to allow himself to become susceptible to the influence of the group upon his behavior; (4) is willing to report the fact and effect of change, or efforts to change, to the group. A fifth criterion might be a willingness to help others in the group setting.

It is quite possible that individuals meeting *none* of these criteria would be good group members. Such individuals, however, will probably tend to be exceptions, whose contributions to group and benefits from it may be less visible than people meeting these criteria, and they will therefore prove more difficult to work with.

The attributes which make a patient a good group member may not be the same attributes which make benefit from group likely. Highly manipulative, articulate individuals, with a flair for the dramatic and a penchant for the spotlight, can help get a group going and may at times oil the silences. However, they may be able to do these things without ever letting the group touch them or without learning from the group experience. For the most part, however, good group members are probably also those who are most likely to benefit from group.

Selection criteria can be summarized as follows:

1. The group leader should accept into group anyone who he thinks can benefit from the group experience and whose

behavior is likely to be at least tolerated by the other members of the group. The best approach is to be inclusive rather than exclusive, and to accept an individual unless there is some clear indication that group would not be appropriate or beneficial.

2. While other criteria will be determined by the setting, the nature of the patient population, the proclivities of the supervisor, and the like, the most important operational criterion is likely to be whether or not the patient is available for meeting at the time you are planning to schedule the group.

Pregroup Screening Interviews

Screening interviews are seldom desirable and frequently necessary. They are seldom desirable because they are quite expensive of the therapist's time, and the patient's; they give both patient and therapist very little information about how each will act during the group meetings, and they constitute a test or examination for the patient who, if he is not accepted for group, must add yet another failure experience to a list which is already long enough to have brought him to the clinic for help. Rejection is always painful, and rejection by those from whom one seeks help is especially so.

But screening interviews are frequently necessary because in a training clinic referrals for group are usually made by therapists who are uncertain as to what constitutes an inappropriate group referral because of their lack of experience. Novice therapists may also have a somewhat greater general propensity than experienced therapists for making illegitimate referrals. This tendency may be even more pronounced if the novice therapists are fearful of confrontation with patients or are not yet in touch with or accepting of their own feelings (i.e., if they cannot admit they don't like a patient).

A screening interview reflects the group leader's (and supervisor's) uncertainty about the ability of the referring therapist to avoid an inappropriate referral. In a training clinic, where the referring therapist is a trainee, he is learning how to make referrals as part of learning how to be a therapist. In clinics where group leaders and referring therapists know each other fairly well, there is much less need for screening interviews. In such instances, the referral source will have some idea of the kind of person the group leader is looking for, and the group leader will be familiar with how the referring therapist uses technical language to describe patient characteristics.

The contract made during the screening interview.[3] The specific manner in which the screening interview is conducted will depend upon the theoretical proclivities and personality styles of the therapists, the needs and expectations of the patient, and the interaction between these patient and therapist factors. In the ideal situation, the therapists will have discussed with the supervisor the type of patient or kind of patient characteristics they are looking for, and will have obtained some guidance in terms of how to conduct the screening interview. Similarly, the patient will be either clearly appropriate or clearly inappropriate for group, and that fact will emerge and be agreed upon by the end of the interview.

In the more typical situation, the group therapists are likely to have only a general, vague notion of what patient characteristics to look for and no notion of how these characteristics might manifest themselves in group. Some supervisors may not conceive of the supervisory process as starting prior to the selection of patients for screening, viewing it instead as beginning with the first group meeting. In those instances, the novice group therapist may not get much pertinent assistance in the conduct of screening interviews and

3. This does not refer to the Transactional Analysis concept of contract. Transactional Analysts have their own pregroup workup techniques and language, and this discussion does not apply nor refer to what they do.

the selection of patients. And finally, in the real situation, as distinct from the ideal, it will be found that very few patients are clearly inappropriate for group: some are almost certainly good risks, and the majority fall into the limbo of uncertainty.

There is a difference between an initial intake interview and one which is held because a referral has been made. In the latter instance, the therapist already knows something, often a considerable amount, about the patient and he should let the patient know it: not in great detail but in brief summary. The patient should also be told what is expected of him during the interview, and the kinds of conclusions which might be reached at the end of the interview. This approach is true of many referral interviews including of course the screening interview for group.

The contract between patient and therapists *pertaining to* the screening interview is that some conclusion (hopefully, agreement) will be reached by the end of the interview about whether or not the patient should attend group. This contract involves structuring and defining the task of the screening interview, and should be made as early as possible during the interview.

The contract made *during* the screening interview involves what kind of group experience the therapists will undertake to provide, some delineation of the problems the patient wants to work on, and the magnitude of the commitment the patient makes to the group and group interaction. The therapists should describe, as specifically as possible, what they expect to happen, at least during the initial stages of group. What is predictable about virtually any therapy group is that people will be tense, anxious, and possibly hostile. These phenomena are sufficiently ubiquitous that telling a patient about them in a screening interview does not constitute a self-fulfilling prediction. What is usually not predictable is how the tension, anxiety and hostility will become manifest in early group interactions, or how much there will be.

Whether or not the problems the patient wants to work on will emerge in the screening interview is open to question. How truthful the patient will be probably depends on many factors, including his fear of rejection, his ability to be open or honest, trust of the interviewers, and so on. In general, patients *are* truthful at this point, and what they describe in terms of problem areas to be worked on can be taken pretty much at face value. The accuracy of a patient's assessment of his problem may be questionable, however, which is one reason that adequate diagnostic work should precede referral.

The surprises come later on, during the initial group meetings, when the problems discussed in the screening interview fail to surface and the patient takes an interpersonal position which has no apparent relevance to what he has said he is coming to group for. The problems and issues discussed in the screening interview (and before that, in individual therapy or evaluation) may not surface in group until the patient feels comfortable or safe about exposing his sore spots.

The contract which is made during the screening interview will depend in part upon what the patient wants from group and in part upon what the therapists think they can offer. Generally, patients wanting insight but no change do not fare well in groups which focus on change. What a group does best is to focus on interpersonal behavior, and within that very broad range it is possible to make rather different contracts with different people in the same group. While a group experience is not all things to all people, the participants may derive quite different emotions and cognitions from a shared group episode, and can reasonably be led to expect such differences.

Although each contract between patient and therapists can (and should) be negotiated on a very individualized basis, there are some "clauses" which should be included in most group contracts. These are:

1. Specification, by the therapists, of what they expect from the patient. Therapists can reasonably expect the patient to (a) come to the group meetings, (b) pay the bill, and (c) make a commitment to change in either behavior, attitude, life situation, or all three. People who are unable or unwilling to make such a commitment to change are not looking for therapy, but may be interested in some other type of group activity, such as a growth or consciousness-raising group.

Note that the list of what the therapist can expect of the patient is not long, nor should it be. We cannot ask much more of the patient than that he comes to group and that he pay his bills. If we expect of him a high level of psychological sophistication, or insight, or the ability to formulate his problems in such a manner that they are rapidly susceptible of resolution, we are asking of the patient the level of expertise which he is paying us to make available to him.

2. Specification, as much as possible, of what the patient expects or hopes to gain from the group experience. If the patient does not know what he expects to gain but has a generalized expectancy of benefit, both he and the therapists will have some difficulty recognizing the point at which such benefit is clearly manifest. Such a patient might do better in a closed group (one which has a finite life) than in an open group (through which patients and therapists rotate although the group itself goes on indefinitely). Not all of a patient's problems are going to be particularly amenable to group influence, and one of the few genuine advantages of the screening interview is that such problem areas can be defined and their later avoidance in group legitimized. For example, problems of physical intimacy in relationships with others are not usually fruitfully discussed in group. A therapy group may become

open and honest, but it is seldom intimate. Problems of dependence and counter-dependence are, on the other hand, probably more appropriately discussed. Thus, a patient's need for and fear of sexual tenderness from a spouse is a less appropriate problem area, for group, than that same patient's conflicts about the spouse's helping with household chores. In a screening interview, the patient can be reassured that the former need not be dwelt upon in group.

What a group contract boils down to is that the therapists offer to make their expertise available in the group setting. The patient, in turn, offers to come to group, to participate in the interaction, to avail himself of the expertise of the therapists and the wisdom of the group. It is not a symmetrical contract, but reflects the adjustmental asymmetry of patient-therapist interactions.

Individual vs. group. Early in the screening process, the therapists will not have a good idea of the type of people who are going to be in their group, and can be rather more open and broad in their selection criteria. At some point, usually at the third or fourth screening interview, the therapists will begin to ask themselves, "How will this patient fit in with those we have already accepted into group?"

This is the starting point of a balancing act of individual *vs.* group interests which the therapists will be wrestling with through much of the life of the group. At this very early stage in the life of the group, the therapists' concerns will be about group interaction, as distinct from and sometimes opposed to the individual's need for group therapy, the amount of benefit he is likely to sustain from it, and so on. Later on in the life of the group, the problems or issues which constitute the individual-vs.-group balancing act will be different.

At this point, the polar conflicts involve the patient who needs group but is not likely to contribute much to it, as contrasted to the individual who does not much need it but is likely to make some major contributions to group interaction. These are conflicts experienced by the therapist, who has rather less of an opportunity to discuss them during the screening interviews than the patient.

Although it is generally true that effective psychotherapy constitutes a peak emotional experience in the life of the patient (and the therapist!), it may also be true that the novice therapist tends to greatly overestimate the magnitude of his impact upon the patient, and to underestimate the patient's ability to escape a difficult or taxing situation by simply dropping out of group. If the group experience does not prove itself to be worth the patient's time, effort, and money, he will drop out. Making a bad guess about how a particular patient will work out in a particular group does not have the same kind of consequences for him that a bad guess by a surgeon or internist might have. If a patient who can offer but little ends up in a group which demands a high level of emotional interchange, he may very well withdraw from group. Such a withdrawal may be viewed as a protective mechanism and, given the circumstances, perhaps healthy. By the same token, an individual who is accepted into group because the group needs him, and who stands to benefit little or not at all, may withdraw because he senses that he is being used.

Somewhere in between these two extremes is the individual who can both contribute to and benefit from group. This is where most people will be found; group and individual interests usually coincide. Even where there is opposition between group and individual interests (and the therapist is in conflict, facing a choice between individual and group), it is sometimes possible for a skilled and experienced therapist to make a contract, during the screening interview, which involves *reconciliation of individual and group interests as one of the goals* for that individual. But the novice therapist who is not experienced in group *or* individual therapy may lack confidence in his skill regardless of whether it is great or small. Therefore, if the novice therapist comes to feel, during the screening interview, that there is or might be a conflict between the best interests of the individual and the best interests of the group, the following guidelines are offered for resolution of the dilemma:

1. If the individual would benefit from inclusion in the group, but seems likely to impair the effectiveness or meaningfulness of the group experience for some or most others, he should be excluded. It is not that group needs have primacy over individual needs, but the needs (and rights!) of each of several people may in this instance prevail.

2. If the group would benefit from inclusion of an individual for whom such an experience would be of dubious benefit at best, the interests of the individual should prevail. In this case, responsibility for the decision may be shared with the patient, who after all has a right to choose how to spend his time.

When the therapists' concern is about harm rather than benefit, the ancient medical dictum of *primum non nocere*— first, do no harm—should be followed. Generally, that will mean excluding the individual from group.

The conflict between individual and group interests is probably most difficult for the therapists to resolve during the formative stage of group—the screening interviews. This is because of the nature of the decision to be made about entry or non-entry into group. It is an all-or-nothing decision, either way: the patient is either accepted or not. The consequences of the decision are therefore greater than later on, when decisions about individual vs. group interests are made in the context of a continuing commitment to come to group, and imbalances can be redressed at subsequent meetings.

Scheduling

Unless you are handed, all at once, a sufficient number of referrals to begin screening, it will probably be difficult to set a definite date for the beginning of group. You then have the problem of what to tell the first few patients who are accepted for group about when the group will begin. If the rate of referral is slow, so that there is some possibility of a lapse of several weeks between referral and first group meeting, it is generally better to set the appointment for screening no more than two weeks before you expect group might begin.

In some instances the appointment for the screening interview might have to be made a month or so in advance. You'll lose some patients that way; interest declines, problems resolve themselves, people seek service at other clinics. But you'll also lose patients if they come in for a screening interview, are accepted, and then have to wait for several weeks before the group starts. If people are going to drop out of the referral pipeline, it is better for them to do so prior to screening, since then that time won't have been wasted and you won't be planning on them coming. The longer the interval between referral and the beginning of group, the more people you'll lose.

If it is possible to do, then, it will generally work best to do the screening interviews one or two weeks before beginning the group. That means setting the date for starting the group before doing the first screening interview. That way, you can tell the prospective patients the time, date, and place the group is to begin, without ambiguity. Group members are more likely to appear for the first session if things are firmed up during the screening interview.

Incidentally, scheduling the screening interviews during the time that the group will meet may save some trouble. If people can't come for a screening interview at 2 P.M. on Wednesday, then probably they can't come for a group that begins at that time either. It's disheartening to get clear through a screening interview only to find the patient can't come at the time the group is scheduled, and restricting screening interviews to those hours minimizes that problem.

In the ideal situation, you'll screen and accept a sufficient number of patients to begin the group on schedule. In the more typical situation, you may experience some uncertainty as to whether to go ahead and start the group because only three, or four, people have indicated that they'll come. It is better to go ahead and meet with those few than to cancel or postpone the group meeting. The clients have set the time aside and have geared themselves up to come to group; they're entitled to some service. It isn't usually possible to do as much with a group of three as with four or five; but cancellation or postponement of a group meeting tends to lessen the group members' commitment to coming and may make your referral sources even more hesitant to refer. So it's better to meet with those three or four, and perhaps to talk with them about their expectations of group. In this instance, the fact that the meeting is held may be more important than what transpires during the meeting.

The Purpose of Groups

Fairly early in the process of beginning to do a group, it may be helpful to consider the purpose of what you are undertaking. The purpose of a therapy group is the facilitation of change in behavior. Such change is usually, although not always, preceded by emotionally intense interpersonal interactions characterized by intimate self-disclosure. The task of the group leaders is to establish and maintain the conditions under which such intense interactions are most likely to occur and, when they have occurred, to move the group toward the facilitation of change in behavior.

Intimate self-disclosure is an individual's (usually verbal) report to the group about how he feels and/or thinks *at this moment* about some topic which is of great importance to him, i.e., in which he is investing considerable feeling. It involves taking an interpersonal stance from which there is no retreat: this is how I feel, now, really and undeniably, about this topic. Later, the individual may report that he has come to feel differently, which may involve a change in his earlier stance but not a denial that he once held it.

The facilitation of change involves an assessment of discrepancies. There may be discrepancies in the way the group member has organized his understanding of what happened in the past; discrepancies between his experience of himself and the way others perceive his actions in the present; discrepancies between where he is now, in relation to his needs, wants, and expectations, and where he would like to be. These discrepancies may be more visible or obvious to others than to the individual who experiences and maintains them; and they tend to be highlighted in emotionally intense interactions in group when the individual engages in intimate self-disclosure.

The assessment of discrepancies by the group cannot occur until the group has certain data about the individual: either about his past, or his present behavior, or his expectations and goals for the future, or some combination of those. This data comes from the individual's self-disclosure and from the group's own experience. When the disclosure is particularly intense and vehemently personal, it may be regarded as intimate self-disclosure. The importance to the individual of subsequent change in behavior may be related to the intensity of the interaction, and to the extent to which self-disclosure is linked to self-esteem, self-evaluation, and one's assessment of one's ability to survive in the prevailing interpersonal atmosphere.

The first task of the group leaders is to establish the conditions under which intimate self-disclosure is most likely to occur. Some specific techniques are offered in chapter 2. The task in general involves the reduction of anxiety and the facilitation of interaction (at first, virtually *any* interaction) in the group. The conditions under which intimate self-disclosure is most likely to occur include: (a) an atmosphere of mutual trust on the part of most (not necessarily all) group members; (b) feelings of warmth and supportiveness within the group; and (c) the confident expectation that self-disclosure will be heard respectfully, listened to empathically, and responded to honestly and gently. Intimate self-disclosure is not likely to occur in a group until these conditions prevail. However, less emotionally intense interactions, and disclosures which are less important to the individual, will occur quite early in the group and are steps toward the higher level of intensity and openness.

Both the content of the disclosures and the way that the disclosures are made may be assessed by the group. On occasion, the content may involve a traumatic event or series of events in the patient's past. More often, the most cogent content in terms of later behavior change is that which pertains to the here-and-now ongoing interpersonal interaction in group. Sometimes the patient has an expectation that catastrophe will occur if he engages in self-disclosure. In this case, it is the expectation more than the content which needs to be focused on, for such expectations wall people off from each other, inhibiting interaction and the consensual validation of one's own experiences. The most common form of this catastrophic expectation is, "If you know what I'm really like, you will dislike (or reject or harm) me." Sometimes the major work of therapy in group involves dealing with this expectation and its ramifications.

Once the individual has given the group the information it needs, either through discussion or through interaction, the group can help him to identify and reassess discrepancies. The group may then help the individual to develop new coping mechanisms (ways of relating) or to a reformulation of the psychological environment in such a manner that the individual feels (and thus becomes) able to derive satisfaction and perhaps fulfillment with the coping mechanisms he already possesses.

Neither intensely emotional interactions nor intimate self-disclosure are of themselves the goal or the purpose of group. Their function, in group, is related to the ability or willingness of the self-disclosing individual to allow the group to influence change in his behavior. Such willingness frequently seems heightened during and immediately following intimate self-disclosure. Reaching a very high level of emotional intensity is difficult work for the entire group. Intimate self-disclosure by one or more of its members has some intrinsic satisfaction and is usually given the explicit approval of the group and the therapists. It is, therefore, tempting to stop at this point, to regard such self-disclosure as the goal of group. There is some evidence that self-disclosure is associated with good outcome (Lieberman, Yalom, and Miles 1973). However, the relationship between intimate self-disclosure and change in behavior may not be at all obvious to the self-disclosing patient. Moreover, although he may be especially susceptible to group influence immediately following self-disclosure, the desirability of taking the next step—toward specification of potential change in behavior—may also not be obvious to him. The therapists should help the patient begin the task of specification of potential change. Specification or description of potential change outside the group, or actual change in behavior during the group session, are the outcomes toward which the intense interactions and self-disclosure are aimed.

The second task of the therapists, then, is to guide the group toward facilitation of change during and after individual self-disclosure. The orientation of the therapists should always be toward change in behavior. The probability of change is enhanced if the therapists direct the focus of group toward that end. The encouragement or facilitation of self-disclosure for its own sake, without a concomitant or subsequent focus on the modification of behavior, may be fruitless and ultimately unsatisfying to the patient, who may come to feel that he has revealed himself for naught except perhaps the satisfaction of the psychological voyeurism of the group.

The purpose of groups: concluding comment. This discussion of the purpose of therapy groups and of the role of intimate self-disclosure reflects some of the assumptions made throughout this book about psychotherapy and psychopathology. An implicit premise of most psychotherapies is that intraindividual, intrapsychic factors are responsible for the patient's suffering. Therefore, the healing process involves change in intrapsychic factors. Laing has suggested that psychoanalytic theory may offer no theoretical constructs accounting for the interrelationship of two people (Laing 1968). (He notes that both projection and introjection are intrapsychic events.) This strong emphasis on intrapsychic psychology has clearly proven fruitful for individual psychotherapy and its validity is not at issue here. Group, however, is above all an interpersonal context. The most fruitful way of conceptualizing psychopathology *in this context* is in interpersonal rather than intrapsychic terms.

The group therapist, then, is concerned with those psychopathologies which are manifest in disturbances in interpersonal relations. What is disturbed involves ways of relating to other people, that is, behavioral patterns. The most extreme disturbances involve gross impairment of the ability or desire to relate with other people, and these grossly deviant behavioral patterns are termed psychoses.

From this standpoint, psychotherapy consists of helping the individual to change the disturbed behavioral patterns. While individual psychotherapy readily offers a means of verbal exploration of alternatives, group psychotherapy provides an interpersonal context in which the disturbed behavioral pattern itself may become manifest. What the individual therapist hears about from his patient, the group therapist (and the group) may see directly. The group therapy setting offers the individual the opportunity to practice altering habitual behavioral responses and to experience different interpersonal responses from others.

The emphasis which the present volume places on behavioral disturbance and behavioral change should not be misunderstood as representing advocacy of a behavior therapy technology. Rather, behavior is emphasized because it is manifest, directly observable by all members of the group, and provides explicit rather than inferential information about other people. Intrapsychic disturbances, such as disturbances in affect, perception, and formal thought processes, are not emphasized here because being intrapsychic they are not amenable to close examination or assessment by the group. Behavior is *public,* while intrapsychic events remain private, hidden, unobservable. Its own observations of the individual constitute the data which the group assesses as it helps the individual explore the discrepancies in his life which brought him into therapy. Intrapsychic events, however compelling, are firsthand knowledge only to the individual experiencing them. The relationship between such events and external reality remains inaccessible to the group except via inference (from observable behavior) and verbal report. Focussing on intrapsychic events may be fruitful in groups; a number of technical approaches to group therapy favor such an emphasis (Shaffer and Galinsky 1974). However, this focus does not provide the common group of experience readily and directly shared by the group which an emphasis on observable behavior offers. The present emphasis on behavior, then, stems from the fact that observable behavior constitutes the directly available experience of the interpersonal context of group. In that context, it is easier to deal with what can be seen than with what can only be inferred.

Chapter 2

Starting the Group

Groups start in silence and solitude. There may be six or eight or ten people sitting in the room waiting. There is tension, nervousness. Usually, there is little movement, little fidgeting. What motion there is, is mostly in the hands and fingers; small, incessant, repetitive. Twisting strands of hair, rubbing the arms of chairs, running back and forth lightly over the fabric of skirt or shawl or coat. Scarcely perceptible, yet constant. The background motion of anxiety.

No one is likely to be looking directly at the group leaders, lest their attention be drawn to him and he gets called upon. Nor are people likely to be doing a great deal of looking at each other. They are, usually, quite cautious initially about giving off non-verbal cues which might be taken as an expression of interest in other group members, or in the group leaders, or as an expression of willingness to initiate the group interaction.

When you do a group, this is the atmosphere that you find yourself in at first. The knowledge that you are supposed to somehow help these anxious, isolated, and awkwardly silent individuals to become a group, and to establish the warm and supportive atmosphere in which intimate self-disclosure will occur—this knowledge is likely to contribute to your own anxiety. Like your group members, your own defenses will probably be operating at full steam.

It is usually of considerable help to you if you know what your defensive style is: the kinds of things you say or do when you are anxious, uncertain, a little or very scared and trying not to show it. Your defensive style is how you act to ward off anxiety or to reduce its debilitating effect on you. It helps you to know what you look like and how you come across to others when you are feeling defensive and are trying not to show it. This is one reason why some experience as a group member is useful for the novice therapist—a sensitivity or T-group being particularly appropriate, the focus of such groups being precisely on how you come through to others, or are perceived by others, and on the discrepancy, if any, between how you think you're coming through and how you are perceived by most others. This knowledge of how you come through at such times may help you to modulate your responses so that you are perceived as you intend and not merely as you assume.

It is also likely to be helpful to you if you are aware of what you do when you perceive that other people are anxious. Before you ever reach the group therapy room, you will have been in many situations where you have sought to reduce or alleviate someone else's anxiety. The situation in that group room full of silent, nervous people will tend to evoke behavior from you which is similar to what you have done in those other situations.

These two vectors—your defensive style and your need, desire, or intent to reduce interpersonal anxiety in others—will influence the way you begin to interact with group. Other factors influencing how you start will include what your supervisor has told you—your own assessment of the interpersonal situation in the room at that moment, and how helpful you find the following sections of this chapter.

What you are facing is probably the most awkward, most delicate, and most anxious moment in the life of the group: the moment when you begin to lead. What follows can be beautiful or disastrous. There is nothing in any book which can tell you precisely what to do.

There are however some guidelines. Your first tasks are to reduce anxiety and to facilitate interaction. Those are the first steps toward the establishment of an atmosphere of warmth and supportiveness. In beginning a group, you will reduce anxiety if you, as group leader, appear to be in charge and know what you are doing, and if you provide the group members with some instruction about what to do and information about what will happen.

But at first you sit there in the silence of the initial group meeting, perhaps looking around at these people who are apparently looking at no one in particular, and who appear mostly calm. You wonder what you should say and which particular moment you should seize upon to begin saying it. Your own anxiety is not likely to be perceived by the group members. The probability is that you appear remarkably calm and confident, both to the group and to your cotherapist. Your defensive style is likely to be taken (or mistaken) by them as a manifestation of your technical approach. In addition, the group is likely to be quite acutely aware of where you are, what you are doing, and who you are looking at—for all that, this wariness on their part may not be obvious to you. Your very first task is to deal somehow with the silence, to get the group moving.

Dealing with the Initial Silence

The silence. The group leaders can wait until the silence is broken by a group member, can break the silence themselves, or, foreseeing that the silence is quite likely to occur, they can, in effect, seize control of it and utilize it to assert and exercise their power. If the group leaders choose to wait until the silence is broken by the most anxious member, the level of group anxiety is high; frustration and hostility are at a peak. Not infrequently, the member who first breaks the silence serves as an initial focus for hostile attacks from other members; or the hostility will turn at the group leaders or at the clinic. The point here is that an initial impassive silence by the group leaders will generally lead to hostile opening interactions in the group. If the hostility reaches too great an intensity, it will frighten patients away, and those who remain will tread cautiously for a very long time — months, in a weekly group — before entering into genuine interactions on risky topics. If the group leaders prefer to function in an initially hostile atmosphere, they can create for themselves the task of conflict resolution and the role of peacemaker or neutral intermediary by waiting until a group member breaks the initial silence.

One of the group leaders can break the initial silence by prodding individual members. He can do so by asking questions, by suggesting that people tell about themselves, etc. If he chooses this course, what will ensue is a series of patient-therapist interactions, one-to-one, but in public, since the other members of the group will be watching as closely as they dare for whatever kinds of cues they typically are used to picking up and responding to.

At this point it is unlikely that the group leaders will elicit any meaningful information whatsoever. As a group begins, the conditions for genuine—let alone intimate—self-disclosure are simply not present. Indeed, the occasional group member who announces that he is going to be open and/or honest, or who begins by revealing ostensibly highly personal and intimate information about himself, is quite likely to turn out to be fairly closed off but able to fake rather well. What is disclosed in terms of case history facts is relatively unimportant. The initially open/honest group member is staking a claim to a particular interpersonal position, and if the group leaders respond at this point to content rather than to structure, they may be making a serious error.[4]

Prodding group members to respond, as a means of breaking the initial silence, is like trying to start a wood fire with a propane torch and no kindling: as soon as the heat is turned off, the fire goes out. The therapists establish a question-answer, teacher-class relationship, and it usually requires not only considerable skill but also time to get themselves out of that role—if they want out of it.

Seizing control of the initial silence may not always be easy to do, but is nearly always worth a try. The group leaders, knowing that the initial silence will occur anyway, can lay claim to it by asking the group members to be silent for a few minutes, to focus or concentrate on their feelings. The group leaders should then add that they will ask each group member to report his feelings to the group.

The purpose of adding this comment is to reduce anxiety. The initial anxiety is produced, in part, by the lack of structure inherent in any new situation. That lack of structure is reduced

---

4. Content refers to what is being said; structure, to what is being done. Structure includes the nonverbal metacommunications about how the content is to be understood, and the flow and play of interpersonal maneuvers and manipulations within group (or dyadic) interactions. A response to structure, in the above example, would be a statement by the therapist that the speaker is staking out a position (the specific wording the therapist uses depends on the situation); a response to content might be to applaud, or doubt, the patient's honesty.

to the extent that the leaders let the group know what they expect to happen. Asking group members to do something which they are likely to do anyway—to remain silent initially—and then telling them that they will be asked to report on their feelings is, in a sense, seizing control of the silence and of giving the situation anxiety-reducing structure.

Some group therapists, and perhaps some theorists, are opposed to the reduction of anxiety or tension in a group session. The rationale offered is that people work harder in group if they are more anxious or more tense (Armstrong and Rouslin 1963). The assumption appears to be that the therapist can help the patient to channel the psychic energy which is keeping him anxious into more fruitful paths. The net effect is supposed to be the reduction of anxiety and the learning of new ways to reduce anxiety—ways which, ideally, are more effective and satisfactory than those the patient had been using.

Yet, the patients in a therapy group have come for therapy and have accepted referral for group because something in their lives is intolerable: anxiety, depression, rage, guilt, grief, and so on; the litany of pain and despair and fear that we call presenting complaints and symptoms. Patients come for therapy seeking relief. To deliberately increase, or deliberately avoid decreasing, anxiety is cruel. The first task of the group leaders is to reduce anxiety, not to nurture it. No theory of therapy regards compassion as a technical error.

Requiring the group members to report how they feel gives them an opportunity to express anxiety without taking any particular interpersonal position within the group, without losing self-esteem and self-respect, and without revealing more about themselves than a willingness to cooperate with the group leaders. The leaders know that anxiety is likely to be both high and ubiquitous; hence, what they are doing, in effect, is asking each individual to report his anxiety. Getting the group going in this way relieves that anxiety to some extent: the admission or acknowledgement sometimes helps, and each member discovers that he is not the only one who is scared. In addition, getting the group going in this way draws an initial commitment, however slight, to interaction with the group, or at least with the leaders.

By giving each member of the group a task he can meet, the leaders also effectively abrogate the initial silence, reducing it to a controllable phenomenon. The exact wording used by the leaders when they ask the group members first to introspect and then to report is not important. Jargon like *introspection* and *selfness* is probably best avoided. If you're worried about how you will sound, try your introductory speech out on your cotherapist before the initial group meeting.

The following is an example of how to start a group in this manner. If you are about to do your first group, you may feel some impulse to memorize this example. The feeling of "Aha! Here's what to do!" can be reassuring, or anxiety-reducing. The danger in memorizing someone else's words, however, is that you perform for, rather than interact with, the other people in the room. It's better to do it in your own words, and to memorize someone else's only as a last resort, if you thereby reduce anxiety to the point where you're at least functional.

Well it's time to start. The way I'd like to begin is to ask you to take a moment or two, and turn your attention inward. Pay attention to how you are feeling right now: what your emotions are, but also to what's going on inside of you: how your stomach feels, and your head, and your arms—if you're feeling full or tense or cold, whatever—pay particular attention to where you feel tense, if you do—and also I'd like for you to pay attention to the feelings that you have, the sense impressions, from the environment: how the chair feels against your back, the way your clothes feel against your skin, the sensual elements. Take a moment or two to look inside yourself and then I will ask each person to share with us, to tell us how you are feeling or how you are experiencing yourself at this moment, how it feels to be here now.

When people have completed the task of looking into themselves, gathering their feelings at this moment, they will generally stir, change position, raise their heads, but the room will still be silent. When people are ready to respond, the non-verbal cues they give off resemble the cues given off in church or synagogue when the congregation finishes a silent prayer. Generally, after a couple of minutes, more than half the group will have finished, and you can ask someone to begin the reporting process.

Getting the initial interactions started in this way will not necessarily set up the question-answer, teacher-pupil structure mentioned above, one reason being that the leaders include themselves in the process, saying something also about how they feel.

It is perfectly all right for a group leader to admit that he's nervous or anxious. Admitting panic, however, or uncertainty about what to do is wrong, for it is likely to further increase group anxiety. The leader may admit uncertainty about what is going to happen, but only in terms of how this particular group—which at this point is still a gathering of individuals— will respond in this situation. Uncertainty about what is going to happen is not the same as uncertainty about what to do. The latter is a reflection on the technical competence of the therapist: you may feel incompetent, but it is a mistake to admit it to the group.

There are, of course, other ways to begin a group so as to exercise leadership, reduce the initial silence to a minimum, and draw from each member some small commitment to group interaction. One is to ask each group member to tell his name and perhaps one other fact. Another might be to structure the time by telling the group the kind of activity they will be engaging in for the next hour or so and then beginning to do it—for example, talking about "life scripts" in the Transactional Analysis fashion. Still another way of beginning is to ask each person what he wants the group experience to do for him, and what his contribution might be.

It is also possible to begin a group by remaining silent and waiting impassively for a group member to break the silence. This way of starting has a lot of tradition behind it (Powdermaker and Frank 1953). But it can take forty minutes and requires a considerable commitment to theory, is liable to prolong anxiety, and is not recommended.

Procedural Rules

At some point early in the initial meeting of the group, it might be helpful to give the group some information about procedural or ground rules. Whether this is more helpful to the therapists in terms of reducing their own anxieties, or to the group members in terms of providing structure and limits, is a moot point. If you are going to lay down some rules (or, more accurately, guidelines) it can be done either before or after the initial silence is broken and should be done before any of the group members attempt some serious work.

We need not discuss at length the pros and cons of starting a group off by giving it some ground rules. Whether you do so or not will depend on your personal preferences and those of your supervisor. The position taken here is that it is generally desirable to offer some guidelines, briefly, and with a minimum of explanation. It is worth doing even if you have already gone over some of the procedures during the pre-group screening interview. However, you are by no means courting disaster if you elect to omit this kind of orientation.

The procedural or ground rules—these guidelines—which are suggested cover three general areas. These are: confidentiality, respect for privacy, and the development of relationships among group members.

Confidentiality. In individual psychotherapy, you are prohibited from talking to others about your patient, except for your supervisor. If you talk with your colleagues about your patient, you will (or should, at any rate) generally do so in such a manner as to make identification of the patient impossible. The patient, however, is not bound by any such prohibition: he is perfectly free to report anything that you say to his friends, parents, spouse, the public. In group psychotherapy, the patient should be asked to accept some of the limitations which are characteristic of the therapist role in individual psychotherapy; that is, to refrain from discussing other group members in such a way that they could be identified by people outside the group.

How you word this request will depend upon your verbal style, your leadership style, and the assessment you make of the audience characteristics of the group members. You can tell the group, for instance, that talking about group outside of group is forbidden. You have no way of enforcing this prohibition, nor any reliable method of determining whether or not it has been broken. A more workable alternative rests on the assumption that people are going to talk about what goes on in group whether you forbid them to or not, and emphasizes that care should (not must) be taken to protect the anonymity of the other group members. Couched as a request, the rule that group members should not talk about others in such a way that people not in the group would recognize them has a greater chance of being heeded than a stern, blanket prohibition. Anonymity, rather than confidentiality, is what we offer our individual patients and is probably all that we can hope that our group members, who are not bound by professional ethics, will grant each other.

Respect for privacy. A very common fear among patients who have been referred for group is that they will be required, during the group sessions, to reveal their most intimate secrets to other group members, and that these will respond with criticism, revulsion, or ridicule. It is not an unrealistic fear: a group is capable of putting considerable pressure on one of its members to reveal what he really does not want to reveal, to discuss what he really does not want to discuss, to engage in exercises he really does not want to engage in. All of these things have happened.

The fear that group therapy sanctions such "mental rape" should be dealt with during the pre-group screening interview, and further reassurances should be given to the entire group at the outset of the first meeting. There are not many things that the group therapists can guarantee: they cannot guarantee patient improvement, or that the group will be exciting or interesting or fruitful. But the therapists can guarantee that a patient's privacy will be respected, and unlike the issue of confidentiality, this is a rule the therapists can enforce. The principle is simple: if a patient indicates that he does not wish to pursue a particular topic or exercise further, the matter is dropped, and dropped without question and without penalty (i.e., making the patient feel bad or guilty for refusing to continue). Efforts on the part of other patients to cross the line, once it is drawn, must be thwarted by the therapists, as gently as possible, but with vehemence if necessary. And once a patient has closed the door on a particular topic, the therapists as well as the other group members must refrain from attempting to break it down.

There is a difference between a door which is locked and one which has rusty hinges. The former, the therapists must respect and protect; the latter represents a situation in which the patient would like to discuss something but finds it difficult to do so. If a patient wants to be drawn out, pursued, or to play

"I've got a secret," he will generally respond differently than if he wants the matter truly dropped. Pursuit is not always bad; rape is. Let the group know this, and let the cotherapists define the difference between the two.

The development of relationships among group members. Some therapists "forbid" group members who do not already know each other to see each other socially, outside the group. The development of friendships among group members is regarded as undesirable since it draws energy away from the group, providing an alternate relationship in which issues better raised in group might be worked out, and since friendships between patients are more likely to meet neurotic than healthy needs. In addition, because of virtual unanimity among group theorists that the development of sexual relationships between group members[5] is virulently destructive to the therapeutic efficacy of group, it is better not to let relationships get started which might turn into friendships and/or seductions.

The injunction against patients seeing each other socially outside of group is, like confidentiality, unenforceable, and if a relationship which is prohibited should develop, it will almost certainly not be reported in group. The main reason for the injunction is that such relationships will influence how people relate to each other in group, and how each relates to the group. The purpose of the injunction can be accomplished at least as well, and perhaps more effectively, by asking the group members to report to the group if a social relationship does arise. The justification for this request should also be made explicit: friendships outside group influence behavior in group, and the other group members can better understand what's happening in group if they are aware of the fact that the friendship exists.

5. Commonly known, in the mental health professions, as "sexual acting out." The term *acting out* refers to behavior of which the therapist disapproves, and which is defined by the therapist (but not the patient) as being not in the patient's best interests.

There is also little point in forbidding patients to go to bed with each other. At the beginning of a group, such an injunction is likely to prove more frightening than reassuring, and if affiliative passions do develop later on, the therapists' rules aren't going to keep people out of bed anyway. Sexual alliances between group members are a type of special problem for the group leaders, and perhaps for the group. They are extremely rare during the early stages of group—the first four or six weeks—and are never very common. (This problem will be discussed further in chapter 8.) Here our point is only that prohibition of sexual or social liaisons need not and perhaps should not be a procedural rule laid down by the therapists at the first group meeting.

There are a number of other procedural rules to which patients can be introduced at this very early point in the group's life. One is a prohibition against physical violence—a commonsense rule, and one which is enforceable. However, the time to tell your patients not to hit each other is not during the first session. Such a statement presumes that the group will reach a level of intensity and involvement which is likely to be inconceivable to people attending their first group meeting. The effect of this prohibition is likely to be frightening, or at least to make people even more cautious about interacting in group than they already were. In turn, that will make for an even slower start.

There are two general principles to follow in laying down procedural or ground rules at the beginning of a group. One is to keep the list very short and concise. You will be talking to a group of very anxious people, and they are not likely to perceive nuances in meaning nor to retain very much information given verbally about events which may not occur at all and which have little salience for them at the moment. The other general principle is that the procedural rules should pertain

primarily to rational, cognitive, unemotional behavior and not
to potentially intense interactions or relationships in group.
Comments about intensity should await the development of
intensity.

Whether you describe the ground rules at the very beginning
of the meeting, while people are still settling in, or wait until
the initial silence has begun is really not important. In either
case, the initial silence is likely to begin, or resume, after
you've listed the guidelines, and some activity, such as that
described in the preceding section, will probably be necessary
in order to get that silence ended and the group begun. The
following is an example of how these ground rules might be
given to a group.

Before we go any further, I'd like to offer three procedural
guidelines that we follow. The first guideline has to do with
confidentiality. We ask that you not talk outside the group
about the other people here in such a way that they could be
identified. What Ken and I say is public; you can quote us.
What you say, what they say, belongs to you and to them.
Don't take what they've said with you outside this room.
That's a guideline and not a rule because we have no way of
enforcing it. You do.

The second guideline has to do with privacy. There is no
requirement here that you expose your deep dark secrets to
the group. Your privacy will be respected, and we will insist
that you respect the privacy of others. You may be asked
about something that you don't want to talk about. It's
legitimate to ask, to knock on the door, once. If the door is
locked, we won't break it down. If there's something you'd
like to talk about but find difficult—if the door's not locked
but the hinges are rusty—we have oil. It's up to you to let us
know whether the door's locked or the hinges are rusty.

The third guideline has to do with significant contacts with other group members during the week. We assume that you're all strangers to each other; we have no way of knowing that for sure until now, until the first group session. If you have some significant contact during the week—more than a hello in passing—then we'd like for you to report to the group the fact of that contact: not what you did, where you went, what you said, but just the fact that there was some important interaction during the week, or that a relationship has begun. The reason for this is that if you have had some significant contact, perhaps started a relationship, outside of group, it will influence the way that you relate to each other in here. If we know that you've met, it will help the group to understand better how you're acting in group. Are there any questions?

Usually there aren't questions: occasionally, a group member will ask for clarification of one of the guidelines.

The initial self-report and presentation of the guidelines are, in effect, introductory moves. When they are completed (and the order in which they are accomplished is not important) the group is, one hopes, ready for the next step, which involves building cohesiveness.

Forming the Group: Initiation Rites

Once the initial silence has been broken, and some verbalization obtained from each group member, it is possible to begin the "initiation rite." An initiation rite may be defined as any activity which causes the members of the group to share the experience of a mildly unpleasant emotion, such as embarrassment. Asking all the group members to stand on their heads would not qualify as an effective initiation rite, because it is silly. Asking them to close their eyes and join hands would not qualify either, because there is no interaction. Hence, interpersonal interaction, and probably the exchange of personal information of some sort, verbal or non-verbal, is a necessary part of the initiation rite.

An initiation rite "forms" a group. Before a group forms, it is a collection of individuals. After it forms, it is a group, and there is something in the room, influencing all of the individual interactions, which was not there before. The formed group is the ground upon which individual interactions occur. The group leaders cannot create the ground; they can only facilitate its creation.

The tactical goal at this time is the establishment of group cohesiveness—forming the group—through the conduct of one or more activities (called exercises) which constitute the initiation rite. Each step toward the tactical goal carries with it an increment of potential unpleasantness (usually, potential embarrassment) in the first session of a group. Therefore, the sequencing of exercises during the initiation rite is of some importance. An exercise which might be perfectly suitable later on in the life of the group, when it has formed and has some cohesiveness, might disrupt a group during its first few minutes by generating more anxiety than embarrassment. The task of the leaders during an initiation rite is to guide the group through activities which are neither innocuous nor anxiety-provoking.[6]

---

6. For present purposes, anxiety may be defined as tense, painful fear of feelings or events; the focal point is the self; if the focal point were an object in the environment, we would speak of fear but not anxiety. Embarrassment may be defined as feeling, or anticipating feeling, awkward, clumsy, inept, in relation to other people. Anxiety involves pain. Embarrassment involves discomfort. In the initial group meeting, discomfort is unavoidable. Pain is not. The reduction, however transient, of anxiety takes precedence over the establishment of group cohesiveness by engaging in initiation rites. Asking patients to do something which is mildly embarrassing is not cruel.

In starting your first group or two, it might be preferable to meet the group with an exercise or two in mind, and to proceed with these unless there are clear indications that they would be inappropriate—for example, if the group starts off at a high level of verbal activity, as sometimes happens. (The initial silence is not inevitable.) The planning of exercises is an activity which serves principally to reduce the anxiety of the therapists, a quite legitimate purpose. However, one of the things you will be learning as you lead a group is how to be an opportunist and to utilize the material generated by group interaction. When you have had some experience in starting groups, the initial go-around, which should yield little more than verbal reports of anxiety, may provide you with some cues as to what kind of group it might be, what it is likely to be able to do, and what might be required to get the group formed. When that happens, you may want to choose a different exercise from the one you had planned, or you might improvise one. But even when you are more experienced, that initial go-around may not provide these additional cues, and going with what you had planned may turn out to be the best course.

Exercises which require only verbal responding are less threatening than those which require physical movement. Asking each person to tell the group the most important thing about him that he would like the group to know is one example. This allows people to talk without requiring interaction. Interaction generally involves some physical movement. Asking people to "pair up with the person sitting next to you" is probably the most minimal physical movement you can ask of a group.

Asking the group, thus paired off, to tell each other something about oneself is a notch up on the scale of uneasiness or potential embarrassment, and is therefore not something which should be used as an icebreaker. It is much less threatening if all the pairs are asked to speak more or less simultaneously than if the verbal exchange is done one pair at a time. Similarly, a non-verbal exercise requiring pairing is less threatening if all pairs do it at the same time rather than in sequence.

The problem with initiation rites which involve pairing and then simultaneous activity is that the leaders are going to lose track of what is going on: what is said, what is communicated, by each individual in the group. However, nothing very significant is likely to be said, since the group at this point is far from the conditions under which self-disclosure might occur.

It may be necessary to go through several exercises which serve to reinforce the group's in-ness, the feeling that it shares something from which others are excluded (or which others have missed out on). The more uptight the group, the more such exercises will be necessary to establish and maintain its cohesion, its formed-ness.

If the first several sessions (or hours, in a marathon session) are taken up by doing exercises in small incremental steps, the danger arises of an expectation by both patients and therapists that the group is an opportunity to play group games—these exercises. Then, if after a number of hours or sessions, the group has not formed, is not cohesive, the leaders must consider dissolving it, re-forming with a different mix of individuals.

Once the initiation rites have been completed, and the thinnest and most fragile and perhaps barely perceptible strands of group cohesiveness are present, the group can begin its various tasks. What those tasks are will depend upon the purpose for which the group is meeting. Note that we speak of group purpose only after the group is formed, and this may not always be appropriate: a special purpose group need never "form" in the sense that we have been using the term here (as synonymous with cohesiveness) in order to get its job done. But our model is the group which is concerned with the modification of behavior and the exercise of interpersonal influence. The tasks of such a group are determined by the interaction of the three focal points of group: the group leaders, the individual members, and the group as a whole.

Determining the Tasks of Group

The tasks we are referring to here are those which arise during each session of the group and which can generally be completed within the session. These tasks stem from the process of interaction among the three focal points of group.

Some theoretical approaches to group hold that the leaders should allow the group to determine its own tasks, even to the point of waiting until the group members realize that the leaders are not going to do anything and that the group will have to discover that there are tasks which need carrying out (Bion 1961, Lakin 1972). In these approaches, the task of the leaders is conceptualized as involving facilitation of the process of carrying out the task the group has decided to undertake. Left to its own devices, the group will finally undertake to establish the conditions under which intimate self-disclosure can occur. The leaders facilitate whatever the group tries, confident that the group will eventually find its way to the proper place. And, indeed, eventually it does.

We are taking a somewhat different approach. Initially, the task of the group leaders is to reduce the anxiety of the group to a level at which therapeutic work can begin. In that sense, the group leaders are facilitators, removing the blocks and barriers to open communication. The first barrier is always anxiety. The initiation rite begins the formation of a coalition against anxiety, a coalition in which the strength of all of the members is brought to bear against the anxiety of each individual. The process of forging that coalition involves the establishment of group cohesiveness. Building group cohesiveness requires an active group leader, rather than one who is reactive or impassive.

A prerequisite to the development of group cohesiveness is the establishment of a bond of common, shared experience, such as that provided by the initiation rite. The realm of common experience can then be extended by the individuals who comprise the group. Usually, this is accomplished by their offering additional verbal information, of a more or less personal nature. Sometimes the information is more personal, taking the general form "My problem is . . . ." Sometimes it is more impersonal, pertaining to group members' vocations or major fields of study or interest. The verbal content is less important than the fact that the bounds of shared experience are being expanded. It is this expansion which constitutes the building or strengthening of the group cohesiveness which began with the initiation rite.

Thus, the first task of a group after completion of the initiation rite is usually the strengthening of cohesiveness. Sometimes this task is taken up in the first session, sometimes not until the second or third, depending upon how long it takes for the group to finish its initiation rite.

Beginning a group is in some ways like beginning a chess game. There are a finite number of first moves and responses, but by the third or fourth move the possibilities are astronomical. Groups usually start in silence, there is usually an initiation rite, and the first task after the initiation rite is usually building group cohesion through shared self-disclosure. However, even before the initiation rite is completed, group interactions are so complex and the possibilities so numerous that the situation is analogous to the fourth move in chess.

That is why cook-book approaches to group are frequently frustrating, puzzling, and unsatisfactory to group leaders: what is happening in the room is almost certainly something not foreseen—or, perhaps, not forseeable. This is one reason why the group leader, ideally, is an opportunist, improvising as the group unfolds.

There are, then, many ways of determining the tasks that a group sets itself in the first few sessions. The Transactional Analysts and the Gestalters have perhaps the easiest time of it: "Who wants to work?" they ask, and if no one does, they may terminate the session then and there (Barnes 1974). But Gestalt and TA are not really group techniques. The group therapist must look to the group as a whole for information—cues— relevant to the group task. If one patient's "My problem is . . ." is followed by a second patient's "My problem is . . ." the task of the group is probably extending acquaintances, and the patients' comments are not functionally different from "I work at . . ." or "I'm majoring in . . . ."

If, on the other hand, that first patient's "My problem is" is met with statements of recognition ("I had a problem like that once, and I . . .") or helpful intent ("Why don't you . . .") the task of the group is to reach some resolution of this patient's initial statement or description of his "problem." Whether the group begins to work on that first patient's "problem" or some later speaker's material is an issue which involves focusing, which we will examine in greater detail in chapter 6. Here, we need merely note that sometimes a group "takes off" after completion of the initiation rite, that when it does so its task is frequently to extend the acquaintanceship of common experience, and that at times that task takes the form of a relatively superficial presentation and resolution of some problem in living.

A more difficult problem for the therapist arises when the atmosphere of the group, after completion of the initiation rite, is one of readiness but uncertainty. The group is silent because it does not know what to do next and is awaiting some guidance from the leaders. The leaders don't know what to do next either, but the pressure is on to do something, because if they also remain silent the readiness of the group to engage in interaction will slip away. Early in the life of a group, silence dissolves cohesiveness.

If this silence of readiness (as distinct from the initial silence) occurs after the completion of the initiation rite, the best place for the therapist to look for cues as to what to do will be the latter part of the initiation rite. Somewhere in that process there will be a thread left hanging, a topic interrupted or incomplete for some reason or another, a theme which is a prelude, an overture, an invitation to later exploration. A comment from the group leader, along the general lines of "Well, now we can return to what you were saying, Mrs. Jones, as we were going around the room earlier," may help things along, and with any luck at all the resulting discussion may take up the rest of the group session. If not, if the discussion peters out or is simply completed, it is legitimate to return to the same area, the latter part of the initiation rite, and take up another thread. This technique will provide material for the first session at least, and perhaps more, and what to do next will be discussed in chapter 6, after a digression into theory.

Ending the First Session

In his description of the initial psychiatric interview, Sullivan (1954) suggests that the patient should be given something, toward the end of the interview, which is intended to make him feel that the hour he has just spent has been worthwhile. Sometimes that is a summary, sometimes a report of the therapist's first impressions. It is poor technique to spend an hour asking the patient questions, and then close with little more than a thank you and see you next time.

It is more difficult, in group, to work toward enabling the patient to feel that the time he has just spent has been worthwhile. This is particularly the case if not much has happened beyond the initiation rite and some tentative interpersonal positioning. However, making the attempt may be more important than in a dyadic session, where at least the patient has had your attention to himself for the hour.

The general rule is to tell the group what your experience of the session has been, how you evaluate it. A comment that this is the way groups generally start, is a minimal summarizing statement; that is preferable to a cool, "Our time is up for today."

Another general rule to follow is to ask the group if there are any questions before the session ends. Usually there won't be. If there are, the questions will probably fall into one of three categories:

1. A question which should probably be taken up by the entire group at the next meeting. Questions about how patients should live their lives, or about the plans the leaders have for group, fall into this category.

2. A question which indicates that the group member had a genuine misunderstanding of something which occurred during the session. The leaders should correct or clarify the misunderstanding if it pertains to them, or allow time for its clarification if it lies between patients. Unless such a misunderstanding is blatantly and undeniably related to the patient's psychopathology, don't interpret it. Not every interpretation which can be made should be made.

3. Requests for information which are legitimate and relatively easy to answer. If the requested information would be of interest to the entire group, give it right there. If (as is

usually the case with this category of inquiry) the question relates idiosyncratically to the patient, take it up with him immediately after group.

Sometimes you may be surprised to find that, although the group has apparently ended, and everyone has stood up, and the door is open, and the like, the patients are clustered around you and/or your coleader. It is as if the group has continued, but in a different plane. You are still on stage; you are still the group leader, and your words carry more weight than those of any of the group members. Yet at the same time you are now in a social situation. There need be no rule against chatting with patients, if you are comfortable with doing so and have some interest in it.

There also isn't any rule against excusing yourself and stalking coldly and imperiously out, figurative white coattails flapping in the wind; but there ought to be. Courtesy and some social graces are never out of place in the consulting room.

Leadership Styles

Starting a group is like starting a journey. The group itself is like an ocean liner; the leaders, tugboats. It requires more effort and skill to get the group going, the liner away from the pier, than once the liner is underway and there is more room to maneuver. As the group begins, as the tugboat moves the ocean liner away from the pier, your leadership style begins to emerge. Style is defined as the manner in which a given task is performed. Leadership style refers to the manner in which the group leaders carry out the tasks that theory tells them are important to carry out.

The effect of leadership styles upon group process and outcome has recently been studied by Lieberman, Yalom, and

Miles (1973). They found striking differences in outcome related to leadership styles. Their study was limited to encounter groups of relatively short duration. It is possible that some of the effects they report—particularly the "casualties" they attribute to leadership style—may be more characteristic of encounter than therapy groups, with their different goals, different time spans, and particularly different criteria for admission to the group experience.

Dimensions of style. A group leader's style is as individual as his personality. Group interactions are multidimensional. There are words or silences, there are nonverbal communicative gestures (posture, facial expression, tone of voice, etc.), and there is the flow or sequence of action, as well as other dimensions. Theory guides the leader's attention along these dimensions, favoring some and ignoring others. But theory is applied by an individual, and his own personality influences the process of its application. Which of the cues in the multidimensional group interaction the therapist will discriminate among is a function of the interaction of personality and theory.

It seems a reasonable assumption, then, and one susceptible of empirical resolution, that there is a relationship between leadership style and personality. If this is so, then there are some leadership styles which are more suited to your personality than others. One of the tasks of a group therapy training program is to help the novice therapist find a leadership style or range of styles which seems most congruent with his general interpersonal style and his empathic and defensive techniques. Style is the background-context within which theory is applied.

There are a number of dimensions which constitute leadership style. For our purposes in this brief introductory work, we will discuss only those which the novice therapist is most likely to have to deal with during his first several group meetings. These are: activity, status, and cue-emission.

Activity. This dimension involves a behavioral pattern which, for want of a better word, might be termed "forthcomingness." The behavioral pattern is largely but not entirely verbal. It includes the willingness of the therapist to actively intercede with the group: to be assertive, to make his presence or power known and felt, to direct the action or divert the focus of group toward particular directions. The highly active leader talks a lot, and both asserts and exercises the power of determining who else will speak, for how long, and (frequently) upon what topic. Activity is a principal, although not the sole, component of charisma.

Some people, including some novice group leaders, are not very "forthcoming." They are, or view themselves as, rather quiet people, content in the main to watch and listen, to use words sparingly, and to participate rather than to influence interaction. Such individuals are sometimes described as shy, and may themselves subscribe to this characterization. The level of emotional intensity in their interpersonal interactions is typically low, but there are exceptions—seldom occurring in the context of a group and only somewhat less rare in the one-to-one situation—which reach quite high levels of intensity and are the more remarkable because they are atypical.

The various technical approaches to group therapy require varying degrees of therapist activity. Gestalt therapy, Transactional Analysis, and some of the conceptual offspring of these approaches (see, e.g., Shaffer and Galinsky 1974) require a highly active therapist. These techniques cannot be artfully applied by reticent or passive individuals. A person who is not particularly active or "forthcoming" socially may experience considerable difficulty and discomfort as a group leader trying to hold a Gestalt group to the growing edge of experience.

Encounter or training groups, and psychoanalytic groups, require passive or impassive therapists. Thus, a person who is regarded socially as having a forceful personality may well have difficulty restraining himself in a group of this type. These technical approaches do not require therapists to be highly active, and in the context of these theoretical frameworks, a reticent style is likely to be defined as competent.

When the interface between interpersonal style and technical approach is smooth, the novice therapist is likely to be perceived—and perhaps to perceive himself—as talented. When technique and personality style do not blend readily, the novice therapist may perceive himself—and be perceived—as being inept or perhaps as having made a poor vocational choice. There is undoubtedly a great deal of self-selection in terms of theoretical and technical approaches—more reticent people seeking psychoanalytic orientations, more active and assertive individuals choosing schools where Gestalt or some similar technique is taught. Nonetheless it is probably true that graduate or postgraduate training in psychotherapy is probably the only time in the professional career of a mental health worker when he may be required to subordinate his personal proclivities to that of his supervisor or clinical director, and to attempt to practice and even gain proficiency in a technique for which he is really not suited.

The above describes the extremes of a therapist's interpersonal style dimension with anchors labeled active and passive. The techniques mentioned can be regarded as requiring one or the other extreme. There are, of course, an infinite number of points in between; it may not be impossible for a reticent therapist to do a Gestalt group or an active therapist to do an encounter group. In attempting to determine where, along this dimension, you should place yourself, you may find that you are trying to fit yourself into a box at one end of the dimension or the other, and not quite fitting either. You are most likely to be neither extremely passive nor extremely active. If you tend to be quiet and relatively impassive in new social situations, this tendency is likely to manifest itself during the first few group meetings; if you tend to be more outgoing and interpersonally active in new social situations, that tendency similarly is likely to be present. Our emphasis here is on tendencies, easily ignored impulses, proprioceptive minutiae which more or less perceptibly influence behavior. Therapists, more than most people, must concern themselves with the minutiae of interpersonal interaction.

There is a common, perhaps ubiquitous fantasy among people who are first learning to do therapy. It is that one must do something *different*—behave differently, draw different conclusions from the same set of interpersonal data—when one is doing therapy. It is as though we put on a figurative white coat, mount a figurative pedestal, and attempt to manifest all those qualities which we lack but desire and which our supervisors possess in full measure. Underlying this fantasy is the knowledge that one's own personal problems are not completely resolved, and the myth that one must be possessed of perfect mental health in order to be a therapist. The novice therapist's fear is that if, while trying to do therapy, he responds as he usually does, his problems will become obvious to both patient and supervisor. So he must do something different.

Thus, the novice therapist may go into a therapy group determined to do something different, suppress what comes naturally, and he may experience the resulting disaster as further proof that his own insurmountable problems render him unsuitable to enter the mental health professions. Or he may go into the first meeting and respond the way he usually does, and then chide himself bitterly afterward for failing so miserably to grasp the rudiments of technique.

The alternative which is recommended in this book is to acknowledge who and what you are, in terms of personality style, and the like; then, if possible, to find a technical approach which is congruent with your style, and a supervisor who appears to be tolerably empathic. If you have selected the training program which is right for you, and the program's admissions committee or officer is perspicacious, the task may not be all that difficult.

Status. This dimension refers to an interpersonal stance which the leader takes toward the group members. At one extreme is the group leader who chooses to regard himself as really just another group member, a colleague in the human experience which he shares with his patients. At the other extreme is the leader who plans doctor, claiming implicitly or explicitly for himself the wisdom of an oracle, the omnipotence of a mythical hero, and the warmth and empathy of a fairy godmother (see, e.g., Kaplan and Sadock 1971). Both of these interpersonal stances (which, at the extreme, may be labelled *collegial* and *authoritarian*) can be readily justified by more than one theory.

Interpersonal distance and interpersonal power are two of the major components of this dimension of leadership style. The collegial approach lends itself to less, the authoritarian to more, interpersonal distance. Similarly, the collegial approach leads the therapist to act as though he lacked the interpersonal power accorded him by the group as an *ex officio* function of his status as group leader. The authoritarian approach allows the leader to indulge in fantasies of omnipotence—that is, of pervasive influence upon and responsibility for all aspects of the patient's life. Both of these extremes represent significant distortions on the part of the therapist.

The therapist cannot readily abdicate his power. His attempt to do so constitutes a pretense, an effort to get the group members to accept something which they know is not so: the group leader is not there for therapy, and he possesses more expertise than the group members about groups, therapy, and therapy groups. To the extent that the group leader subscribes to the myth of collegiality, he will generate anger, anxiety, and sooner or later some real doubts as to his competence. Some theoretical approaches to group technique hold that the group leader is merely a special sort of group member, and that the work of the group is done when the members have accepted the leader as one of the group (Golembiewski and Blumberg 1970). Such approaches emphasize the innate or inherent ability of people to resolve their own problems through "group process" or learning how to become one's own therapist (Whitaker and Lieberman 1964). Thus, the collegial approach may appear attractive to therapists who espouse a humanistic point of view, for it allows them to *remain silent* in the belief that the group itself will facilitate self-actualization.

Similarly, this approach may be attractive to therapists who believe firmly in the development of insight as the goal of therapy, for it allows them to *remain silent* as the group works through transference phenomena and extends the sphere of ego functioning.

The collegial approach is not the same thing as the therapist's passive stance. The collegial stance may be subdivided into passive-collegial and active-collegial. In the passive-collegial approach the therapist remains, for the most part, inactive. In one sense, he pretends to be a patient. The resulting group interaction is likely to be slow and aimless, with expressions of confusion and uncertainty on the part of the group and with a rather high level of anxiety which can easily turn into defensive hostility. Theories which lend themselves to the passive-collegial style presume that this type of group interaction is inevitable and ubiquitous. It isn't. (See, e.g., Lakin 1972.)

An active-collegial approach is one in which the group leader actively espouses the role of a group member, and abdicates not only his expertise but also his ethics. Some of the horror stories to be found in the literature on encounter groups may be based on groups in which the leader took this approach.

The authoritarian approach represents the opposite extreme. The passive-authoritarian leader acknowledges the interpersonal power and wisdom accorded him by the group. He exercises that power in primarily non-verbal ways: through bearing and manner. This type of leader does not speak; he interprets. Because of the wisdom attributed to him by the group, obscurity in his comments may be mistaken for profundity. However, he interprets only rarely, and then generally emphatically. If you tend to sit back and take stock of the situation before commenting (in a social situation), you may find this type of leadership style attractive. This style has been described by Horwitz (1964).

The active-authoritarian approach will tend to reduce interaction among group members. The result is a group process which consists of a series of one-to-one patient-therapist interactions. Some active-authoritarian group leaders will explicitly prohibit group members from commenting until the particular patient-therapist dyad in the spotlight (or "hot seat") has completed its work.

The highly active authoritarian leader makes maximal use of the interpersonal power accorded him by the group. He can thus forge from the group setting a powerful tool for the facilitation of intimate self-disclosure and then cue the group to respond supportively, like a Greek chorus celebrating the victory of a tragic hero.

The novice group leader will find that his stance falls somewhere among these approaches: it is unavoidable. While the group leader's activeness is likely to be strongly influenced by his social and interpersonal skills and style, the status he chooses depends upon less personal factors. These include the social psychology of the clinical setting in which the group meets, the theoretical proclivities of the supervisor, and the magnitude of the difference between leader and members in age and socio-economic class.

Cue-emission. This dimension is defined as consisting of the amount and kind of information the group leader offers about himself to others. Self-disclosure usually refers to the verbal report of facts about one's self, about one's current or past feelings and activities, and as such constitutes one kind of cue-emission. Of greater importance to the flow or process of group are the nonverbal cues which a therapist may emit while he or someone else is talking. These cues consist of information about what the therapist may be feeling (or, perhaps, thinking) about what is being said.

Some people have expressive faces, and you can sometimes tell (or, put more accurately, you can sometimes guess) what such people are feeling or thinking about you by their facial expression. Usually, such a person's body language is also expressive, and so there are a number of nonverbal cues which comprise an ongoing commentary about how your comments are being received or the other person's comments are intended to be taken. D. D. Jackson (1960), among others, has described these nonverbal cues on the part of the *speaker* as meta-communication: information about the verbal message which assists the listener in interpreting and understanding the communication. We are more concerned here with the nonverbal and verbal cues (in that order) emitted by someone who is *not* speaking, namely the group leader, as he attends to what is going on in the group. An individual who utilizes facial expression, posture, and (when speaking) tone and volume of voice to communicate affect in an ongoing communicative process is defined here as a cue-emitter. A glance or two at him and you can pretty well guess where he's at.

At the other end of this dimension are those individuals who are cue-suppressors. Their facial features are less mobile, their facial expressions and body language harder to read. They do not typically engage in verbal self-disclosure. A cue-suppressor is not inattentive. He may be quite attentive, and may give off a variety of non-verbal signals, including eye contact, which indicate that he is listening. But he will give no indication, verbal or nonverbal, of *how he feels* about what you're saying: whether he's bored, listening politely, thinks you're dull or brilliant, or wholeheartedly agrees with your position and empathically understands it.

Most novice therapists tend to be cue-suppressors, whether this interpersonal style comes naturally to them or not. For one thing, the predominant affective component of the novice therapist's response to a patient or an interaction in group is likely to be anxiety accompanied by uncertainty, and it is unthinkable that this feeling should be communicated to (or discoverable by) the group, one's cotherapist, or one's supervisor. A second factor favoring cue-suppression is that many theoretical approaches to group (or individual) psychotherapy virtually require the therapist to be a cue-suppressor. Those orientations which regard the group leader as a facilitator of group process are somewhat less demanding of cue-suppression and may at times require some self-disclosure, verbal or other, of the therapist. On the other hand, there are some approaches to group which require (or allow) intense emotional interchange between patient and therapist. Therapists who are cue-suppressors will have a more difficult time engendering this kind of interaction.

If possible, you should find out before doing your first group where you stand as a cue-emitter or cue-suppressor. A sensitivity or T-group is a good place to have learned this kind of thing about yourself. Your knowledge of which pole you're closer to may help you to understand why people in groups you lead react to you the way they do, as well as what effect you are likely to have on the process of the group-as-a-whole. If you tend to be a natural cue-suppressor, you will probably be more comfortable with a technical approach which does not require a high level of emotional intensity on the part of the therapist, and you should probably avoid techniques which place a premium upon such interactions. If you tend to be a natural cue-emitter, the process of learning how to do groups will include becoming comfortable enough and confident enough in group to stop suppressing cues and to allow your more typical interpersonal style to become manifest.

Leadership styles. Concluding comment. Implicit in the preceding discussion is a general principle which is sometimes difficult for novice therapists to accept. This is the principle that what fits you best, what you are most comfortable doing, is likely also to be the most effective therapeutic style for you. If your tendency is to be verbally forthcoming and dominant in social situations and in work or school settings, then probably you're going to be most effective as a group leader following a technical approach which facilitates a high level of verbal activity on your part and which views therapist control of group process as theoretically correct. On the other hand, if you're quieter and prefer to follow rather than to lead discussions, or to follow empathically but not verbally or overtly, there are some technical approaches that you'd probably best avoid.

While the particular style you choose (or discover) will influence what happens in group, there are a few phenomena that are ubiquitous. Denying that you're exerting leadership influence (as in a collegial role), or claiming that you're influencing events remote from the group interaction (as in a highly authoritarian role) is to carry these ubiquitous factors to an unrealistic extreme. What happens in the former is that a hostile type of interaction is likely to follow; and what happens in the latter is that transference phenomena are facilitated. Furthermore, generalizations based on the group interactions which result from these therapist stances are likely to be distorted.

If there is any therapist response which is invariably correct it is a response based on reality. Sometimes that is also the most difficult or frightening response for a therapist to make; the novice therapist may not yet have discovered that the group member is even more frightened of reality than he.

Chapter 3

The Role of Theory

It is possible to go through all of the work of starting a group—finding time and space, a cotherapist, a supervisor, doing pre-group screening interviews, and getting through the first session or two—without paying very much attention to theory. The mechanics of getting a group started are usually determined by the exigencies of particular clinical settings, and are more closely related to budget and architecture and tradition than to theory. Once the group has started, however, some theory is necessary. This chapter is a digression into theory. It is intended as an initial orientation for novice group therapists, and to precede, not supplant, the more thorough and enduring orientation toward theory which evolves during the course of supervisory conferences. If you are still involved with the mechanics of assembling a group, you may wish to skip to chapter 6, and return to chapters 3–5 later.

Theory performs a roadmap function: it tells the clinician what to expect, what is likely to happen, what the destination or goal is, and how to determine when it has been reached. A corollary of this roadmap function is that theory helps the clinician reduce the complexity of the therapy situation to understandable proportions by directing his attention toward some events and away from others. Thus, theory performs an explanatory function about what is happening, a guiding function about what to pay attention to, and a predictive function about what is likely to happen next. It also performs a validating function: if you can interpret what is happening in terms of the theory, you are likely to feel that you understand what is going on and that your ability to correctly assess the situation is good.

Problems occur when the explanations offered by the theory seem irrelevant or trivial; when the events predicted by the theory fail to occur even when correct technique is followed; and when events occur about which the theory is silent. These problems show up in the supervisory session as the student learns to apply theory and as he experiences the interaction between theory and practice. In this chapter, the interaction between theory, observed events, and supervision is explored, and the role of theory discussed.

Validity, Utility, and Fantasy

Theory is an organization of data into a pattern which accounts for relationships among observable phenomena and predicts relationships or phenomena not yet observed. The function of theory is to elucidate relationships among phenomena. The purpose of theory is to further the goals of its science. These goals include the prediction and control of those phenomena which fall under scientific purview: observability, replicability, and communicability.[7] It follows that the goals of

---

7. If you're compulsive, the best place to find a brief and lucid discussion of this point is in the first chapter of an introductory textbook of psychology.

a science of behavior include the prediction and control of behavior, goals to which behaviorists explicitly subscribe.

However, most theories involving human behavior remain at the explanatory stage, venturing little into prediction and less into control. There are, for example, numerous theories (or, more precisely, proto-theories) of schizophrenia which seek to explain various aspects of schizophrenic behavior without in the least offering guidance or suggestions to the clinician whose task is not to control but to heal. There is, therefore, a difference between those theories which seek to understand and explain, and those which seek to understand and to heal. The former are likely to meet the formal criteria of science. The latter are more likely to be useful to the clinician, because that is what they are intended for.

A theorist who attempts to offer an understanding of human behavior, reality, and psychopathology is rather like the proverbial blind man encountering an elephant. Every theorist, without exception, selects some part of human behavior for explanation, and ignores the rest. Proto-theorists may acknowledge that they are attempting to account for only some part of the elephant, but major theorists seem to assume more or less implicitly that their slice is the whole.

As a result there are some events which are not accounted for, not even mentioned, by a particular theory, and which are therefore difficult if not impossible to fit into the conceptual framework of that theory. The failure of any theory to account for most or all significant human behaviors has led Hall and Lindzey (1970) to liken theory to a set of blinders, directing our attention toward some behaviors and away from others, though no less significant.

The breadth and complexity of human behavior is probably beyond the scope of any one person's understanding. The theory of behavior which is truly comprehensive has not yet appeared. When it does, it is likely to be the work of many minds, a ponderously slow accretion of data and proto-theories over a very long period.

The clinician chooses not to await this truly comprehensive theory of behavior before attempting to alleviate the suffering which stems from psychopathology, and he is confronted with a plethora of theories, some of which make more sense than others. Some theories are structurally elegant, stemming from and supported by research and empirical data; others lack such elegance, have equivocal empirical support, or, like psycho-analysis, do not readily lend themselves to experimental scrutiny. Yet, it is the less elegant, less confirmable theory which frequently appears to address itself cogently to the realities of emotional suffering and its alleviation, the more scientifically respectable theory defining more modest and less ambiguous behavioral events.[8] How is the clinician to choose between validity and utility?

The answer is that the clinician should, whenever possible, use the theory which makes the most sense to him. Each theorist makes some assumptions about the basic nature of people, about how things really are, and these assumptions guide the theorist toward addressing some aspect of behavior while ignoring others. Freud, for example, assumed that man is a savage beast. Therefore, affiliative and cooperative behavior required more explanation than hostile aggressive behavior. In addition, Freud's emphasis on unconscious processes led him to develop an entire theory of behavior based on the assump-tion that *things are not what they seem.* Maslow is represen-tative of a group of theorists who assume that man is basically

8. The gap between scientific respectability and clinical utility has narrowed in recent years, as the behaviorists have taken their token economies and schedules of reinforcement out of the laboratory and into the clinic. Their success is undeniable; the questions raised here about their limited scope remain. Some of the proverbial blind men encountered only the tail of the elephant.

good and who therefore must explain violence as an aberration. Berne (1964) dwells on Parent, Adult, and Child, while the Gestalters (e.g., Perls, Hefferline, and Goodman 1951) seem fascinated with the digestive process. The theory which makes the most sense to you is probably one written by a person whose basic asumptions about reality, and perhaps whose interests, are similar to your own. A theory which dwells on some aspect of behavior you consider unimportant or improbable may reflect implicit assumptions about reality which are different from yours. A theory which does not make much sense to you is not necessarily a poor theory; it is only less meaningful to you.

The position taken here is that theory need not be true—that is, empirically verifiable or verified—to be useful. Fantasy is not true, in the scientific sense of that word, yet it is useful. Some theories are mostly fantasy, and, like fantasy, are useful in making sense out of highly complex phenomena—such as a therapy group. A theory of groups which is presented in the following chapter is based on Freud. Whether Freud's theory is more fantasy than fact is not at issue here. It is a useful theory to many clinicians whose implicit assumptions about reality and about people are perhaps similar to Freud's.

In graduate schools in the various mental health professions, and in practicum training centers, the trainee is seldom asked which of the various theoretical frameworks is most congruent with his own experience or his own inclination. There is, of course, a great deal of pre-selection: a student who is enamored of Maslow as a result of undergraduate exposure is not likely to seek out a predominantly psychoanalytic training center for graduate work—or, if he should stumble into such a place, to be accepted by it. Nonetheless, it is not uncommon for a trainee to be confronted with a theory which is foreign to his own conception of interpersonal reality, and to be required to learn and to practice techniques based on assumptions which are essentially alien to him. Indeed, graduate or postgraduate training is probably the only situation in which the trainee is reinforced for doing something which is incongruent or disparate with his construction of reality.

If you find yourself in such a situation, you may find that challenging the theory espoused by your supervisor generates rather more heat than might be expected in such a purely rational setting. That is because you may be challenging in some sense his construction of reality, *and he yours.* The most beneficent results of such a challenge may well be a recommendation, from the supervisor, that the trainee seek therapy, and a privately held conviction, by the trainee, that the supervisor is narrow, rigid, and a bit daft.

The Influence of Theory Upon Practice

The influence of theory upon practice is exerted primarily during the group session. As the group interaction unfolds, theory guides the therapists' attention toward some events, away from some events, and is silent about yet others. The events which the theory focuses upon are those which it can explain; the events which it does not alert the therapists to are those which that particular theory does not or cannot explain—perhaps because these unexplained or undescribed events did not fit into the theorist's implicit assumptions about behavior and reality, or because, though perceived, he regarded them as unimportant.

Most theories of group therapy draw the therapists' attention toward the same classes of events and types of behavior (Shaffer and Galinsky 1974). The events to which the therapists are led are (a) interpersonal, between patient and therapist; (b) interpersonal, between patients; and (c) intrapersonal, when the patient explores his own psyche, but in the presence of others. Theory may be regarded as drawing the therapists' attention to certain cue dimensions, such as verbal and non-verbal communications and the relationship between them; to the sequence of events in the group; and (within the dimension of verbal communication) to the content and function of verbal activity. Considerable overlap exists in the cue dimensions that various theories define as important in the practice of group psychotherapy.

Where theories differ is in the importance assigned to the various cue dimensions, and, within a particular cue dimension, to the type of response regarded as theoretically correct. Some psychoanalytic group psychotherapies, for instance, assign an almost overwhelming importance to the cue dimension of verbal communication, while a number of other theoretical approaches (of which Gestalt is perhaps the best known) place less emphasis on verbalization and more on experiencing in the here-and-now—what the analysts might call abreaction. Within that cue dimension, the psychoanalyst listens to the verbal content in order to detect illogical or irrational reasoning (Foulkes and Anthony 1965). When a Gestalter listens to what a patient is saying, he may listen less to the content, less for illogical premises, and more for the emotion conveyed by tone of voice.

In sum, theory defines, for the therapist, (a) which cue dimensions to attend to, and in what order of importance; (b) how to discriminate among cues (e.g., if verbal, then whether to attend to content, semantics, or tone of voice); and (c) having discriminated appropriately, how to interpret or understand the cues which have been selected as most meaningful.

From this standpoint, it might be said that the first task of the therapist is to teach the group the language of the theory he is using. In order for the therapists to do this, the events which are most readily explained by the theory must first occur. The therapist may be regarded (by his supervisor) as skilled to the extent that he facilitates the occurence of such events. The Gestalt therapist whose patients begin, after two or three months, to report dreams is in fine shape; the psychoanalytically oriented therapist, confronted with patients' dreams after the same length of time, should not yet respond to them.

Therapists encourage, in group, the behavior which theory tells them should occur. This encouragement may be subtle, as when the cue-suppressing group leader suddenly (but nonverbally) shows heightened interest in what a patient is saying; or it may be quite open, as when Gestalters and transactional analysts take some time to teach theoretical concepts during the group sessions.

The therapist's second task, from the standpoint of theory, is to convince the group that the types of interaction which the theory deems important are in fact important. In order to do that, the therapist must himself subscribe to the importance of the event. For instance, theories (and therapists) which assume that hostility mediates interpersonal interaction until libidinal ties are established must convince the group that intragroup conflict is inevitable, natural, and necessary, and that one task of the group leader is the resolution of such conflict. That is not a particularly difficult task, for it is relatively easy to generate conflict in a group, and interpersonal conflict is observable behavior.

A more difficult task for the group leader is to convince the group that *things are not what they seem* (the psychoanalytic formulation), that unconscious motivations are present, and that what may appear to be a trivial interaction in group is actually quite significant because it reveals or portends some unconscious mechanism. Even if you believe that sort of thing, it's hard to sell. Analytic group therapists may wait six months or so before venturing a heavy interpretation of that type. If you don't believe the theoretical formulations and your supervisor does, the best thing to do is to change supervisors, if that is possible. It's difficult to sell someone else on something that you yourself don't believe in; patients will quickly pick up your lack of enthusiasm for a technique you don't like, and your inability to produce or facilitate the kinds of interaction that theory says are important may be taken by your supervisor as a reflection on your general competence.

If you approach group work with a clear theoretical bias, and therefore some notion of what ought to happen, you will be confronted with the discrepancy between what *is* happening and what *ought* to happen, with no clear idea of how to get from what is to what theory says ought to be. In these circumstances feelings of frustration, ineptness, and stupidity are not uncommon among novice group therapists.

The situation is somewhat similar to that of individual psychotherapy, when the patient seems to be into something which theory doesn't readily account for. You know that the patient should be talking about something else, you aren't clear on how to get him to do so, and you envy your colleagues whose patients are producing material which is easily handled by the theory you're learning to apply. For example, your patient may drone on and on about how to catch fish. Your theory says he ought to be talking about his feelings, and the path from fish to feelings is not immediately obvious to you, although you may expect that it will be obvious to your supervisor later on. An analogue in group might be a session where most of the members seem quite earnestly interested in discussing the local zoning ordinances.

The dilemma that this kind of situation puts you in is that you'll have to say something to get the patient back on the right track because if you don't, if you remain silent, the entire remainder of the session will have been spent on something peripheral or irrelevant. Yet the very theory which propels you into verbal activity fails to tell you what you ought to say: this situation seems to have been unanticipated by the theorist.

The influence theory has upon practice seems then limited to generalities, to general principles, to abstractions, while what you have to deal with in the group session (or in individual psychotherapy) is concrete and specific. Novice therapists may be tempted to make theoretical statements during the sessions, stretching logic a bit in order to fit theory to events. If you try that approach, try to restrict yourself to statements which are logical derivations of theory, you'll find that you're working very hard, that you're defending your theory to your patients, and that the discussion gets farther away from where you want it to go in spite of your efforts.

This problem arises from the assumption that theory and practice are closely allied, that there are a finite number of theoretical statements and practical situations, and that the task of the therapist is to memorize as many of the former and experience as many of the latter as possible. It is true that one role of theory is to reduce the complexity of group interaction to manageable proportions, but it is incorrect to infer that complexity can be reduced to a finite number of statements each of which produces a specifiable result.

In addition to its reductionistic role, theory serves as a focal point or framework for the development, in the therapist, of a *point of view.* The application of theory is comprised not of technical interventions, but of statements and actions by the therapist stemming from the point of view generated by the theory. If you can find, reconstruct, discover, or deduce a point of view, an attitude, a *set of implicit assumptions about behavior and reality* which is consistent with theory, then it will be considerably easier to decide when and how to intervene therapeutically—what to say and when to say it.

Theory, we assume, represents the point of view and reflects the implicit personal assumptions of the theorist. In order for the theory to make sense to you, therefore, it is necessary that you hold some of those same assumptions. In addition, an intimate familiarity with the theory is necessary if that theory is to serve as a focal point for the development of a point of view which, while your own, is also consistent with that of the theorist.

The influence of theory on practice, then, is manifested in two functions. The first is an ordering or guiding function, defining what the therapists should look for and respond to in group, and approximately in what order. The second function is to serve as a nucleus and stimulus for the development of an attitude or point of view from which therapeutic interventions may stem.

The Influence of Practice Upon Theory

Practice influences theory after the group session, during the supervisory interview. At that time, the tasks of the group leaders include accounting to the supervisor for what happened in group in terms of the theory espoused by the supervisor. If things went as the theory predicted, this is not a difficult task. The initial silence, followed by hostility, which results from passivity on the part of the therapists, is easily described in terms of group members' dependency, hostility, and hostile dependency, for example.

What is more difficult to account for is an event or behavioral sequence in group which does not readily fit into the framework of the theory but which the group clearly spent a good deal of time and energy on. Theory tells what should have happened; the tape (or notes or memory) tells what did happen; the task of the supervisor is the reconciliation of the two. While the number of options available is probably infinite, they probably fall most frequently into one of the following three classes:

1. The group members are said to have failed to come to grips with problems defined (by theory and supervisor) as important. They are not yet ready for the insight or interpretation or experience (etc.) which the group leaders have correctly visited upon them. This leaves both the group leaders and the supervisors in the right, and the group members to be blamed, and to be regarded as somewhat more immature than one might have expected.

2. The group dwelt on a point which theory regards as irrelevant or unimportant because of a technical error by the therapist. This formulation needs no further comment.

3. The behavioral sequence may be redefined as important. Theoretical concepts may have to be stretched to cover the event and accomplish such a redefinition; thus does practice influence theory. Discussion of a zoning ordinance, for instance, may be seen as resistance, avoidance, or as a symbolic attempt to establish ego boundaries. The possibilities are limitless.

What makes them so is the nature of the data with which the therapists work. Most behavior is ambiguous and susceptible of many interpretations. The very theories which are useful to the clinician because they address the quality of experience are similarly susceptible of many interpretations precisely because they reflect the ambiguity of experience rather than an attempt to quantify it. The greater the ambiguity of theory, the more it can explain and the more susceptible it is to the influence of events. The ambiguity of theory, however, the elasticity of its concepts, need not necessarily reflect loss of validity; in interpersonal relations, truth is a judgment, not a datum.

Concluding Comment

In the natural sciences, and to some extent in the social sciences, the interaction of theory and practice involves the design and performance of experiments. Theory generates hypotheses, that is, performs a roadmap function. Experiments test hypotheses, and empirical data determine whether or to what extent the hypotheses are supported. Theory is then modified to conform to empirical findings.

In the mental health professions, each therapeutic intervention is rather like an experiment, whether that intervention is the administration of medication, the application of a schedule of reinforcement, or the comment of a therapist during a group or individual psychotherapeutic session. That experiment tests an hypothesis stemming, ideally, from some theoretical point of view. The result tends either to support the hypothesis or not.

However, theory is not modified to conform to empirical findings. It may be *distorted,* that is, applied in an erroneous or deviant fashion, but it is not modified. Psychoanalysis is not significantly different from the way Freud left it, nor is Gestalt from where Perls left it, nor any of the other theories upon which some psychotherapeutic interventions might be based.

These theories behave more like philosophy than like science. Philosophy is noncumulative. Science is a cumulative enterprise, and a scientific theory which fails to undergo major modification over the course of several decades is either highly venerable or highly suspect. It is because we are closer to philosophy than to science that we find truth in judgments rather than empirics.

The judgmental truth which prevails is, therefore, that which is most convincing. Theory provides a conceptual context within which judgments are made, and the context lends credence to these judgments. The point of view advanced here is that behavioral episodes such as those which occur during therapy groups are inherently ambiguous, and thus will support a number of interpretations of "what really happened."

To attempt to place any particular interpretation somewhere along a continuum of *correct* or *incorrect* is fallacious, except in the context of theory. The theory itself derives its power not from accuracy (i.e., empirics) but from its ability to convince people and thus to form a pool or consensus of judgments about reality.[9]

If there is no ultimate truth in interpersonal relations, but only opinion, then the clinician must function in a situation which is inherently and unavoidably ambiguous, and in which certainty will forever elude him. It is this inherent uncertainty and ambiguity of the therapy situation, combined with the awesome responsibilities of the helper role (as he perceives them), which so terrifies the novice therapist. The problem is compounded in group therapy. There, any consensus reached by the group about what really happened may be deviant relative to the rest of society. But it is more powerfully convincing to the therapist in the group because such a consensus is, by definition, the pooled judgment of a number of people. Few novice therapists have the *chutzpah* to say, to a room of six or eight or ten other people that things are not what they seem, or, in effect, to hold that their judgment of reality is better than that of the six or eight or ten people put together.

The first task of the novice clinician faced with doing therapy is to confront his terror and to function effectively in spite of it. To the extent that the sources of that terror are the ambiguity and uncertainty of the therapy situation, whatever steps the clinician takes to reduce ambiguity will reduce anxiety. Theory provides a way of reducing ambiguity in the therapy situation. It also provides a set of judgments, preformed and readily available, about those aspects of reality which are reached through judgment and experience rather

9. Thus, Sullivan's concept of consensual validation.

than through experiment and the accumulation of facts. If those judgments embodied in theory do not make intuitive sense to the clinician, are not congruent with his own experience of reality, then theory cannot function as a roadmap (you have to trust a roadmap if you're going to use it); it contributes to rather than reduces ambiguity, and at best fails to help the clincian reduce the terror of the situation of uncertainty combined with responsibility which appears to be characteristic of psychotherapy.

If, on the other hand, the theory does make intuitive sense to the clinician, it may serve to reduce ambiguity and thus anxiety to tolerable levels, and to buttress the clinician's own sense of reality. Theory in psychotherapy is ultimately a set of judgments offering to the clinician consensual validation of his own experience. Theory cannot offer certainty, although some theories provide that illusion; but the validation of one's own experience is requisite to the maintenance of sanity. The role of theory, then, is to help the clinician to maintain his own sense of interpersonal reality, and to help him to make that sense of reality prevail when there is nothing else to buttress it and the edge of the abyss looms near.

Chapter 4

The Application of
Freud's Theory of Group Psychology

Few group phenomena occur with invariant regularity. Some facets of group experience, however, occur with sufficient frequency to require explanation. Here, we will consider some of these. They are:

1. The source and nature of the interpersonal power accorded the group leaders by the group members
2. The development of the atmosphere of warmth and supportiveness in which intimate self-disclosure can occur
3. The willingness of the individual to allow the group to influence him, and
4. The willingness of the group members to help one another

In our discussion we will also take up other group phenomena, such as scapegoating, the factors underlying group cohesiveness, and the like. The purpose is to offer the group therapist some conceptual tools with which to make sense out of quite complex sensory input in the group sessions.

The facets of group experience which concern us here are not limited to therapy groups, but occur in other types of groups as well (see, e.g., Lieberman, Yalom, and Miles 1973, Shaffer and Galinsky 1974). Our theoretical model is, therefore, not limited to groups explicitly designated as psychotherapeutic, but may also apply to others.

This theoretical framework is based on Freud's theory of group psychology: *Group Psychology and the Analysis of the Ego* (1922). That theory, although intricate, is not complex, utilizing only a few theoretical concepts to explain a number of group phenomena. Derived from Freud's theory, our framework does not lend itself readily to the development of specific therapist interventions—a point to which we will return at the end of this chapter—but is rather intended to facilitate the development of a point of view from which technical interventions can be formulated.

Interpersonal Power of the Group Leader

Let us distinguish at once between the power of the group leader to influence the course of events which occur during group, and the power he may have to influence events which occur outside group. We may call the former, leadership functions, the latter, therapist functions. While the group leader has considerable power to influence events which occur during group, his ability to influence patients' behavior outside of group is much smaller and, at best, is only one of many influences upon the patients.

The group leader is accorded some interpersonal power *ex officio*. In the group session, he is an expert, utilizing his expertise for the benefit of his patients. Initially, the patients assume that the group leader is expert. Generally, they hold this assumption unless (and until) the patient possesses so much evidence to the contrary that he can no longer deny it. The group leader, that is, is generally given the benefit of doubt and must actively disprove his competence before the group member is willing to reassess it.

Like the kind of interpersonal power accorded by a client to any expert practicing in his field—doctor, lawyer, television repairman, forest ranger—so is the group leader's; his ability to influence events in the group is no more than the ability of a plumber to influence the activity of a family while he is repairing the kitchen sink and they are in the kitchen.

It is possible, then, to account for the interpersonal power of the group leader in terms of the structure of the situation, that structure being essentially a client-expert relationship. This formulation omits, however, *the intensity of emotion* which the group leader is capable of arousing within individuals or within the group. This ability of the group leader might be attributed to transference phenomena: the group leader is perceived as powerful in the same way that the group member's parents were perceived. Freud, however, does not take this route. He attributes this power of the leader not to transference, but to identification. Let us look briefly at how Freud arrived at this conclusion.

Freud's starting point was the individual group member. Of particular interest to Freud were two characteristics of group membership: the intensification of emotion, and the impairment or reduction in the level of intellect. Freud wrote:

> We started from the fundamental fact that an individual in a group is subjected through its influence to what is often a profound alteration in his mental activity. His emotions become extraordinarily intensified, while his intellectual ability becomes markedly reduced. . . . We have heard that these often unwelcome consequences are to some extent at

least prevented by a higher "organisation" of the group; but this does not contradict the fundamental fact of Group Psychology—the two theses as to the intensification of the emotions and the inhibition of the intellect in primitive groups. [1922, p. 33]

Freud's "primitive groups" refer to the degree of the organization of a group, whether it has come together for one meeting or several. In the quoted passage, he is referring to a crowd or mob. A therapy group of six or eight or ten patients similarly lacks organization; there are no subgroups,[10] and patients do not differ in rank or position. The "two theses" are at least potentially present in a therapy group and may, as Freud seems to be suggesting, be a function of its lack of structure. No other similarities between a therapy group and a mob are expressed or implied.

Having identified the phenomena he wishes to discuss, Freud then turns to a consideration of group cohesiveness. He suggests that the power which holds the group together is that of the libido, that group ties are libidinal ties. As Freud was not a particularly careful theorist, defining the technical terms of psychoanalysis in somewhat different ways in different contexts, it is pertinent to quote the definition Freud used in this context:

Libido is an expression taken from the theory of emotions. We call by that name the energy (regarded as a quantitative magnitude, though not at present actually measurable) of

10. Or, at any rate, there shouldn't be. Transitory subgroups may arise (based on sex, age, common experiences, etc.) and disappear within a single group meeting. If two close friends are inadvertently placed in the same group, what tends to get focussed on is the relationship between them: seldom is that in their individual contracts, and seldom is it beneficial to the rest of the group.

those instincts which have to do with all that may be comprised under the word "love." The nucleus of what we mean by love naturally consists (and this is what is commonly called love, and what the poets sing of) of sexual love with sexual union as its aim. [1922, p. 37]

Freud applies the concept of the libidinal basis of group cohesiveness to the Catholic Church and to an army. He finds that the concept works (that is, explains certain phenomena) in both types of organization. Of particular interest for present purposes is his emphasis upon the necessity of the leader of the organization to love each member of the group equally. The "leader" of the Catholic Church is Christ, and of an army its commanding general.[11]

Freud speaks of this love by the leader as being an "illusion," but states that

Everything depends upon this illusion; if it were to be dropped, then both Church and army would dissolve. . . . [1922, p. 42]

Thus far, Freud has suggested that cohesiveness among group members is attributable to a libidinal tie, and that the love of the leader equally for all members is also in some sense libidinal. With these concepts, it is already possible to account for a number of phenomena which are fairly characteristic of groups—the warmth and supportiveness which tend to occur, and the warm and loving glow which is typical of the last group session. Lieberman, Yalom, and Miles (1973) report this afterglow as having occurred in all of their 15 encounter

---

11. Strachey's translation has "commander-in-chief," which clearly has different connotations for American and British readers.

groups, but as being absent in two "leaderless" groups which listened to encounter group tapes.

At this point in his exposition Freud takes what he himself calls a digression to consider a type of emotional bond between people which is not so directly (or blatantly) sexual. Libidinal cathexes are not the only bonds which bring people together. Freud introduces the concept of *identification* as a type of emotional tie; indeed, he suggests that it is the first or original form of an emotional relationship with another person.

The formation of this tie involves a complex process. The first step is *introjection* of the admired (or desired) object: the boy wishes to be like his father, and so introjects his conception of father: What would father do, say, etc., in this situation that I am now in? The process is fairly devoid of nuances, since it occurs initially in children who are in transition between the anal and phallic stages of psycho-sexual development. The second step involves equating of the introject with the ego: I am like him, we are at one with each other. (The pathological form is, we *are* one: I am my father. It is the non-pathological form, the I-am-like-him formulation, which is pertinent to our understanding of group behavior.) The end-point of Freud's disquisition is the suggestion that the members of a cohesive group have all performed the same mental work: they have introjected the group leader, and the introject is equated with, or takes the place of, not the ego but the ego-ideal.

Although Freud did not address this specific point, it may be helpful to remember that it is not the group leader who takes the place of the group member's ego-ideal, but rather the group member's concept of what the leader is like. Introjection is not veridical, either in the child or in the adult. The group member's perceptions of the leader will of necessity contain some gaps and some distortions, because it is not possible to know another human being completely and fully. If the group leader is bland, impassive, and cue-suppressing, opportunities for distortion and gap-filling by the group member are maximized. The ways in which the introject is distorted and the ways the gaps in information about the introjected object—the group leader—are filled are functions of the group member's personality. The process of distortion which occurs here may be regarded as projection; but it is not the ego-defense mechanism of projection which stems directly from libidinal involvement with the cathected object, but, rather, the projection which accompanies the first step of the process of identification: the formulation is, "This is how I think you are, this is what my information about you leads me to infer," rather than "This is a characteristic which I need for you to possess" (e.g., strength, wisdom, forbearance, etc.). It is this type of projection, the projection attendant upon the introjection-identification process, which psychoanalytically oriented group therapists have labelled *transference,* and have sought to foster.

The introjection of the group leader by the group members, and the equation of the introject with the ego-ideal is the first step of a two-stage process. The second step is the recognition by the group members that their ego-ideals are identical. Such recognition is the basis for the identification of group members as *we,* upon which group cohesiveness is built. Freud puts the matter quite succinctly:

A . . . group . . . is a number of individuals who have substituted one and the same object for their ego-ideal and have consequently identified themselves with one another in their ego. [Freud, p. 80]

Freud goes on to account for the individual's willingness to become susceptible to the influence of the group by referring to his theory of the Primal Horde. We need not follow him thence. Instead, we now return to the tasks we set ourselves at the beginning of this chapter: to account for some characteristic, if not ubiquitous, phenomena of groups.

The source and limits of the interpersonal power accorded the group leaders. The interpersonal power accorded the group leader can be understood in terms of the introjection, by group members, of the group leader, with the introject taking the place of the ego-ideal. The function of the ego-ideal, put simply, is to visit praise or reproach upon the ego for actions taken or contemplated. The ego-ideal is the source of many, if not all, of the injunctions against action which the ego seeks to take in order to satisfy strong instinctual drives. When the ego-ideal is supplanted by the introjection of an external object, this external object (in this case, the group leader) is able to exert considerable control over the individual. Because the individual does not discriminate between the introjected leader and his own self, reproach from the group leader is experienced in the same manner as reproach from one's own ego-ideal. (In the latter case, as Freud notes, the result may be mania; in the former, melancholia or depression.) The group leader is also in a position to give or withhold consent for any number of activities which are prohibited to the individual by his own ego-ideal, and with this consent, the group member can engage in actions which he would not normally engage in when alone or in a social situation without feeling guilt, remorse, or shame. But when the group member's survival is at stake, when he feels that his survival is threatened by a particular request from the group leader, he will simply refuse to obey. Nevertheless, he will feel bad about himself as a result, and nevertheless, he may magnify any hint of reproach from the therapist well out of proportion.

We now have also the theoretical tools to account for the phenomenon of *scapegoating.* Scapegoating is most likely to occur when the group members have introjected the group leader, substituting him for their ego-ideals, and have identified with one another. If the group leader is critical of a group member, and especially if the leader is critical and hostile, the other group members will frequently turn on the one who has been thus singled out. This is the clinical, observable phenomenon called scapegoating, and it can drive the victim out, out into the cold, out away from the we-ness of the group in much the same way as the Biblical scapegoat was driven away from the tabernacle and into the cold and barren desert, there to perish. (There is some evidence that scapegoating can result in genuine emotional injury to the victim—e.g., Lieberman, Yalom, and Miles 1973.)

The group leader, by attacking, sets an example; it is as though he grants permission to the others to attack; and perhaps the attack of the group serves both as a kind of ingratiation and to distract the leader away from attacking other group members: I am with you, I am like you, I too attack your enemies; therefore don't attack me.

The group does not need to see an actual attack by the group leader. Rather, the group has what amounts to an uncanny sense of who is in favor, who is in disfavor. Group members are as adept at picking up subtle cues as is the group leader; the difference between them is that the group leader has some obligation to report rather than to act on what he sees.

In effect, the group leader speaks with the loudest, most powerful voice in the group. Consequently, what the group leader may issue as a mild reproach or a faint disapproval may be heard by the group member (and the rest of the group) as though it were the severest of condemnations. This tendency of the group to amplify nuances places the group leader in something of a quandary: the group leader must be able to challenge, question, in some sense perhaps find fault with, the patient's conception of reality, or with the patient's mechanisms for dealing with reality; yet, if the leader does make the challenge, he runs the risk of making of the patient a scapegoat, who will be attacked by the other group members.

Thus the group leader must be aware that the group will tend to magnify and exaggerate his comments, and that any comment which has even a remotely negative tone may invite scapegoating; he must watch for any signs of attack from group members; and he must come to the rescue of the patient. Such rescue will not usually be perceived by the group as favoritism, but rather as an extension of the protection by the group leader of each member of the group unconditionally. The perceiving of this protection is likely to lead to a decrease in tension rather than to an increase in sibling rivalry. (The latter might be expected if transference rather than introjection and identification factors mediated group cohesiveness and the interpersonal power accorded the group leader.)

If the group leader does not come to the rescue, the group, sooner or later, will do it, will do his work for him. But as Freud said, when the group leader does not love all the group members equally, the group dissolves: if you allow the group to attack and don't protect the victim, you will in effect be showing the kind of negative favoritism which may impede or even dissolve group cohesiveness.

To summarize: the interpersonal power accorded the group leader during the initial few sessions of group may be attributed to the structure of the situation: he is the expert to whom patients will listen precisely because they are soliciting, and in most instances paying for, the leader's expertise. Soon, however, the process of introjection begins. Through this process, the group members' perception of the group leader gradually takes the place—in what Freud refers to as "the mental apparatus"—of the group member's ego-ideal, and thus the leader's power over the individual becomes similar, or perhaps analogous to, the power of the ego-ideal. Principally, that power is one of giving or withholding permission. When the individual follows the dictates of the introjected leader, approval is granted, and that approval is experienced, by the ego, as love or enhanced self-esteem; when disapproval is experienced, it is experienced in the same manner as disapproval by one's own conscience, by feeling loss of love, lower self-esteem, and/or guilt.

The development of an atmosphere of warmth and supportiveness. We now turn to a consideration of factors affecting group cohesiveness. As we saw in chapter 2, the first bonds which form a group are those associated in some way with initiation rites. The sharing of mildly embarrassing experience appears to serve as a kind of permission for the group members to begin to interact. Within the Freudian framework we are utilizing here, this initiation rite phenomenon must be an ego function: we share the common experience of suffering (the information elicited by the group leader when' he breaks the initial silence of group by asking each member to report on his or her feelings) and of working together in somewhat unpleasant circumstances (the initiation rite).

Probably the initiation rite is more complex than this formulation. Here, we wish merely to point out that the initial working together of the group, the initial "we-ness," is an ego function stemming from the perception or awareness of a shared experience: the forerunner of the later identification (which is based on the same perceptual mechanism) through the awareness that other group members share the same ego-ideal, i.e., the introjected group leader. The theoretical formulation, "I identify with you because we share the same super-ego," is not an especially compelling one if it is conceptualized as pertaining to a dyad. In a larger group, however, the shared permission which constitutes the functional manifestation of the introjection of the ego ideal can begin to intensify the phenomenon of identification through the kind of feedback loop which Freud described as he was accounting for the phenomenon of contagion in crowds, church, and the army.

This feedback loop is composed of the following links: (a) the perception or awareness by the group member of some internal affect; (b) the perception in others of the manifest signs of a similar emotion in the first group member, (c) whose behavior then reflects this intensification, which (d) intensifies the emotion and its behavioral manifestations in others, and so on. The entire emotional experience is further intensified if it occurs in a context where a group leader has given permission to each member of the group to allow the feelings into consciousness and has approved of their visible manifestation.

We may now address ourselves quite directly to one of the problems which we set ourselves at the beginning of this chapter: namely, to account for the atmosphere of warmth and supportiveness in which intimate self-disclosure is most likely to occur. The establishment of group cohesion is a prerequisite. The psychodynamics of the group may be understood in terms of the introjection of the group leader, and the substitution of the introject for the ego-ideal of the group members, followed by identification of group members with one another. The group members have thus yielded a critical faculty to the group leader. In so doing, they also acquiesce in his leadership.

The identification of group members with one another, based upon this acquiescence, is not sufficient to establish the desired conditions of warmth and supportiveness. In some types of groups, as, for example, classes in school, or athletic teams, where the emphasis is on competition rather than cooperation (as in swimming or gymnastics), and of course (as

Freud pointed out) in the military and the church, cohesiveness may be based on introjection and identification, but the atmosphere may be hostile and suspicious. In such instances, the permissions given by the leader may involve hostility and aggression, while the shared identification may be based on such emotions as fear and hatred of a common enemy. Freud apparently felt that the cohesiveness of groups characterized by this type of emotion was not as strong as that of groups where the identification was associated with warmth and supportiveness. Our point here is merely that group cohesion is a necessary, but not sufficient, condition for such an atmosphere to become manifest.

In a group, if the permissions given by the leader involve hostility and aggression, the prevalent atmosphere will reflect those permissions. In order to establish and maintain the desired atmosphere of warmth and so on, the group leader must "love" all the group members equally. To some extent, permission for the group members to be friendly may stem from a general attitude, on the part of the group leader, of warmth, empathy, and positive regard for all of the group members. However, the manifestation of such an attitude toward the group as a whole is not sufficient: the group leader will have to demonstrate his "loving" attitude—patience, empathy, and warm regard—toward one or two specific group members. Which group members in particular receive this "love" is in one sense not important; what is important is that the other group members feel that they have an equal chance of receiving this "love" from the group leader, an expectation that they will in fact receive it if they so desire, and that the other group members identify with those who have directly and specifically received the loving attention of the group leader. This identification with one who is loved has some observable behavioral concomitants: in posture, facial expressions, body movements, tone of voice, and the like, and thus is susceptible of intensification through the feedback loop mechanism of contagion described above.

Thus, the penultimate step in the development of the atmosphere of warmth and supportiveness involves approval of the egos of the group members by the introjected group leader functioning in place of the group members' ego-ideals. The ego feels loved, esteemed, worthy, and perhaps, at times, elated.

The final step involves the identification of loved egos with one another: we are worthy, we share together esteem and love; and if the formulation is that we love and *identify* with one another, then to love another is also to love oneself. It is the latter permission (ultimately, permission to love oneself) which, in a therapy group, the leaders may be able to give so powerfully (along with the help of the process of intensification of emotion among the group members) that intimate self-disclosure becomes possible, and change is facilitated.

Thus, it appears that intimate self-disclosure occurs only when the individual group member loves himself enough to display himself, enough to feel confident that others will love him too, and when he loves others enough to share the gift of his intimacy with them. The task of the group leaders, in this regard, is to help the individual reach a point of self-love, and to help the group reach the point where it can tolerate the intensity of intimate self-disclosure. When the group member has some considerable investment in self-hate (as in schizophrenic patterns of adaptation), considerable skill may be required of the therapists in order to bring a group to this point.

We have taken Freud's concepts of introjection and identification considerably farther than he took them in his book on group psychology. We have, however, but followed a path which Freud might have taken if his interests had led him

thence. Freud, incidentally, did not feel that serious therapeutic work could be undertaken in group.

Willingness of the individual to be influenced by group.
What remains in this analysis is to account for two phenomena
which frequently (but not invariably) occur in group: the willingness of the individual to allow the group to influence him,
and the willingness of the individual to attempt to help others.
Freud was so inner-directed that he could apparently conceptualize one person allowing himself to be influenced by others
as some kind of pathological state. Yet his concepts of introjection and identification lend themselves readily to accounting
for these phenomena. The individual accedes or succumbs to
the influence of group because of the introjection of the group
leader and the identification of group members with one
another on the basis of the shared introject. The formulation
is, we are in this together, we have a common goal, common
interests, a common ego-ideal. It is as though one part of the
individual's mental apparatus (the ego-ideal) becomes equated
not only with the group leader, but with the other group
members. Thus, when permissions are given, some of those
permissions come from the group functioning as an agent of
the group leader. *We* is a powerful concept when identification
is involved: consider the intense emotional reaction of crowds
at sporting events who identify with the teams of professional
athletes: we are winning, they say, and that "we" is available
for the price of a ticket.

Willingness of the individual to attempt to help others.
Somewhat difficult to account for theoretically, this is nonetheless quite common in groups. The extent to which one individual is willing to help another, in the rather special ways that
help can be given in group, is related to some extent to group
cohesiveness and group atmosphere. When the group has
reached the atmosphere of warmth and supportiveness in

which intimate self-disclosure can occur, the help that is given through the interaction of helper and helpee may be considerably more intense emotionally than at earlier—or later—stages of group. Sometimes that help may consist of a willingness to role-play another group member's parent, sibling, spouse, or fantasy; sometimes it consists of working with, rather than rejecting, behavioral patterns or assumptions about other people which are outrageously unworkable. The problem for theory is why an individual who comes for help himself and who is (in some clinics) paying for it should be willing to subsume his own interests to those of another, should take time, effort, thought, and emotional energy away from himself and bestow them upon another.

Here, too, the concept of identification which has stood us in such good stead thus far must again be called upon. The identification of group members with one another is never complete; that would be as pathological as the formulation noted above, *I am* my father; here, the pathological formulation is, We are one person. To the extent that group members identify with one another, love for one another is also self-love, and thus the willingness to exert oneself for another becomes also exertion for oneself. To the extent that identification is incomplete, the helper may be projecting his own needs, problems, and solutions, onto the other group member: in other words, to infer a greater similarity than actually exists, basing the inference on perceived similarity. Thus role-playing, for example, becomes a powerful tool for the group. The group member who volunteers to role-play another's parent may at first say figuratively, "I am playing at being your mother," but this frequently changes to "I am playing our mother," and then to "I am playing my mother who is like yours." Freud, who was a basic pessimist about human nature, tended to attribute helping behavior to self-interest, and we see here that he gave us the conceptual tools—which he himself did not use in this particular way—to understand patients' willingness to help each other in group as a manifestation of self-interest.

A concomitant of the above is that, as with intimate self-disclosure, the individual must love himself sufficiently, must possess enough sense of self-worth, to offer to help another. Patients with schizophrenic adaptations may feel unable to be of help to others, and this perceived inability may allow, or enable them, to deepen their self-hate. Patients who are depressed may also find helping others quite difficult until depression begins to lift.

However, just as with self-disclosure, there is a range of behavior which is helpful. The steps taken along this range may be small early in the life of the group, and for some individuals, the steps may remain small. They still count.

Concluding Comment

In chapter 3, we suggested that one function of theory was to reduce the complexity of a group therapy experience to manageable proportions. Freud's theory of groups is not simple, but like all of his theories, it is reductionistic. Given Freud's assumptions about the structure of the mental apparatus, a few additional concepts—introjection and identification in particular—seem sufficient to account for a considerable number of group phenomena.

Nonetheless, Freud's theory of groups, as applied here to therapy groups, is a proto-theory, for it is not an exhaustive and encompassing accounting. In particular, the theory does not readily lend itself to the construction of therapist comments; it does not make it easier for the group therapist to decide what to say about what is going on. It also does not offer a theoretical language which the therapist should attempt to teach the group. And that's why it's a proto-theory: it lacks direct clinical applicability, and is a language of therapist and supervisor but not therapist and patient.

The theory does, however, offer some guidelines for types of intervention, for what kinds of things to do and to avoid doing, as in its emphasis upon treating group members equally, and in its alerting the therapists to the dangers and mechanisms of scapegoating.

The theory presented in this chapter can serve as a kind of framework, a skeletal structure, which can be translated into whatever theoretical language therapist and supervisor share. Clinical theory—which is another way of saying a therapeutic point of view—is best learned in interaction; competence in therapy comes from supervised experience, not from books. What has been presented here is a foundation. What is built on that foundation must depend upon the interaction between the supervisor and the therapist seeking to understand and to heal.

Chapter 5

Other Theories of Group Psychotherapy

This chapter briefly examines several other theories of group psychotherapy from the standpoint of the procedural problems facing the student: what to do, what to attend to, what to do with what is attended to, and when to do it. These problems coalesce into questions of interpretation of what is going on, and whether the therapist should initiate or respond to interaction, or remain silent; whether the therapist should respond to the individual or to the group; whether the group should focus on the immediate situation of here-and-now or the more abstract and distant there-and-then of individual personal history. Some comments are also offered about the type of setting in which each theory is typically taught; about the way the techniques are practiced; about the way the practitioners of each are trained, as of the late 1970s. Shaffer and Galinsky (1974) present a more detailed examination of theories of group psychotherapy.

Psychoanalytic Theories

As Grotjahn (1977) has observed, there are at least three different kinds of analytic group therapy. One involves primarily the analysis of the individual in the presence of the group, and is exemplified by Wolf and Schwarz (1962, 1971). A second involves psychoanalysis of the group as a whole, which Grotjahn attributes to Moreno but Horwitz (1977) more correctly calls "holistic" and attributes to Ezriel (1973). The third involves analysis *by* the group and is identified primarily with Foulkes and Anthony (1965). All of these approaches use the language of psychoanalysis, and tend to draw analogies, between the group situation and individual psychoanalysis which that language reflects. Theories which use terms like *transference, working through, resistance,* and *group* or *free association* are regarded here as psychoanalytic, though this classification is by no means universal.

Wolf and Schwarz

Of the psychoanalytic theorists, Wolf and Schwarz (1962, 1971) follow the analogy between individual and group psychoanalysis most closely. They view most interpersonal interactions in group as though they were transference phenomena. Wolf and Schwarz emphasize the importance of historical and intrapsychic factors, and explicitly caution against group oriented interventions or interpretations (1971).

However, Wolf and Schwarz do not advocate the adoption, by the group therapist, of the typically passive role of the individual psychoanalyst. Instead they suggest that the therapist open the first session of group by announcing the importance of speaking freely, that he mention the usefulness of reporting dreams to the group, and that he request that group members respect the confidentiality of what is discussed.

If the group is silent, the therapist might engage in a technique called "going around" (originated by Wolf), which consists of each member saying whatever enters his mind about each other member in turn (a process Wolf and Schwarz describe as "a kind of free association"). But they point out that the group therapist must also know when to remain silent himself.

In this type of group, the analyst attends to the interaction between himself and the patient, as well as to the interactions among patients. However, he does not offer interpretations of or about the group as a whole. Wolf and Schwarz regard such interpretations as technical errors, perhaps because there is no analogous type of interpretation in individual psychoanalysis. Just as the individual analyst interprets many of the patient's interactions with him in terms of transference, Wolf and Schwarz understand group interactions in terms of transference. Patient-therapist interactions are regarded as manifestations of parental transference, patient-patient interactions as sibling transference.

The analyst begins the task of understanding and interpreting what is going on in group in terms of the hypothesis that *things are not what they seem.* The patient's thoughts, feelings, and actions in the group toward another group member, or the analyst, are not really reactions toward that particular person at the present time, but are manifestations of unconscious motivations with historical determinants— transference reactions. Wolf and Schwarz acknowledge that "the search for unconscious motivations and processes leads patients away from the here-and-now and into the there-and-then, into historical determinants" (1971, p. 250).

The task of the analyst is to gather evidence that unconscious determinants are influencing the patient's behavior, and to present this evidence when the patient is likely to agree with it. The task of the analyst doing individual psychoanalysis is similar.

If the patient does not agree with the interpretation, he is said to be resisting. Wolf and Schwarz allow for the possibility of incorrect technique—interpretations may be premature—but suggest that such errors may be a reflection of the therapist's own pathology. The group does not allow the analyst's distortions of reality to go unnoticed, but may call attention to them. In this way the group offers protection to its members from the "blind spots" of the analyst. While there is no analogue in individual psychoanalysis to this protective group function, Wolf and Schwarz regard it favorably.

The group analytic techniques advocated by Wolf and Schwarz are, then, in many respects similar to those used by the classical practitioner of individual psychoanalysis. In both individual and group analysis, the interactions are predominantly verbal, there is focus on intrapsychic phenomena, and present interactions are interpreted in terms of transference. In addition, there is an emphasis on rational verbal communication in the group, with the analyst actively moderating the intensity of affect expressed or manifested in the group.

Wolf and Schwarz are careful to defend psychoanalysis in groups as being distinctly different from individual psychoanalysis, despite the similarities of the techniques, and, further, as having its own advantages. While in individual psychoanalysis the patient's transference reactions are directed toward the analyst alone, in the group there are transference reactions to other group members as well. Thus the intensity of the transference is diluted, and the patient may be able to become more objective about his transference behaviors more easily (i.e., may be able to accept transference interpretations sooner) when the tranference involves several people rather than an intense focus on a single person. The protective function of the group is also important, as is its lower cost to the patient than individual analysis. Wolf and Schwarz emphasize that treatment in depth is possible in group just as it is in individual analysis, the *sine qua non* being the exploration of unconscious intrapsychic phenomena.

Ezriel

The "holistic" psychoanalytic approach to group was developed by Henry Ezriel at the Tavistock Clinic in England following World War II. In this approach, the therapist assumes the existence of a *common group theme* or problem. All of the spontaneous verbalizations of each group member are regarded as embodiments or manifestations of the common group theme. The individual, therefore, is regarded as speaking not for himself but as a spokesman for the common group theme or tension. These group tensions result from the interplay of unconscious fantasies which the group members project upon one another.

The task of the therapist is to detect the common group theme, to present it to the group, and to clarify the idiosyncratic reaction of each individual in relation to the theme. The therapist is not supposed to respond, in group, until he knows what the theme is and has formulated his intervention. Consequently, if the therapist is asked a question, *any* question, early in the life of the group, he is unlikely to respond in any way. There will be no eye contact, no shifting of position toward the questioner, nor any other sign that the question has been heard: the therapist continues to look attentively at the group. Even apparently trivial questions—is it too warm in here, does that light bother you, is someone sitting here—will not be responded to. To an unsympathetic observer, the therapist may appear to be suffering from a disturbance in consciousness. When the therapist finally does break his silence, he addresses the group rather than any individual, and efforts to get him to respond to any one group member will again be disregarded. Horwitz (1977) has suggested a modification of this technique to allow the therapist more freedom to address individuals and to intervene at an earlier point, perhaps before he has completed his formulation of the group theme and each individual's relationship to it.

This way of leading groups is intended to foster transference. It structures the relationship between therapist and group members such that he seems impervious to them. He remains silent and unresponsive until he has figured out everything about what is going on, and he is permitted to take quite a long time to do that. He neither initiates nor responds to group interactions; but once he has decided what to say, he may interrupt whatever else is going on. Then he continues to ignore the individuals who address him. This approach is likely to provoke irrational responses from the group members toward the therapist. These responses are understood by the therapist as manifestations of transference, whether he comments on them or not. Not surprisingly, considerable dissatisfaction with this approach has been documented, along with some evidence that it is not particularly efficacious (Horwitz 1977). The Ezriel approach continues to be among those taught in England; in the United States, the Menninger School of Psychiatry is among its foremost proponents.

Foulkes and Anthony

There are many similarities between the techniques advocated by Ezriel (1973) and Foulkes and Anthony (1965). Both are variations of the same general psychoanalytic theme; both emphasize group themes and regard the individual as the spokesman or mouthpiece for these themes. They differ mainly in the emphasis placed on transference and on their willingness to deal with individual as well as group themes. Foulkes and

Anthony emphasize the discrepancy between manifest and latent group themes. At the manifest level there is interpersonal interaction, the sharing of common experiences, and facilitation, by the group as well as the leaders, of self-disclosure. But, as with other psychoanalytic theories, *things are not what they seem*. There is an underlying, latent level of interactive patterns which the therapist must keep track of. At this underlying level, the therapist is felt (by the group) to be omnipotent and perhaps omniscient. The group wants the therapist to be in charge, solve its problems, and tell each group member what to do. The group wants to be led, and attributes considerable leadership power to the therapist. The source of this power is transference rather than identification: the group members attribute authority to the therapist in a manner resonant with their attribution of authority to other (usually parental) figures in their past. As we have seen in the preceding chapter, Freud accounts for the power of the group leader through the process of identification; he comes to be regarded as indistinguishable from some aspects of the group member's superego.

Since the power attributed to the group leader in the Foulkes and Anthony model is unrealistic—as all transference phenomena are unrealistic—it is important that the therapist avoid even the semblance of exercising this power; he must avoid being directive. He must also thwart the group's dependency needs, which are similarly based on unrealistic (and unconscious) assumptions of group member helplessness and therapist power. Passivity and nonresponsiveness on the part of the group leader is thus elevated to a positive virtue. But Foulkes and Anthony recognize that there are times when therapist silence is inappropriate, and emphasize the importance of intervening at appropriate times. Considerable technical skill is required for the prudent exercise of silence, and for the drawing of accurate inferences about the latent level of group interaction from careful observation of what is manifest.

Psychoanalytic Theories: Concluding Comment

The three psychoanalytic theories of group psychotherapy summarized above are similar in their emphasis on intrapsychic phenomena—unconscious and historical determinants of present behavior—and in their tendency to understand much or all of what is going on in terms of transference. They are verbal-cognitive theories, regarding rational understanding as desirable and irrational affect as undesirable. While these three theories differ in the emphasis placed on individual vs. group interactions, on the level of activity permitted the group leader, and on the timing of interventions, these theories are more closely related conceptually to each other than they are to nonanalytic theories. Similarly, the techniques based on these theories have a greater resemblance to one another than to most of the nonanalytic techniques.

To some students, the group techniques advocated by Wolf and Schwarz, Ezriel, and Foulkes and Anthony may seem cold, barren, intellectual, and unemotional. Indeed, the student standing at some distance from these psychoanalytic viewpoints might raise the question as to why anyone—patient or therapist—would subscribe to such methods. The followers of these approaches, in turn, look down upon the nonanalytic group therapies. Wolf and Schwarz comment:

Certain group therapists who are inadequately analyzed are inclined, usually overzealously, to join one or another prevailing movement, no matter how senseless or extravagant. They are usually affect-addicts given to the practice, misperceived as therapeutic, of expressing their feelings in and out of group therapy and of advocating the ventilation of emotion as a way of life for their patients as well. They are critical of reason in themselves and others because it seems to them to be too cold, detached, and unfeeling. They idealize affect as the only legitimate vehicle for communication. [1971, p. 273]

This comment contains three components characteristic of the attacks made by proponents of various theoretical schools upon their rivals. These components are: (1) the personal problems of the rival practitioners have led them to espouse the rival technique; (2) the technique is not therapy or not therapeutic; (3) the technique differs significantly from the critic's own preferences in terms of emotional intensity. Attacks of this sort flourish in the absence of empirical data on the relative accuracy and efficacy of the various theories.

The student coming from a school with a psychoanalytic orientation into a clinical setting espousing some of the nonanalytic theories may find himself in a more highly charged emotional atmosphere than his classroom experience had led him to believe tenable in practice. Conversely, the student coming from a nonanalytic academic environment into a medical setting for clinical training (for that is where the psychoanalytic orientations are most likely to be found) may find the permissible level of emotional intensity lower than anticipated, the pace of therapy slower, and the patients perceived as more fragile. When discrepancies of this sort occur between academic preparation and clinical training, it is not unusual for the student to feel some sense of disorientation and even of betrayal. Such feelings are less likely when there is a close relationship between the academic and clinical faculties, or when both settings espouse the same theories.

Yalom

A refreshing exception to the polemics and intolerance which characterize much of the discussion of professionals about each other's theories is Irvin Yalom. A psychiatrist, he has written a scholarly and influential work on group therapy (1975). Although not a pure empiricist, he employs research findings to buttress his theoretical position and attempts to allow research data to influence clinical practice—a rare effort outside behavioral circles.

Yalom's theory uses many psychoanalytic concepts and some of the terminology of psychoanalysis. However, he does not place great emphasis on the analysis of unconscious dynamics, transference, or the development of insight. The past is important only as it elucidates here-and-now inter-personal interactions in group. The theory may be regarded as neo-analytic; Yalom describes it as "interpersonalist-integrationist" because of his focus on dyads or subgroups combined with an emphasis on group process:

Yalom describes ten curative factors in group therapy, a somewhat more complex and detailed view of what is effective than that presented here. The simpler view of the present volume—that intimate self-disclosure is facilitative of behavior change—seems an easier framework for an introductory text; those students desirous of greater cognitive complexity will find it in Yalom.

Although he offers numerous clinical examples to illustrate his points, Yalom does not get very specific about the technical operations of the group leader, the title of his book *(The Theory and Practice of Group Psychotherapy)* notwith-standing. But we infer from his descriptions and comments that he favors a rather passive leadership style, though clearly one far from the monumental impassivity advocated by Ezriel and Foulkes. Silence, for Yalom, is not necessarily a virtue, nor is a markedly active, initiating stance. He suggests attending to the group process especially when it may lead away from the "corrective emotional experience" and toward the development of "antitherapeutic group norms." He also comments that it is important not to lose sight of the individuals. Coming as he does from a psychoanalytic framework, he finds it necessary to defend at length his orientation to here-and-now interactions, and the result is an excellent discussion of the relationship between such an orientation and there-and-then material.

The student who wishes to compare Yalom's work with the present volume will find considerable overlap in point of view as well as some slight differences, particularly as to the level of activity of the group leader and the interpersonal distance the leader maintains from the group along the authoritarian-collegial dimension. A further major difference between the two volumes is that Yalom's is not an introductory text.

Behavior Therapy in Groups

At the opposite end of the spectrum from the analytic therapies are the behavior therapies. If there is any overlap between these two sets of theories, either in terms of theory or technique, it is not readily apparent. The behavioral group therapist must be active and authoritarian, and it would probably help if he were cue-emitting as well. Behavioral approaches are ahistorical; they focus on here-and-now and the immediate or short-term future (i.e., a week from now). The group focuses on concrete elements of observable behavior, redefines those elements in such a way as to facilitate change, and provides reinforcement for the patient when he either manifests change or reports its occurrence.

Among the most prolific and influential behavior therapists are Wolpe (1958, 1969) and Lazarus (1968, 1971). In addition to the excellent summary in Shaffer and Galinsky (1974), the student may find the recent work by Rose (1977) a good introduction to these theories. The student who is not well versed in learning theories will find it difficult to attempt to lead a behavior therapy group. By contrast, the student who is not well versed in psychoanalytic theories may have an easier time leading a psychoanalytically oriented group, for the very simple reason that the first several sessions of such a group are likely to be characterized by silence, so that he may have as much as a month to do the background reading.

All of the behavioral approaches require an active leader. The sessions tend to be programmatic, requiring detailed preparation by the leader. Some groups may begin with a period of deep muscle relaxation (Wolpe and Lazarus 1966). The patients are asked to get as comfortable as possible, or perhaps to lie down on pallets on the floor. The therapist then instructs the group members to alternately contract and relax various muscles until a state of general relaxation is achieved. The group members then resume their places in comfortable chairs. The relaxation period is not characteristic of all behavior therapy groups. Another part of the group session is taken up by patients reporting on problem behaviors they have worked on during the preceding week. Each patient then decides, with the therapist's guidance, what to work on during the coming week, how to work on it, and what reinforcement is available as the behavior changes. The therapist may give "homework assignments," which are usually instructions to the patient to try some new behavior. People who are shy, for example, may be instructed to initiate some interaction—such as saying hello—with one stranger during the week. The patient may be offered the opportunity, during the group session, to practice the new behavior. Other patients may be asked to play the role of "stranger" (in this instance) or of other people toward whom the patient wishes to change his behavior. The patient can then rehearse the new behavior in a relatively safe environment, and experience immediate positive reinforcement from the group for having done so. The availability of this social reinforcement, and the ability to engage in role play/rehearsal techniques, appear to be the major differences between behavior therapy in groups and in individual therapy.

Behavior therapy in groups is most likely to be practiced by psychologists, with an occasional medically trained individual developing competence with these techniques. The theory and practice of behavior therapy is most likely to be encountered by the student in psychological clinics which are part of, or affiliated with, academic departments of psychology.

Gestalt Therapy

The psychoanalytic group therapies and the behavioral therapies are the older, more entrenched, and more conservative of the group techniques. What makes them so is, in part, their acceptance by academic as well as clinical settings; graduate-level course work in one or the other of these therapeutic approaches is available to the student mental health professional in schools of medicine, psychology, social work, and nursing. Some techniques have not yet gained such acceptance by the graduate or professional schools and are taught principally in institutes founded by the originator of the theory or by his students. Psychodrama is one such technique. It is of such theoretical importance that Shaffer and Galinsky (1974) devote an entire chapter to it; yet the technique has not gained wide acceptance and the student is not likely to find himself in a setting where psychodrama is the only group technique being

taught. It is not discussed here principally for this reason.

Gestalt therapy, which has gained considerable popularity in
recent years, has not yet gained much academic respectability
perhaps in part because some of its practitioners are ambivalent about seeking it. Frederick S. ("Fritz") Perls is regarded as
the founder of the Gestalt therapy movement. It was during his
three years in residence at the Esalen Institute in Big Sur,
California (1966-1969) that Perls and the Gestalt therapy
movement gained national prominence. He died in 1970.

Gestalt therapy uses some of the language of academic
Gestalt psychology, but there is no real relationship between
them; the therapeutic techniques are not based on the experimental or theoretical work of the Gestalt psychologists. The
student interested in learning more about Gestalt therapy who
buys Kohler's *Gestalt Psychology* is in for a surprise. The
Gestalt psychologists were, principally, German academic
psychologists interested in some perceptual phenomena which
could not be explained either by the early behaviorists or by the
neurophysiologists of the 1920s and 1930s.

Gestalt therapists tend to be highly intuitive people, highly
skilled clinicians, with great tolerance for ambiguity. Highly
individualistic and spontaneous, they have not developed a
single core of theory; in this they differ markedly from the
Transactional Analysts (discussed below). Rather, the
Gestalters are as heterogeneous as the psychoanalysts and the
behavior therapists. It is probably more accurate to speak of
the Gestalt theories in the plural. Of these, there appear to be
two main streams. One is that of Perls himself (Perls 1969),
which is being carried on principally by Simkin and his asso-
ciates in Southern California and (to a lesser extent) by
Shepherd and Fagan in Atlanta. The other, a more group-
oriented approach, stems from the Gestalt Institute of

Cleveland and the works of Erving and Meriam Polster (1973) and Joseph Zinker (1977).

What Gestalt therapists seem to have in common is an exceptionally strong emphasis on here-and-now experiencing. They strive for a heightened awareness of this moment, not in isolation, but in relation to other moments in the past and to potential moments in the future. *Experiencing* is a positive virtue; talking about, instead of experiencing, is not good: *aboutism* is a bad word in Gestalt terminology, perhaps on a par with resistance in psychoanalytic terms.

The basic Gestalt technique is *counterphobic:* directing the patient's attention toward those feared or distasteful thoughts and feelings which he usually tries to avoid experiencing. The Gestalt therapists always move toward that which is repressed or feared, never away from it. Analytic therapists might search for connections between present and past fears; behavior therapists might look at patterns of reinforcement; Gestalt therapists ask the patient to intensify the experiencing of whatever the patient has been trying to avoid experiencing. A patient who says that he is afraid to start crying because he thinks he will never stop is encouraged, by a Gestalt therapist, to cry as hard as he wants for as long as he can. Of course, he stops sooner or later, and usually far sooner in a therapy session than if he were alone. A patient who is afraid to express anger because he might hurt someone is encouraged to go ahead and express his anger, with suitable precautions being taken by the therapist against injury to the group or damage to the furniture.

When the patient accepts the therapist's encouragement and permission to go ahead and experience that which he fears, the result is frequently an intensely emotional experience followed by a peaceful, relaxed, quiescent state. Cognitive restructuring and the development of insight may occur during either the heightened emotional experience or the quiet aftermath. The patient, having experienced and expressed something which he had previously been trying to avoid, loses some of his fear, sees that avoidance is not as necessary as he had thought, and thus becomes more open to experiencing.

Gestalt therapy is most commonly practiced in three ways: in dyadic psychotherapy, in one-to-one patient-therapist interactions in the presence of a group, and in groups. Perls used the one-to-one in group model. This involves a "hot seat" which is occupied by the patient who wishes to "work." The other group members sit by and watch, waiting their turn. The therapist may ask the audience to remain silent until he has finished working with the patient, and to refrain from commenting at all about the dyadic interactions. The Gestalt therapists of the Cleveland Institute tend to practice a more group-oriented approach. They may at times use the "hot seat," but will also comment directly to the group as a whole, enhancing awareness (experiencing) of the group process itself.

The student seeking to learn more about Gestalt therapy, and to obtain training in it, will probably have to do so outside of the formal training mechanisms set up by his graduate school or residency program. Gestalt therapists offer introductory workshops virtually anywhere in the world where one or two dozen people can get together, organize the workshop, and pay the fee. In keeping with the general looseness and spontaneity of the Gestalt movement, there are few organized training programs leading to certification of Gestalt therapists, though the number of such programs is increasing. The major Gestalt training centers are in Los Angeles, Cleveland, and Atlanta, with newer centers springing up in several of the major cities of America.

Transactional Analysis

Transactional Analysis (TA) is a theory which, in the late 1970s, is enjoying considerable popularity. Its major theoretical textbook, Eric Berne's *Games People Play* (1964), is still the best introduction to the theory. It reached the best-seller lists and should be read if one is to be aware of the major trends in the mental health professions today.

A typical TA therapy group resembles a behavior therapy group in several ways. Both are programmatic; the group leaders initiate and guide the interaction. There is usually a chalkboard or flipchart for the leaders' use. TA group leaders are generally active in teaching TA theory to group members and are more willing to discuss the relationship between theory and technique than are therapists of other theoretical persuasions. In both behavior therapy and TA groups, there is considerable focus on behavior change: what is the current problem as the patient sees it, what changes are desired, how might the changes be accomplished, when will they be implemented, and how will the patients know when all of this has been completed? Contracting for change is an important component of both TA and behavior therapy.

The similarities, then, include focus on present problems and immediate solutions to them, and on the systematic application of reinforcement for behavioral change either observed in the group or reported by the patient during the session. Where the techniques differ is in the amount of help the patient gets from the therapist and in the greater orientation of TA toward historical factors. TA therapists tend to rely on the patient to provide solutions to the problems which brought him into therapy. Behavior therapists may assist patients in constructing response hierarchies leading systematically but in small steps toward resolution of problems. TA therapists tend to understand the patient's current problems in terms of past learning and try to help the patient see things that way also; they encourage new learning but do not direct the new learning as systematically or precisely as do the behavior therapists.

The TA therapist going in to lead a group must be intimately familiar with the theory and must be prepared to be quite active. At times, the group may resemble a class, as when the leader teaches theory, instructs the group members, and writes their responses on the flipchart. Because the theoretical language of Transactional Analysis is extensive, capable of encompassing virtually any situation, it is possible to translate virtually any patient's comments into TA language. Of the predominantly verbal therapies, TA is probably the most unambiguous.

At least some of the appeal of TA theory stems from the simplicity of its structure and its language. It is easy to teach to groups of unsophisticated laymen, can be understood by children, and uses language which is more acceptable to people of lower socioeconomic strata than the languages of psychoanalytic or Gestalt theories. It is also powerfully oriented toward rapid and unambiguous change in painful interpersonal situations. The appeal of a theory which promises simple, fast, effective relief is not difficult to understand. It is likely that the theory delivers what it promises when it is used by skilled and talented practitioners, but that is true of most theories.

Because of its lack of ambiguity, the simplicity of its terms, and its emphasis on teaching, the technical operations of Transactional Analysis are not difficult to learn. Indeed, the technique can probably be learned more readily than any other by people who have little talent for psychotherapy. Training in TA is most commonly offered by certified practitioners or by institutes. The guild structure of the International Transactional

Analysis Association (the certifying agency), with its own seminars, examinations, and experience requirements, may make TA difficult for university departments to incorporate into their training of mental health professionals.

Transactional analysis as a therapeutic technique is practiced by psychiatrists, psychologists, social workers, and psychiatric nurses. It also attracts people from other fields, most notably the ministry, and ITAA certifies their clinical competence if they pass its examinations. The particular attraction of TA for ministers may have to do with the exhortative quality of the technique. *You can change if you want to* is a central tenet of the technique, and statements by patients in group of an intent to change are greeted like the minister greets the sinner who professes salvation at a prayer meeting.

Sometimes there are environmental and interpersonal factors over which the patient has no control. Failure to change these factors is occasionally attributed by some TA therapists to the patient's lack of desire or commitment to accomplish such change, and that is cruel. Both the potential cruelty of TA and its prayer-meeting oversimplification of human potential have recently been discussed by Kopp (1977).

Concluding Comment

There are many more theories of group therapy, as for example the focal conflict theory of Whitaker and Lieberman (1964). This brief chapter was not intended as a survey of the field, but as an introductory glance at the theories the newcomer to the mental health professions might most likely encounter or hear about.

There is considerable disagreement among various theorists. On occasion, group therapists, their supervisors, and their teachers indulge in name-calling and derogatory remarks about theories they do not practice. Such remarks seldom see print; they occur most often in casual, informal, and unguarded conversations—after class, perhaps, or in response to questions, or in the social hours at the annual meetings of learned societies. For all of their informality, however, the message to the student is clear: my theory is good, theirs is bad; mine works (makes sense, generates effective interventions), theirs doesn't. In this informal teaching about theory, the other theories are seldom presented accurately, so that the more reflective student may wonder how it is that grown men (the other theorists) could so enthusiastically embrace patent nonsense.

These other theorists do so, of course, because their theory *works for them:* it fills the functions of theory discussed in chapter 3. Close examination of rival theories may reveal surprising similarities between supposed antagonists, or may make it clear that they are addressing quite different aspects of complex group phenomena. Theories make sense within their own frames of reference, and it is only from outside the theory that some interpretation may seem nonsensical or trivial. Most theories the student is likely to encounter can generate effective therapeutic techniques and interventions, given the intelligent application of technique by a competent practitioner

These are murky waters for the student seeking truth, certainty, and effective psychotherapeutic tools. In the informal teaching of theory and technique, research supporting the efficacy of the other theorists' approaches tends to be dismissed as methodologically unsound or as trivial. Ultimately, belief in the efficacy of one's own theory and techniques, and in the foolhardiness or irrationality of any other, takes on the character of a moral creed. The opinion that those others ought not to be doing what they are doing, ought not to be calling it therapy, is ultimately a moral judgment. That is, judgment about theory comes to be based on terms of good vs. bad and right vs. wrong rather than on evaluation of its usefulness, helpfulness, and effectiveness with patients. That it is a moral rather than an intellectual judgment may account for some of the tenacity with which theoretical positions are held, and for the vehemence of the response of some supervisors when the student questions those positions.

The popularity of theories varies from time to time. The analytic therapies and the behavior therapies have proven durable. The newness of other theories makes their durability difficult to assess. Proponents of any theory seldom hesitate to tell students that rival theories are now fading. Such predictions may be of considerable importance to the student who risks years of study and effort as well as thousands of dollars to gain competence in a therapy which may pass from the scene and the marketplace. Perhaps the most important issue is not durability but the extent to which any theory helps you to become a good therapist with enough credentials so that the patients you know how to help can find you. Theories come and go; competence is never out of style.

Chapter 6

The Second Session: Procedures and Issues

The second session will probably begin like the first: in silence. The group members assemble silently in the waiting room; they barely acknowledge each other's presence; they walk wordlessly into the group room. There, they sit still, as before the first session, not looking at anyone in particular, waiting for the group leader to begin. This silence is best understood as a reaction of the group members to the newness of the situation, a manifestation of their uncertainty as to how to proceed and of their unwillingness to interact intensely with people who are still strangers. Such a silence calls for therapist intervention: letting the group remain silent is not particularly therapeutic. Later on in the life of a group silences may have a different function, and it may be inappropriate to break them.

One way of breaking the silence is to introduce new group members, if there are any. If there are one or two new members, the group leader should do the introduction. Introduction of the new patient does not involve revelation of the patient's case history. The concern of the group is likely to be about how the new patient will relate to each of the group members. Why the new patient might relate in this way rather than that is of greater concern to the therapist than to the group.

With three or more new members, however, you have, in effect, another initial session of the group. You may wish to follow the procedure for starting which is outlined in chapter 2. Each newcomer is likely to assume that he is the only one, that everyone else in the room already knows each other and knows what to do. Therefore, you should indicate that there are several new members and who they are, and then ask each person, including those who were present last week, to introduce himself.

An example of what the group leader might say in order to start the session is:

> I think we should start. We have two new members today, Pat (indicates with gesture) and Dave. I'd like for each person to say your first name, and to tell us how you're feeling right now. Would you (turning to person next to him) please begin?

The specific wording is not very important, and should suit your own style. Asking each person to say his or her name is part of the introduction of the new members. It also serves to remind the other group members of names which may have been forgotten or never learned because of the high anxiety which is characteristic of the first session.

If there are no new members, the therapist may ask for a brief verbal report from each group member at the beginning of the second (and subsequent) sessions. This serves several functions: it gives each person an opportunity to bid for the group's attention and perhaps for its solace; it allows patients in acute discomfort some opportunity to let it be known; it allows some significant event or interaction during the past week—if any—to be stated. To the group leader the survey provides some clues as to what to do next.

Instead of asking one of the patients to initiate the survey, telling his name and something of what he is feeling at this moment, the group leader himself could go first:

> I'm Meade, and I'm feeling a little nervous, and glad that we're finally getting started.

In going first, the group leader is providing a model, and the patients are likely to give the same kind and amount of information. The advantage of modeling is that it provides cues and thus makes it easier for the group members to respond. In addition, gross deviations from the model are interpretable as significant. The disadvantage of going first and providing a model is that thereby the therapist defines the verbal field, and may evoke rather less information than would have been elicited with less guidance.

If there is no modeling, typical responses fall into one of three categories: (a) a response indicating anxiety; (b), a non-committal response; (c), a response which is cognitive and not affective, like, "I feel that last week was a really good start and I'm ready to go on." Challenging such an un-affective response is not likely to be fruitful because of the high level of anxiety of the group; furthermore, such a challenge may be perceived by the group as criticism, and criticism, however gently worded, does not alleviate anxiety. The therapist's first concern must be to reduce the anxiety which inhibits interaction in the group, and to do so as rapidly as possible. Therefore, non-committal or primarily cognitive comments from patients during this initial survey of the group should go unchallenged.

After the survey has been completed—and it should include both group leaders—the group's attention should be directed toward the patient who has won the bidding for that attention. If there is one, it is generally easier for the therapist; it is harder if there have been no bidders at all and the group again has fallen silent.

How do you get the silent group moving? What on earth are you supposed to say now? *What does the book say?* The book, or at least this one, says that at this point your own anxiety is likely to be at least as high as that of the patients, the difference between you and them is that you're generally somewhat better at doing something to reduce anxiety than they are, and that this is what you should do before you go on.

You begin with some topic that has been left over from the first session, for example. Leftover topics are those which someone—either patient or therapist—has indicated during the first session would be taken up again at this time. Yet there are very few topics potent enough to hold a group's interest from one week to the next, even in a group which is cohesive and has been meeting for several months. So it is not likely that a leftover issue will occupy much of the group's time or energy during its second session. Once again, silence. It will be difficult for the therapist to avoid the feeling that he should be doing something, even when his supervisor has counselled explicitly against breaking the silence. The position taken here is that most silences, particularly those during the first few meetings, are not likely to be therapeutic, and that it is incumbent upon the therapist to break the silence if the group does not.

What begins to happen, in the flow of the experience of the group, is a sequence or patterning of events. We will label the sequence *engagement, process,* and *closure.* Engagement involves a casting about or seeking after some topic for discussion and exploration, or reaching a decision about what to do next. Process involves the actual doing of whatever this next is. Closure involves reaching some conclusion about what is or has just been happening, including perhaps the conclusion that the process cannot be completed at this time and will be resumed in the future. We will discuss each part of the sequence of group experiences below. Here, we emphasize that the issue of engagement may arise as early as the second session of group, when the group falls silent after the therapist's opening moves and the therapist must decide what to do next and how to do it.

There are many ways of beginning to engage with a group. Theory and the guidance of your supervisor are the best sources of information about what to do next, until your own experience with groups tells what works best for you. Analytically oriented therapists, and those who follow a group process model, generally make no attempt in the second session to engage with the group, and they remain silent, impassive, waiting to be called upon. Gestalters and Transactional Analysts tend to be somewhat less inactive, stating their availability for "work" or asking simply, "Who wants to work?"—and then waiting until something happens. The approach suggested here is to try to determine which of the group members is most ready (or least unready) to respond, and to invite engagement with him. The invitations are likely to be relatively easy ("Warren, what would you like to do today?" or "Martha, you look nervous. Would you be willing to tell us a little about that?" or, simply, "Ken, go ahead."). Determining which of the group members to begin this kind of interaction with is what is difficult; how to determine that is a procedural problem with which the group leader must frequently wrestle.

Determining this is but the first of many situations which will require the exercise of interpersonal sensitivity, perceptiveness, or talent (these terms are intended to be synonymous) by the therapist; it is one of the more difficult circumstances in which the novice group therapist will find himself. None of the group members have given any indication that they want to engage with the group, your cotherapist is of no help, and you do not have your supervisor's permission to allow the group to remain silent. What you face here is to some extent a phobic anticipation, an expectation of difficulty. Yet this silent, impassive group does occur in reality, although probably not as often as therapists fear it will.

As you look around the room, you are likely to see what you saw at the beginning of the first session: there is not much eye contact; people look at the walls, or off into the indeterminate distance, or at the floor, or at their hands. The room is still, except perhaps for the small movement of hand or foot that is like the twitching of a waiting cat's tail. Yet there are differences in patients' readiness to engage with you. How to find them, how to find the right door to knock on when all of the doors look alike?

The answer to that difficult question is most likely to be found in the very small, almost imperceptible cues that people emit, more or less inadvertently, through posture, gesture, facial expression, and movement. When the group interaction is verbal, changes in characteristic speech rhythms and syntax, as well as in tone of voice, may provide the therapist with hints as to the affective state of the individual or the group. In the silent group, look now at the way people are sitting. It is reasonable to assume that the person who looks poised for action probably is, and you knock first on that door. The patient who sits curled up into herself, legs crossed, arms folded, hands grasping her own arms, may be more prepared to defend than to interact. Sometimes a very slight movement of the shoulder—as though some motion was started and then inhibited before the patient was irretrievably committed to it—is all the indication that you'll get.

What therapists who are interpersonally sensitive sometimes experience at times like these involves a rather complex and swift intermix of perception, intuition, and cognition. The perceptions are most likely to be visual, and involve your concentrating on the smallest details of visible behavior. Intuition, which is subjective and potentially idiosyncratic, is difficult to describe. It generally includes perception and interpretation of one's own internal processes, an awareness of minute changes in the magnitude or location of tension or fear or arousal; it may include perception of a particular affective state and is usually not verbal. Cognition is the verbal rational component of subjective experience. Talent in psychotherapy involves integration of all of this into a verbal formulation or a behavioral interaction.

In general, the group therapist faces three major procedural problems. These are (a) what to pay attention to, (b) what to do about what is paid attention to, and (c) when to do it. The most reliable domain for the therapist to seek answers to procedural issues—what is happening and what to do next—involves the structure of group experience. Structure refers to what is going on in groups; content refers to what is being said. What Whitaker and Lieberman (1964) refer to as group process is one aspect of structure. Frequently, the therapist is uncertain as to whether to attend to structure or to content. Structure is the surer path; something is always going on in group; there is always structure. There is not always content. The therapist who relies on verbal content either has a difficult time with a silent group, or has a theory which tells him that silence is golden. Usually, the result of the latter is that the therapist is uncomfortable even though theory says he needn't be.

In the remainder of this chapter, we will describe the experience of a group session in terms of its structure. We will look at the interrelationships between structure and the decisions the therapist must constantly be making about what to attend to, what to do about what is attended to, and when to do it. Although the discussion will focus primarily on the second session of an outpatient group, we will not restrict ourselves solely to that session. A number of the issues and procedures are applicable, with little change, to subsequent sessions and, with perhaps more modification, to some types of inpatient group as well. (For more specific information about the latter, see chapters 9 and 10.)

Structure: An Overview

Structure refers to nonverbal ways of relating, to the usually unspoken "rules of the game," and to ways in which people implicitly agree to organize their shared experience of reality. The experience of living, of relating with another person or people, is smooth when there is consensus about structure, and uncomfortable when consensus is lacking, or when someone does not know the implicit rules. What the sociologists call roles, and role expectations, come under our definition of structure. In one sense, people become group members because they are experiencing difficulty of some sort with the implicit consensus about structure within their shared experience of reality. If we define structure more simply as what is happening in the interpersonal world (as distinct from what is being said), then we can say that people become patients when their version of structure differs from that of people who are important to them, or when their version of structure is painful, intolerable, or confusing.

Group therapy re-creates, in microcosm and in a somewhat artificial atmosphere, a social structure to which patients can relate, a structure which is quite susceptible, as though *in vitro,* to the patient's manipulations (and the therapist's). Clarifying the structure of experience in terms of antecedents and consequents, in terms of alternative courses of action, or in terms of the magnitude of deviance which the patient may wish to embrace or reject, may be one of the most important therapeutic tools of group psychotherapy.

In social interactions people tend to ignore structure, and frequently lack the conceptual tools to deal with it. Consequently structure, although always characteristic of interpersonal interaction, is seldom discussed. It is an exercise of the therapist's ingenuity to do so in a manner which can be readily understood by patients who may lack psychological sophistication. And it is an exercise of the therapist's sense of therapy as an art form to direct the group's attention to structural issues at a time when it is most likely to make sense to the group members.

Episodes

The group session tends not to be a unitary experience, but to fall into topics or "pieces of work" (the Transactional Analysis term, sometimes also used by Gestalters) or what we will call here *episodes*. If a group session is likened to a book, episodes are the chapters. An episode is a series of interactions which are concerned with the same topic. The interactions which comprise an episode may be verbal, nonverbal, or both; may include exercises, role-playing simulations, or spontaneous discussion; and may, in some of the more complex episodes, include all of the above. An episode is preceded by a period of casting about or deciding what to do next—what we have earlier termed *engagement*—and ends with closure. What happens between engagement and closure is the therapeutic work of the group.

Engagement

We have already described the situation in which the therapist must do most or all of the work of engaging with the group and has little help either from his cotherapist or from the group. That is the situation of the silent, cue-suppressive group. The solution suggested was to use small behavioral cues as indicators of who might be willing to respond, and then to invite or call upon that person. If the first person you call on demurs, try a second, and even a third. If you have followed the guidelines in chapter 1 on the selection of patients, the probability is very high that one of your first three tries will succeed.

However, there is always the possibility that none will, and you may get three demurers in succession. If that occurs, the next step is to try an exercise which will involve the entire group, either simultaneously, in pairs, or in triads. The exercise may either be intended as tension-reducing or as mildly embarrassing—a second initiation rite. Introducing such an exercise might go something like this:

> Sometimes it's hard for a group to get started. That might be because we still don't know each other very well. I'd like for you to turn to the person sitting next to you, to pair off, and to tell your partner one important fact about yourself. Then the other person should do the same: tell one important fact about yourself. Then I'll ask each person to tell the group his partner's name and what he learned about him or her. Are there any questions?

Some additional instruction might be necessary to get the group members paired off. If there is an odd number of people in the room, one of the group leaders should include himself in the pairings.

If need be, the entire second session might be taken up with this kind of activity, and beginning to engage individual patients might not occur until the third session.

At the opposite end of the problem spectrum from the silent group is the group which starts off with a high level of verbal activity; that is, during or immediately after the initial survey of names and feelings, one of the patients announces that she has a problem that she would like to talk about:

> My problem is that nobody likes me in the dormitory that I live in. They are all very cliquish there and they all know each other from high school. I try to be friendly with them but they just ignore me. I don't know why.

What follows, in such a group of college students, is a discussion of dormitory life. The group agrees that dorm life is difficult, that people are unfriendly, and that roommates, in particular, are hard to get along with. The conversation might then go on to other familiar gripes about college life: the food, the unfairness of the professors, difficulties in relationships with parents. Depending on your theoretical orientation, this type of verbal material is either rich or sparse. If this is your second session as well as the group's, you are likely to feel so relieved that the group is not silent that you don't really care about whether what's being said is the theoretically right kind of thing.

Usually, when a group takes off like this in the second session (and sometimes in the first as well), nothing much comes of it in terms of behavioral change. The conversation is most likely to be social discourse, not different from the superficial, polite, and conventional talk which strangers or acquaintances engage in to while away the time. The function which this kind of talk serves in a therapy group is to allow the group members to become better acquainted, and less fearful of each other and of the group as a whole.

Generally it will not be regarded, by one's theory or one's supervisor, as a technical error to remain silent while this kind of conversation goes on. We know that sooner or later the conversation will end: sometimes with a conclusion, a feeling of closure, but more often with a kind of dwindling into silence like the flame on a match which gets smaller and smaller and then disappears into a wisp of smoke. How long it takes to reach that point will of course vary; in a really talkative group, it may take several sessions. But what is important is that almost always the less active the therapist is in the early sessions, the higher the probability that when the group does begin its work the atmosphere will be hostile. Waiting until the group has decided that it wants to do something more than engaging in social discourse has the advantage of leaving the responsibility for its choices—including the choice of getting into therapeutic work—with the group itself. But waiting that long has also the disadvantage of taking up a significant amount of time. The dilemma for the therapist is whether to intervene in a conversation in which everyone appears interested, or to wait until the group members themselves either lose interest or realize that what they are doing is not fruitful in terms of why they are there in group.

The first step in resolving this dilemma is to ask your supervisor. If that's not feasible, consider what would be congruent with your supervisor's theory. A third alternative, and the one favored here, is to define social conversation in the first few sessions of group as a means of avoiding interpersonal engagement. Since you are here for exactly the opposite reason, you should intervene as soon as practicable so as to help the group through the process of engagement and into the work of an episode. The amount of anxiety reduction and enhanced cohesiveness which results from social conversation in group is simply too expensive of the group's time.

The particular form of intervention must, of course, depend upon the particular circumstances, group composition, and therapist personality and style. Sample comments include, "This is interesting but it isn't what we're really here for," or a simple, direct "We're wasting time," which disparages, however, whatever genuine interest and commitment there may have been in the conversation, or "I wonder what the difference is between what we're doing here now and what we would be doing if we had met socially outside of group?" However it is said, the result of the intervention is most likely to be a sudden silence. What happens next is likely to be closer to the process of engagement.

At a midpoint between the silent group and the talkative group is the group in which there is a series of one- or two-sentence statements by several individuals, in fairly rapid succession, but with no apparent or real relationship among them; the comments are sequential in time but not in meaning. This is, in effect, a series of one-to-one interactions, usually patient to therapist, but occasionally between patients. Some of these comments may be a kind of whistling in the dark, saying *anything* in order to avoid silence; other comments might be a bid for the therapist's attention, or the group's.

Structurally, what the group is doing is skimming lightly over topics and people, with the spotlight of the group's attention not staying in any one place for more than a moment or two. This kind of verbal skimming, which we are describing as occurring early in the second session, may occur later in the life of a group as well, either at the beginning of sessions or between episodes. The problem for the therapist is in deciding which of the patients' statements to respond to, or make some effort to pursue in more detail, or whether to respond at all.

When there is a series of interactions which follow one another temporally but not logically or associatively, the sequence is unfocused, and might be viewed by those with psychoanalytic inclinations as a group analogue to free association. From that point of view, the correct therapist response is to wait, remain silent, until the underlying thread of meaning which connects the apparently unrelated associations has become visible. When you follow this strategy in the second session, what will usually happen is that these comments will peter out, a lengthy silence will occur, and the next interactions will probably be hostile. But it is better, we think, in the second session at least, to intervene, to pick up on the topic most likely to get the group where you want it to go. Topics which are most likely to help move the group toward the establishment of an atmosphere of warmth and supportiveness are those which involve interaction between group members here-and-now, about something that is happening between or among them at this point in time. Whatever topic you choose, at this early stage, is less important than *choosing;* your task at this point is to help the group to engage, settle on a topic, and begin its work.

There are many ways to do this. One is to say something like, "I'd like to stay with this topic for a bit. Dennis, you mentioned last week that you had sold your car and I wonder how you felt when Jim said just now that he bought one just like it?" If the spotlight moves on too quickly, it is sometimes necessary to move it back to where you want it:

> John, I'd like to hear more about your new girlfriend, but first I'd like to get back to what Dennis was saying about selling his car. We'll come back to you in a few minutes.

Probably the worst thing that could happen at this point is that you choose a topic that no one is particularly interested in, it peters out where you had hoped that it would flourish, and people may briefly experience some faint boredom. The consequences of a wrong choice are clearly not momentous, and you will have ample opportunity to try again. The best thing that could happen is that the group begins to actively pursue the topic you have guided them toward, they work as intensely as a group can during the second session, you feel bright and competent, and your supervisor smiles at you and remembers your name.

We have described some aspects of the process of engagement with groups ranging from silent to active. When the relationship between successive interactions in group is clear, the flow of experience is smooth, and the chain of associations is easy to follow, it is evident that one comment is a response to the one which preceded it, and a stimulus to the one which follows it. When the group devotes its attention to a single topic in this manner, its experience is focused on that topic. An episode is a series of focused interactions. The group is engaged when the series of focused interactions has clearly begun.

Process

How the group does its work—or, more accurately, how you conceptualize the way the group does its work—depends on the theoretical model you are following and the technique you are trying to learn. In TA and Gestalt groups, work begins when a contract between patient and therapist to "do a piece of work" is established. In psychomotor groups, the process of engagement is played out between the individual and the therapist, and when that process is completed, construction of the psychomotor structure (the unit of work in this technique) can begin. In psychodrama, there is a rather analogous process of engagement and construction of a living tableau in which role-playing occurs. And so on. Each theory, each technical approach to group, has its own terminology for its unit of work.

The goal of the work of an episode is to facilitate change in behavior. As we noted in chapter 1, change in behavior is frequently (although not always) preceded by intimate self-disclosure. The tasks of the therapists include facilitating intimate self-disclosure by establishing within the group a safe and supportive interpersonal environment, providing the group with some conceptual tools with which the relationship between intimate self-disclosure and change in behavior can be clarified, and keeping the group's attention and level of emotional intensity at a point where these things can occur.

During the process of an episode, one problem confronting the group leader is whether to attend to individual interaction or to the group as a whole. To some considerable extent, theory and the group supervisor will offer guidelines. Those techniques which are not group therapy at all, but the practice of individual psychotherapy in public, direct the therapist's attention toward individual interaction and away from the group. Even within this type of technical approach to group, there is considerable variation in the application of techniques. Some Gestalters, for example, attend to group as well as individual processes. Thus, the technique itself need not be a definitive determinant of the extent to which the group leader focuses on individual interaction or on the group as a whole.

The quandary facing the novice therapist is that of determining the extent to which he should attend to individuals, one at a time, as opposed to attending to the group or allowing the group to address itself to a particular individual. The more experienced therapist and supervisor will have already determined for themselves the answer to this kind of question. What is suggested here is that the issue of individual "work" vs. group work resides in, and is ultimately resolved through, personality factors more than through technical or theoretical approaches. That is, you do what you are most comfortable with. In a new situation, it is difficult for you to know beforehand what you are going to be comfortable with, and that sense of your own comfort is something which will evolve as the situation progresses and as you gain experience.

The tendency of the novice is to confront this aspect of process rather ambivalently. On the one hand, what you are used to doing, know how to do, and are relatively comfortable with is probably some form of individual psychotherapy or counseling. On the other hand, you know you are in group, and that in group something different is supposed to happen than in individual therapy. The issue is, how far do you go with an individual in group, how personal do you get, how intense do you allow the interaction to become before acknowledging that there are other people in the room and that they must be attended to?

The answer offered here (by no means the only answer, nor the only correct one) is that a group experience, an episode, should be as much a unitary experience as possible, and should involve the entire group, even when that involvement is nothing more than attentive interest. When other people in the group seem bored, listless, restless, impatient, stoic . . . it is possible that you have delved too far into idiosyncratic material that is neither of interest nor of use to the rest of the group. Losing sight of the group is easier than losing sight of the individual; losing sight of either fails to lead toward or maintain an atmosphere in which intimate self-disclosure of intense emotions can take place.

If there is little in the interaction of one or two patients that is applicable to the group, the group begins to lose interest, cohesion is diminished, intensity is low—except perhaps for the individual who is in the spotlight. If you find yourself in this kind of situation, or beginning to get into it, one way out is to simply shift the spotlight by asking other members of the group how they feel about what the individual who's been in the center has been saying. Another is to suggest to the patient that what he is getting into might better be explored in individual therapy—where it can be explored in greater detail than is possible in group.

The Gestalt technique of dream interpretation leads the therapist readily into getting too much into material that is neither of interest nor of use to any other group member. (The Gestalters themselves take the position that other group members benefit vicariously from this intensively individual focus—see Simkin 1972.) A number of other technical approaches also facilitate getting in too deeply with one individual—techniques which reflect the assumption that group psychotherapy is really little more than individual therapy in public.

We believe that group therapy is considerably more, and is quite different from, individual therapy. From a phenomenological viewpoint, dwelling on non-generalizable idiosyncrasies leads to a lot of dull, boring hours for other group members. While group is not an entertainment, it ought not to be dull. From the viewpoint of Freud's theory, as described in chapter 4, dwelling extensively on the minutiae of one group member to the detriment and boredom of the others is an error, since it reflects favoritism by a group leader who should love all group members equally.

On the other hand, many times it is quite fruitful to explore the experience of one individual in some detail. Such explorations are most likely to be fruitful when (a) the verbal content of what is being discussed involves experiences which are not uncommon, and with which other members of the group can at least empathize; (b) what is being discussed pertains to the individual's present life, present circumstances, issues he is currently dealing with; (c) what is being discussed pertains to what is happening here in this room now—that is, the feelings of one group member about another, or others, or the group as a whole. Intimate self-disclosure is always a here-and-now phenomenon, and in this sense is different from a confession, which pertains to the past: *Here I stand* is a more powerful and compelling statement than *there I stood.*

Group leaders whose personal preferences involve maintaining a focus on here-and-now may find themselves inexorably drawn into there-and-then, slow, low-key interactions. A phenomenological approach may be helpful at such times: there isn't really any there-and-then, there is only here-and-now, and a patient dwelling upon the past is doing so in the present *for present purposes.* Even the recounting of dreams in group can be understood in terms of the individual's pattern of relating to the group-as-a-whole at this time and as a means to some present goal.

This situation, of a patient recounting a dream in group, serves to highlight once more the dilemma which group theorists and therapists have been struggling to resolve virtually since the beginning of group treatment: whether to focus on the individual or on the group. A student of Gestalt (as distinct from an experienced practitioner, who may be more flexible) would focus intensively upon the dream, ignoring the group process; a group-process orientation would lead toward a more rigid here-and-now orientation, focusing on the effect of re-counting the dream upon the group, and ignoring the content of the dream. What we advocate here is to delve as far into the dream as seems of general interest and application, and leads to some point of closure with the dreamer. (Usually, in dream work, there are a number of quite legitimate stopping points.) Then, in order to bring the episode to a close, the group leaders should shift the focus back to the group, to the effect on the group of the dreamer's recounting.

The group leaders control the spotlight of the group's attention. If the leaders follow a model of therapist impassivity, they may allow the group, or some of its members, to control the spotlight, and determine what the group will focus on and for how long. It is better when the group leaders actively control the spotlight so that the group does not divert attention from what needs to be done. Within each episode, the group leaders should attend to the three focal points of group: the leaders, the members, and the group as a whole.

Before leaving this discussion of process, one additional point needs to be made. It is that in any textbook dealing with the technique of psychotherapy—individual or group—there are necessarily a lot of sentences which start with the phrase *the therapist should*. The present work is, alas, no exception. The novice mental health worker, and the aspiring graduate student, may find the list of *shoulds* so long that attainment of the status of therapist seems out of reach. The picture of the therapist which emerges is of someone impossibly wise, unimaginably intelligent, unfailingly kind, the epitome of virtue, and the reincarnation of Hippocrates.

Therapy *is* a complex art. There *are* a lot of shoulds. No one knows, let alone remembers, all of them. Sometimes a therapist will know what he *should* do, and be uncertain of how or when to do it; that is true of experienced as well as novice therapists. At best, you are going to be considerably less than perfect. Aspiring to perfection is one thing; thinking that you have to be perfect before you're any good is something else. You're probably going to do less well than someone with more experience; that doesn't mean that you'll be ineffective. If you allow your own humanity and humaneness to prevail, the inevitable errors in technique are likely to be forgiven by your patients and ultimately by your supervisors.

Closure

Closure is the conclusion of an episode. It is the feeling or awareness that this "chapter" has ended, that the "piece of work" has been done, that the process has been completed. In groups where therapists work one-to-one with patients, closure is the point at which the patient leaves the "hot seat" and returns to the outside of the circle. It is the point at which contact is released, the final measures or coda of a movement of a symphony.

Reaching closure involves coming to a conclusion, and then tying any loose strings that may have been left during the process of interaction. Sometimes the conclusion that is reached is that a particular topic cannot be further pursued at this time, that the patient has to go out and think about what has happened, or to try to make some changes in his behavior or his environment before pursuing the topic further. That kind of agreement is as valid as any other as a kind of closure, an ending of an episodic process.

After closure, there should be a pause before beginning the engagement process again. If the work which was brought to a conclusion was brief or of low intensity, the pause need not be more than a moment or two; if the work was intense, the pause should be longer. It is the pause between movements of a symphony, and should have about the same duration. At times, patients are eager to begin their own work or to shift to a topic of their own choosing, and they may intrude on the pause after closure with another patient. Ask them to wait. Therapy is an art form, and has its pauses as any art form which occupies time rather than space must have.

Closure is one of the ways episodes may end. Others are:

1. When there is an interruption in the flow of experience of the group session. Sometimes time runs out and the session must end before closure is reached. On occasion, there may be

other interruptions, such as a phone call or message which must be responded to by the group leaders, or a group member. A different kind of interruption, and a more significant one, is the intrusion of a new topic before the old one is really finished. The group leaders are then faced with the sometimes difficult choice between insisting on reaching closure or some other resolution of the old topic, and allowing the intruder to seize the spotlight. The general principle of the Gestalters would probably be to go with the energy, to allow choice to be dictated by whichever topic is most potent. In general, they are right. But sometimes it is necessary to protect a less potent, less intense interaction until it has played out. For example, a bland, reticent, low-key patient may have the spotlight, working slowly but as rapidly and intently as it is possible for him on some issue of little importance to the group, when some verbal bickering erupts between other group members. Making sure that the group stays with the low-key episode until it is concluded is the correct response here from the standpoint of theory presented in the preceding chapter. The group leaders must "love" all the group members equally, the less interesting as well as the more vivacious.

2. When the topic is dropped without reaching closure. One reason for dropping a topic is that the group reaches an impasse (also a handy Gestalt concept), and either cannot or will not mobilize sufficient energy (interest) to break through it. Another is that the individuals involved in the interaction may choose not to pursue the episode to closure. This occurs most frequently when such pursuit would result in a greater degree of intimate self-disclosure or a higher level of emotional intensity than the members involved in the interaction are ready for at that time.

3. When a topic just peters out, dies for lack of interest, dwindles to silence. This type of ending, which is somewhat

more common early in the life of a group—and early in later group sessions—marks a minor theme or episode, never a major one. The quality of the subsequent silence is similar to that of the silence following closure: it is the pause before the taking up of a new chapter.

After closure has been reached and the group pauses, there is a period of transition; the group is between episodes. In later sessions people shift positions, stretch, yawn, refill their coffee cups. In the earlier sessions, there usually is too much background anxiety for much motoric movement to occur during the transition from one episode to the next.

The engagement process which now follows may be regarded either as part of the transition or as part of the next episode. Sometimes the process of engagement is longer; the group is casting about, the spotlight is wide and searching. Sometimes there is more immediate entry into the process of an episode; occasionally a group will get stuck in the engagement process. The amount of work the therapists have to do to help the group through the transition from one episode to the next generally decreases markedly after the first two or three sessions.

Sequence of Episodes

In the first few sessions of group, there is probably no relationship between one episode and the next. Closure is achieved, there is a transition period, and then the group begins to seek to engage again. After the third or fourth session, the sequence of episodes generally stops being random. The verbal content of successive episodes may appear unrelated, and the interactions may center around different people; yet, as the group leaders listen, observe, and interact, a pattern of sequential episodes may begin to emerge, each of which is complete within itself.

This is not to suggest that *things are not what they seem,* and that a discussion of real estate (for example) may really refer to the impending vacation of the therapist (Whitaker and Lieberman 1964). One task of the therapist, whether in individual or group therapy, is to help the individual or the group to bring into central awareness that which was at the periphery of awareness—dimly sensed, almost lost, half-formed. The group members may themselves sense that there is some underlying connection between episodes. Seizing and acting upon this awareness constitutes an exercise of the technical skill and expertise of the group leaders. If the group members could do it themselves, they wouldn't be in group.

At what point do you begin looking for underlying themes? In terms of time, a good rule of thumb is about halfway through the second group session. You will have to discover for yourself what signals will alert you to look for some underlying theme or continuity in a series of apparently unrelated episodes. If you work primarily intuitively, then it is going to be a feeling—a feeling that things are not quite making sense, a feeling that the group is skirting some issue, a feeling that the interaction is heavier, stiffer, more difficult than the verbal content would justify (but this is rare)—a feeling that *something else is going on.* If you function primarily on a cognitive level, you'll be looking for a set or sequence of cues along some cue dimensions—and probably not those which are most obvious, such as tone of voice, posture, verbal content, etc. Until you learn what your own rules are for attending to group process issues, what signals alert you, a safe rule to follow is to hypothesize that once the introductions are over and the group has begun its work for that session, all episodes are related. Part of your task as group leader is then to formulate hypotheses as to what the underlying theme might be. The hypothesis which seems to account for most of the data in the most parsimonious manner should be offered to the group.

Note, again, that a therapist intervention of this type is *not* of the general form, "things are not what they seem." That formulation denigrates and emasculates the validity of the group's experience. Rather, the therapist intervention here is of the general form, "in addition to what we've just been talking about, something else is going on." The experience of both the group and the group leaders should, if the interpretation is correct, contain an element of feeling that something which was on the periphery has now been made central. The response of the group will generally be something like, "Oh, yeah, I see, now that you mention it," while the subjective experience may be somewhat akin to the "aha" experience which some Gestalters describe as insight.

It is not always possible to discern the patterning of a group session, and sometimes it is possible to discern it, but not possible—or desirable—to point it out. If the underlying pattern involves an intensity of emotion—either positive or negative—which the group is not yet ready to deal with, then wait. As a rule, a group is ready to deal with intense emotion—particularly conflict between group members—only when some resolution of the conflict seems attainable.

Therapist interventions of the general form, "something else is going on," are probably the most difficult to make. Such interventions are seldom made by novice therapists, especially when the cotherapist is a supervisor or has more group experience. They are the kinds of interventions that you have to be pretty well buttressed by theory to make (see chapter 3), because what you're doing is making a number of inferences based in part upon theory and in part upon the sequence of episodes, and the relationship between your interpretation and your own awareness of immediate sensory input may be very tenuous indeed—as though you were making an interpretation *almost* out of thin air. Failure to take a risk of that magnitude cannot be considered a technical error or shortcoming on the part of anyone with less than a year's experience in doing groups.

The purpose of making this type of intervention—pointing out the underlying themes and the connection between episodes—is to make available to the patients information about structural influences on interpersonal interactions, information of which they may have been only dimly aware. *The underlying themes which relate episodes in a therapy group constitute evidence of structure underlying group interaction.* Such a structure is more readily available to the group's attention than is the structure underlying interpersonal interactions in the social world *in vivo.* The clarification of the relationships between this underlying structure, and the content and interactions within those episodes which comprise the group experience, may enable the group member to see more clearly the relationships between antecedents and consequents, the way some choices become easier than others, or the magnitude of deviance from the unspoken consensus about structure which he may wish to correct. In sum, the clarification of the underlying structural themes of a group session provides the group member with a new source of hypotheses accounting for and predicting interpersonal behavior.

As a group continues to meet, it generally becomes easier for the therapists to identify the underlying themes which successive episodes have in common. Work on the underlying themes continues, however, to be more difficult than work on themes that are overt. The difficulty stems largely from the degree of abstractness and the intangibility of the structure. Sometimes a major part of the mental work the therapist must perform involves identifying the underlying themes and then presenting them to the group in a way which makes them less abstract, more tangible, and so susceptible of examination and resolution.

At some point, this infrastructure begins to persist and to last more than one meeting. After a group has been meeting for some months, it is sometimes possible to characterize the major themes, including the themes of the infrastructure, which this particular group is concerned with. The themes which transcend group sessions and are prominent and persistent enough to characterize a group's entire life span will generally be found to include those interpersonal problems which most people in our culture struggle with: themes of love and hate, of intimacy and tenderness, of power and control, of pride and fear, of need and deprivation, of survival. Each group concerns itself with some of these themes—seldom with all, and the varying emphases it gives various themes are what make each group unique.

These themes are not themselves the underlying structure of group; they are in a sense the content, the concerns about which people evolve structured ways of relating. When those ways of relating are unsuccessful, they may be called symptoms. For the group therapist, a symptom is a behavioral pattern in interpersonal relations; defining symptomatology as indicative of an intrapersonal disease process tends to deflect the therapist's attention, and the patient's, away from the interpersonal environment of the therapy group.

Concluding Comment: On Timing

Our main concern in this chapter has been with the three major procedural problems facing the group therapist: what to pay attention to, what to do with what is attended to, and when to do it. All of these issues involve timing. Timing is a critical variable in therapy, difficult to teach and to learn, yet central to the effectiveness of therapuetic interventions. Poor timing robs a potent interpretation of its impact.

Good timing helps to make a group session an experience of artistry. A sense of timing, in group therapy, is learned by trial and error more so than in individual therapy. The task of the supervisor is to help the student to see that errors in timing are not fatal and that the course of events may be slowed but is seldom stopped by poor timing. The artistry of therapy is knowing when to work hardest at helping patients to find what is true.

Chapter 7

The Cotherapist Relationship

In chapter 1, we discussed briefly some factors relating to the choice of a cotherapist. In this chapter, we will examine some aspects of the relationship between cotherapists which are likely to be of particular concern to the novice.

It has been assumed, more or less implicitly, throughout this book that groups are, and should be, led by two therapists rather than by one. Cotherapy is viewed by a number of people as desirable only in training situations (Davis and Lohr 1971, Berne 1966), and the psychoanalytically oriented workers in particular warn against countertransference and competitiveness between cotherapists (MacLennan 1965).[12] Yalom (1975) is in favor of neophyte therapists of equal status doing groups, while Berne favors the novice functioning as assistant therapist with his supervisor—what is also recommended here.

As we saw in chapter 1, the ideal is a short group with your supervisor as cotherapist, followed by a longer group with a

12. The author is indebted to Judy Southerland for making available to him her excellent review of the literature.

friend—of equal status and experience—as coleader. Thus, your first experience as a group leader should be in the position of assistant therapist. Usually, as an assistant, you go through four distinct stages. In the first stage, you will feel in awe of your cotherapist, who appears confident, relaxed, knowledgeable, and infinitely resourceful, and you yourself will feel quite puzzled as to what to do or say, are nervous or anxious, and feel utterly unable to come up with any comment worth uttering. Some beginners get into a vicious cycle of feeling incompetent; they upbraid themselves because they are silent; because their cotherapist does all the work, leads the group, and does so without any help.

In the second stage of such an assistantship, you begin to have some idea of what cues your cotherapist is paying attention to, begin to see what he does with them, and, toward the end of this stage, may be able to predict approximately what he will say or do. Post-group discussion facilitates this process, and videotape, if it is available, allows you to focus in some detail on the relationship between what your cotherapist perceives as happening in group and what he does about it. As you begin to feel that you have some idea of what is going on, you may find that you are talking more, and if you are an especially bold person you may even initiate some interaction. If you tend toward being intropunitive, however, you may still upbraid yourself for not carrying your share of the load.

Implicit in these first two stages is the notion that everything that your supervisor-coleader does is *right,* and is done with a skill and flair and ingenuity which you cannot ever hope to match. If your supervisor has had a great deal of group experience, the perceived unattainability of his level of competence is likely to be greater than if he has only two or three years of experience. The tendency of novice therapists is to forget that it takes time, effort, and a great deal of supervised experience to develop skill and smoothness in group therapy. It can be painful and frustrating to have to learn to walk when your supervisor is loping along, graceful as an antelope, and apparently without effort.

In the third stage you see what needs doing, formulate how to do it—what you want to say, and to whom—and then hesitate until your cotherapist goes ahead and does it. At first, your cotherapist goes ahead because he's faster at seeing what to do—or, rather, because it takes you longer to get there than it does him. Or you find that you're getting there at about the same time, but it is as though the words stick in your throat: what if you said the wrong thing? With your supervisor as cotherapist, the consequences of saying the wrong thing, or of sounding *dumb,* might be serious, since he also is evaluating you and his evaluation may have considerable bearing on your life. Low self-confidence, uncertainty, and cautious weighing of words before speaking may become magnified, with the result that you become even more hesitant than usual (or, if you're not usually hesitant, you find yourself being so now) and you have another opportunity to upbraid yourself for lacking all of those qualities which your supervisor possesses in abundance.

Here again the post-group discussion is an essential component of learning how to do groups. As we said in chapter 6, a lot of paragraphs, in treatises on technique, begin with *The therapist should.* Here, there is *The supervisor should—.* The supervisor should be supportive of the "assistant therapist" and should encourage the development of self-confidence. In the post-group discussion, the supervisor should encourage the student to take risks, and perhaps should explore with him some of the consequences of saying the wrong thing. Students frequently anticipate catastrophic consequences of errors in timing, in conceptualization of what is going on, and in the application of technique. Errors are seldom catastrophic when you work on a short-term basis with outpatients. If your propensity for making catastrophic errors were as high as you fear, you would probably not have been admitted to the program of clinical training you are in. Your supervisor knows these things, and these also he should communicate to you, as frequently as necessary, during the post-group discussion sessions.

The fourth stage is one in which you are initiating interactions, are guiding the group at least some of the time, and find yourself working with, rather than passively assisting, your cotherapist. You are perceiving what is going on and what to do about it quickly enough that your cotherapist can now afford to wait for you to formulate and take appropriate actions. And then there comes the time, in the post-group discussion, when your supervisor says something like, "I'm really glad you did what you did with Joan. I hadn't seen that, hadn't thought of that, and you did really well." You are adding your voice and your skills to his, at least some of the time, and you may begin to feel that you're carrying your weight. You may still feel utterly lost at times, but the sense of being able to at least know what is going on and what your supervisor-cotherapist is likely to do next prevails.

How long it takes you to get through these stages depends in part on the group, in part on your supervisor, and in part on you. If the group is a good one, verbally active, not too hostile, not too intense, and without a great deal of psychopathology, it will be easier than if these characteristics do not obtain. If your supervisor facilitates learning as well as healing, he will gradually relinquish his senior position, and will not only allow you, but will help you, to grow. And if you have talent and your self-esteem is not pathologically low, you will find it possible to take risks and thus build self-confidence earlier than if you had little talent and risk-taking were therefore associated with failure. To get from stage 1 to stage 4, from silent awe to cotherapy, frequently takes about a school year. It may take you less time, or more. In any event, the pace is not solely dependent on you. Doing two or three different groups during the same time does not seem to speed up the process of growth. Time is important; it takes time to integrate the complexities of a therapy group in such a way that they become manageable and manipulable.

When the group is not a good one, or the supervisor does not facilitate learning (worst is a supervisor who is competitive), or you are convinced that you have been admitted to the training program through some quirk of fate or clerical error and that your best hope of getting through lies in your remaining as silent as possible, you will learn less, and you will go through these four stages more slowly. Particularly if your supervisor is competitive, or too narcissistic to allow you your own space in group, you are unlikely to get to the point of doing cotherapy, of being truly a cotherapist. And that's a shame. However, these four stages are not a necessary part of learning how to do groups. If your first experience is with an equally virginal cotherapist, you won't go through them at all; you'll have a different set of problems. The issues of growth in technical skill and in self-confidence will be experienced differently and perhaps more slowly. But sooner or later you're likely to end up at the same place, having survived one group and ready to do another.

Political Relations Between Cotherapists

When you have no (or little) experience in doing groups, it is difficult to know how to choose a cotherapist because you don't know what will work: you don't have much information on which to base a decision. While there is enormous variation in the way people interrelate, there are some attributes of dyadic relationships which tend to decrease the unpredictability of how any two people will work together. These attributes might be called structural, but since we used the term *structural* in a different sense in the preceding chapter, we will call them "political." Political relations between cotherapists refer to those aspects of the relationship which are likely to be transpersonal and largely independent of technical competence and specific therapeutic techniques. Politics is what happens generally, regardless of who you are or what you're trying to do in group.

Senior-junior. Let us consider a senior-junior cotherapist pair, such as the supervisor-student, senior-junior model just discussed. (Senior is defined here as older or more experienced, while junior is defined as younger or less experienced. Generally, age and experience go together, but this is, of course, not always the case.) If we consider the gender of the cotherapists, there are four possible pairings:

	senior	*junior*
a.	male	female
b.	male	male
c.	female	female
d.	female	male

The most facilitative, or least dysfunctional pairing, is likely to be (a), because it involves the sex-role stereotype for male-female, junior-senior relationships in our culture. Same-sex pairings—b and c—lend themselves more than the others to competitiveness. This is not to imply that such pairings always result in competition, only that if there is going to be strain in the cotherapy relationship, competitiveness is probably the most likely way for that strain to show. The competitive senior therapist will most likely show how wise, skilled, and loving he is, and the junior therapist will most likely look at this kind of behavior as narcissistic, as though the senior therapist were saying "Look how wonderful I am, and love me, not him." The competitive junior therapist will probably be perceived by the senior as challenging his authority; the senior therapist will most likely apply the epithet of transference, and interpret the younger therapist's competitiveness in terms of problems with authority figures.

The potentially most dysfunctional pairing is (d), because it is the most deviant from sex-role stereotypes. However, the senior female therapist may be regarded by the group, and by the male junior cotherapist, as a maternal figure who is protective and nurturant toward her younger colleague—one functional solution to the political problems inherent in this relationship. If female therapists are seen as powerful, hostile, and aggressive by the group, while male therapists are perceived as protective, nurturant, and submissive, it may take the group somewhat longer to become cohesive than if the therapists are behaviorally closer (or are perceived by the group as closer) to the conventional sex-role stereotypes. Thus, the consequences of hostile-aggressive and cool-aloof behavior are somewhat different, initially, for male and female therapists. Once the group is cohesive, the difference in consequences disappears.

Superior-subordinate. Consider the cotherapist pairings where one therapist is also the other's administrative superior. Examples include teacher-student, charge nurse-nurses' aide, and the like. The difference between this type of pairing and the preceding one is that while the preceding one primarily concerns experience and clinical supervision responsibilities, this superior-subordinate one refers to line management responsibilities not defined by clinical competence. Once again, pairings are not particularly dysfunctional if the administrative superior is also the senior or more competent member of the dyad. Again (d) has the greatest potential for dysfunction because it is most deviant from sex-role stereotypes; however, with the weakening of the link between gender and authority which is occurring in American society, the (d) pairing is less sex-role deviant than in the past and its potential for dysfunction therefore may be less.

The problem appears if the subordinate is, or is perceived by the group to be, more competent than the cotherapist-administrative superior. Then the administrative superior most likely will feel threatened, and the subordinate therapist will feel frustration and contempt. These are difficult feelings for cotherapists to discuss openly, particularly for the subordinate member when, because of the power differential, the superior may be able to influence promotions, salary increases, or course grades. (This problem is independent of therapist gender. Difficulty because of gender is not inevitable.)

One implication here is that a young therapist with little or no previous group experience can come into a therapy group and function more effectively, more competently, than a therapist-administrator with considerable previous group experience. Competence is difficult to define (and to measure!). The fact is that people enter training for the mental health professions with quite different aptitudes. Success in an institutional setting is not necessarily related to clinical aptitude, or ability, or success, and so it may indeed come to pass that a novice student with considerable aptitude for group therapy may find himself paired as cotherapist with an administrative supervisor (instructor, charge nurse, field placement director) with significantly less clinical talent. It may take several months for the differences in aptitude to become apparent. If the student is exceptionally talented, the differences may not become apparent at all.

The first question for the student is, what do you do if you perceive yourself more competent than, but are subordinate to, your cotherapist? If your cotherapist is also your supervisor, it may be best to follow the First Rule, which is survival, and remain silent. Some supervisors in this situation will recognize and applaud your talent. But it is difficult for supervisors, or for other teachers, probably, to avoid feeling threatened by students whose aptitude is higher than their own. When people feel threatened, they frequently attack. The most vulnerable point, in this instance, is your own competence, of which because you are a beginner, there is little evidence. Therefore, the cotherapist-administrator will most likely assault your competence, and you will need to do all you can to retain your faith in yourself, in your perceptions of what is happening in group, and in your ability to draw rational and realistic conclusions based on those perceptions. In this kind of situation, what you will need is some social support—from your spouse or colleagues or even from your own therapist. Clinical training may produce transient situational stress sufficiently severe to warrant entering therapy, and the support available from this source may be especially meaningful if your competence is under assault by supervisors who are threatened by it.

Another set of superior-subordinate cotherapist pairings involves role-reversal. Consider, for example, the nurses' aide who is a coleader of an inpatient group on a psychiatric ward in a teaching hospital, and the psychiatric resident physician who rotates through the ward in his first year as is likely, and is having his first major encounter with psychopathology and psychotherapy. This resident will be junior in experience and perhaps in age. The major problem is the role-discrepant behavior which the less experienced member of the pair is likely to engage in, appropriately enough, during the group session, and the carry-over of that role-discrepant behavior into the relationships on the ward. The junior therapist tends to be a bull in a china shop, and the senior therapist may seethe silently because of the potentially harmful consequences of confrontation. One way to avoid this type of situation is to refuse, if possible, to do cotherapy with people who are more experienced than you in group but elsewhere are your subordinates or juniors. On the other hand, a nurse's aid who is willing to confront psychiatric residents, when confrontation is appropriate, may have a great deal to offer, in addition to her group experience, since she spends considerably more time with the patients than the resident.

Nurturant-cold. Another way that cotherapists differ, and are perceived by the group to differ, is along the dimension of a nurturant supportive vs. a cold, indifferent, interpersonally distancing stance. There are three possible pairings here: both therapists are nurturant, both are cold, and one is nurturant and the other is cold. When both therapists are cold and aloof, there may not be much dysfunction between them, but the potential for a dysfunctional, noncohesive, hostile group is high. When both therapists are warm, nurturant, and interpersonally approaching, there may be some potential for competitiveness, especially if both are strongly approval-dependent, but this is probably the easiest pairing once the therapists have learned how to work together. When one therapist is nurturant and the other is cold, the potential for dysfunction in the cotherapy relationship is greatest. To the nurturant therapist, the cool, aloof therapist is likely to look inept, uncaring, hostile, and judgmental. To the cool therapist, nurturant behavior may look sentimentally gushing, inappropriately rescuing, and dependency-fostering. These are epithets that people occasionally hurl at each other, or comments they make to their friends or spouses, when there are such major differences. Such epithets may be more or less accurate. What happens in a cotherapy relationship, as in a marital relationship, is that small differences in the way that people relate are perceived by the cotherapists as major. Those perceptions are then generalized, usually in an unfavorable way, so that it seems that your cotherapist is not only cold and indifferent to you but also, and much more so, to the group.

In this pairing of nurturant-cold, which may also be described as affective-rational, gender is not relevant. The group will assign sex-role stereotypes. The more nurturant therapist will be assigned maternal, the less nurturant therapist paternal attributes. Even in the pairing where both therapists are nurturant, the group will pick up differences in magnitude of nurturance, and accordingly assign sex-role stereotypes. Thus, it is quite possible for a therapist to be perceived as maternal in one group and paternal in the next.

Political relations: concluding comment. Some contributors to the literature on cotherapy recommend that cotherapists should be of equal status (Rosenbaum 1971, Yalom 1975), while others (Berne 1966) advocate a junior-senior split. The student, however, is seldom able to choose his ideal cotherapist. Some cotherapist pairings work better than others because of what you are rather than who you are, and because of what you are relative to your cotherapist. The more closely you and your cotherapist approach sex-role stereotypes, the less likely you are to have to deal with issues involving sex-role stereotypes. Thus, political relations are likely to be smoothest when the senior therapist is male, more competent than you, experienced, and superior in the organizational structure. Strong, competent, active females face the greatest potential dysfunction in cotherapist relationships when they are paired with weak—easily threatened—passive males. Such men are sometimes intolerant of competence because it threatens them, and may feel particularly strongly threatened if, as sometimes happens, they confuse competence and masculinity. They also may attack. There are many ways in which a cotherapist can attack his partner; they are the ways one knows how to attack spouse, sibling, and colleague. These attacks, which may range from non-support when support would be appropriate, to verbal confrontation in the group's presence, render the relationship dysfunctional.

This discussion of "political" relations is not intended as a set of predictions. Some cotherapist relationships, of whatever nature, go smoothly from the outset. When cotherapists differ in experience, authority, and nurturance, then issues of competence, power, and responsibility, or caring, are likely to arise. These are the issues to look out for. There are other sources of stress in cotherapy relationships, and other ways that these stresses manifest themselves. If you find yourself locked in battle, or wishing that you were, perhaps a look at the relationship in terms of these "politics" will help you to account for the particular form and intensity of the differences between yourself and your cotherapist.

Interaction of Leadership Styles

In chapter 1, we described three main leadership dimensions: active-passive, authoritarian-collegial, and cue-emitting/cue-suppressive. Let us consider these from the point of view of the cotherapy relationship.

In this context, *active* means verbal activity, *passive* means verbal reticence. The three co-therapist pairings are: active-active, active-passive, and passive-passive. It is possible for two verbally active therapists to dominate the group, particularly if the group is composed of quiet or non-verbal or impassive patients. These cotherapists can become (or appear) more interested in their relationship with each other than with what is happening in the group. This seems to happen without the therapists' being aware of it, and it is not difficult to handle if supervision is adequate and competent—that is, both frequent enough and pertinent. When one therapist is verbally active and the other more quiet, the situation is potentially dysfunctional unless the therapists' expectations of each other are clear. If both are expecting to share the verbal load about equally, both will be unhappy with the unequal verbal output. If both accept that one is quiet and other more prolix, and that this is all right, problems are less likely to occur.

Perhaps it should be noted that the more talkative cotherapist is not necessairly the more influential or dominant. A relatively quiet cotherapist can have a powerful influence on what occurs during group. Indeed, there is a certain amount of sex-role stereotypy available to the group; female cotherapists may be perceived as more talkative, males as more powerful. These differences in power may be enhanced if the female therapist is in a position of lower status or power, such as in doctor-nurse cotherapists. The group tends to listen very carefully to the relatively few words uttered by the more quiet therapist, to respond more readily to his suggestions, and to challenge him less. This situation is potentially dysfunctional since the more verbal therapist may perceive himself as doing the bulk of the work while his more quiet partner gets the bulk of the credit. Issues of competence and of support come to the fore: the more verbal partner tends to feel that the quieter one should express verbal agreement more frequently, and that silence indicates non-support.

When one cotherapist is active and the other passive, or impassive, passivity may nevertheless be interpreted (by the group as well as the cotherapist) as warm acceptance and acquiescence: passivity and aloofness are not necessarily synonymous. However, if both therapists are passive or impassive, they are both likely to seem to the group cool and aloof rather than acquiescent and accepting. There has to be something to accept before acceptance can occur, and if neither of the cotherapists offers anything, then neither of them can readily demonstrate warm, acquiescent behavior. (The description of the cold distant cotherapist pair in the preceding section of this chapter fits this situation.) The converse, two active therapists, is not the same as two nurturant, interpersonally approaching therapists, since verbal activity can cover a number of spectra, only one of which involves interpersonal warmth.

If cotherapists differ greatly, such as the *authoritarian-collegial,* the result is likely to be disaster. The extreme would be a situation where one therapist wears his white coat into the group room, announces "I'm Dr. Butterfield," and sits in a chair, while his cotherapist comes in in bare feet, blue jeans and T-shirt, sits on the floor, and says, "I'm Fred, and I'm here to help." Of course, this great a discrepancy in behavior is quite unlikely, and manifest differences in approach of this sort will have been resolved before the group begins. However, conceptual differences, which are more difficult to spot and deal with, may not be greater than those underlying this caricature.

Some similarity of cotherapist leadership style is, therefore, desirable. If the discrepancy is noticeable but manageable, the more collegial therapist will probably be better liked by the group, the more authoritarian therapist more respected—provided that the level of competence is roughly similar. This dyad is workable as long as the more authoritarian therapist prefers respect to affection from his patients, and the collegial one prefers the converse. If there is much difference in level of competence, the more collegial therapist may look indecisive, the more authoritarian therapist may look arrogant, and the prevalent affect between them is most likely to be contempt.

Since a great deal of the communication which goes on during a group session is behavioral rather than verbal, cotherapist pairs which are *cue-emitting* are likely to have an easier time communicating during group than those pairs which are *cue-suppressing*. A therapist who is impassive, authoritarian, and cue-suppressing is likely to have a difficult time in cotherapy relationships unless the technique espoused by both, and by the supervisor, calls for this leadership style. A verbally active cue-suppressing therapist is one who lets other people know how he feels about what is being said through his verbal responses and not through facial expression, tone or inflection of voice, or body movement. Since the message rather than the medium is critical in cotherapy teamwork, the verbally active cue-suppressor is a workable coleadership style.

Leadership styles: concluding comment. Our earlier section on "political" relations concerned issues linked to power rather than to personality. This section, on style, is more closely linked to personality than to power. People discover, rather than choose, leadership styles. You may discover that your style lends itself readily to cotherapy, or it doesn't, or even that it does not lend itself easily to group work. An important part of learning how to do group is to learn how to function effectively within the constraints of style. Few training programs can provide the kind of flexibility and diversity of theoretical and technical approaches which will allow you to make this kind of discovery about yourself. In the United States in the late 1970s, Continuing Education workshops on group therapy techniques provide an opportunity for the group therapist to become at least acquainted with a wide variety of techniques and leadership styles, and sometimes also with the chance to practice some new approach for a brief time. The workshop format, which usually requires minimal investment by the sponsoring school or training program, can acquaint you with the range of what is possible, and thus facilitate your discovery of who you are and what works best for you as a therapist.

Cotherapy Teamwork

In this section, we will consider three ways that cotherapists may function as a team: (a) attending to the same person or the same stimuli; (b) attending to opposite, or very dissimilar, aspects of the group experience—as when one therapist focuses on an individual and the other attends to the group process; and (c) functioning at different levels of abstraction, with one taking a more concrete, the other a more theoretical stance. In any group session, both therapists are likely to find themselves in all three positions, regardless of their personal preferences and of whatever they have agreed to as a team. These three styles of collaboration, which we will term *similarity, complementarity,* and *parallellism,* are characteristics rather than inviolate contractual arrangements.

In order for both therapists to attend to the same person or the same stimulus dimension at the same time, there must be considerable overlap in their assessment of the situation and in their awareness of the possibilities of what to do next. Reaching the point where you're both working on the same thing is probably the most difficult part of the process; once there, it is possible to proceed effectively even though you may not be in agreement. Reaching that point involves a decision, usually without verbal communication, based on where you think your cotherapist is going, on your assessment of whether or not he wants you to join in, and on the subjective evaluation of your own ability to join in effectively at this time, with this patient. The situation is less critical if the focus of attention is broad, involving several group members rather than one or two; in that case, your participation is from the standpoint of one who shares leadership responsibilities rather than from the standpoint of one member of a team working toward the same goal in a particular episode of group life.

There are three ways that cotherapists can readily function as a team in focusing on the same individual or topic. (There are, of course, more than three ways. These are likely to be among the three which are easiest for the novice therapist to perceive.) The first is for both to take virtually identical interpersonal positions; the second is for one therapist to function as a moderator of the interaction between the other therapist and the patient or the group; and the third is to function as a modifier or alleviator of the interaction, a buffer rather than a facilitator.

An example of two therapists taking identical interpersonal stands is:

Dr. T.: Betsy, you looked like you were going to say something a moment ago.

Betsy: No, I was just thinking about something.

Dr. M.: Would you like to tell us about it?

Betsy: I don't want to take the group's time.

Dr. M.: Why not?

Betsy: It's not important enough.

Dr. T.: You feel that you're not important enough for us to pay attention to?

Dr. M.: Or be concerned about?

Betsy: No, it's not that—it's just that, ah, I'm afraid I'll bore you.

Dr. M.: Are you afraid that we'll be bored or that you'll be embarrassed?

Betsy: Oh, I hadn't thought of it that way. Both, I guess.

Here both therapists are working to engage Betsy in episodic
work. Dr. M's addendum to Dr. T's comment—"Or be concerned about?"—is the critical phrase, requiring rather deft
timing in order to add rather than intrude on Dr. T's question
or Betsy's answer. It is this addendum which indicates to the
group, and to Dr. T, that Dr. M is right there with him, at the
same point and working toward the same goal.

This example is not particularly dramatic or intense; it is
characteristic of the earlier sessions of a group. Later on, the
interactions can become considerably more intense, and the
cotherapy team working in tandem like this can function like
hammer blows landing in rapid succession on a patient's reluctance to engage—or on a patient's privacy, or on a patient's
defenses. Teamwork is a powerful tool. Your eagerness to
reach a particular point, to get somewhere with a patient or
with the group, can divert your attention away from how
you're getting there—away from your impact on the patient.
This sometimes happens because when you and your cotherapist are in tandem, functioning as a team and engaging
synergistically with the patient, it feels good—the teamwork,
working in harmony, the timing going well, as though you and
your cotherapist were playing a duet or performing a complex
dance together. The first time that this feeling of teamwork
occurs, that you are *together,* that you both know what's happening and what to do, is such a feeling of relief and of
pleasure (that things are happening as they should) that it is
easy to lose sight of the impact of your statements on the
patient. Such an outcome is by no means an inevitable result of
two therapists working in tandem and taking identical interpersonal stands. Because of the potency of teamwork of this
sort to influence interpersonal interactions in group, a little
extra attention to process, a little extra caution, is usually a
good idea.

One of the most useful functions of a cotherapist is to serve as a
moderator when one therapist is involved in intense emotional

interaction with a patient or with the group. Anger and sexual desire are the emotional states which are most easily handled by the cotherapist when one therapist is the target. The moderator can help the patient to explore his angry feelings without sounding defensive. The patient can usually hear the moderator more accurately, and is less irrationally fearful of retaliation since the moderator is not the target of his hostility. What the moderator does, in effect, is give the patient permission to be angry and to discuss his anger. If the therapist who is the target of the anger tries to give this permission, what tends to come through to the patient is that the target therapist does not take the patient's anger seriously: "Oh, it's all right for you to be angry with me. Let's talk about it." If you take someone's anger seriously, then you're not usually going to sanction it. One way of defusing anger which is aimed at you is to interpret it as a transference phenomenon. The therapist working alone might say, "I understand that you *feel* as though you're angry with me. In similar situations in the past, who did you feel angry with? Who does this remind you of?" The cotherapist acting as moderator can more easily move toward resolution of the interpersonal situation in the present before going on to generalize. In the following example, the cotherapists are Doug and Anne. Both are rather quiet; Doug tends to be more outspoken than Anne, who has a very soft, gentle manner. The patient is a rather aggressive graduate student named Paul. The example is fictitious but based on an actual group interaction.

Paul (to Anne): You don't like very many people, do you?
Anne: What do you mean?
Paul: I mean, you don't get very involved here. As far as I'm concerned, we're just like bugs under a microscope. You sit there and observe us and you really don't give a damn.

Doug: You're angry with Anne.

Paul: Damn right I am.

Doug: What's that about?

Paul: She just sits there, never smiles, never gets rattled, always says "And how are you feeling about that" and never says anything about how she's feeling—shit like that.

Doug: You feel that she doesn't really care, that she's just an aloof observer.

Paul: Damn right. And I resent it.

Doug: If Anne were to get upset, would you feel that she was more involved with the group?

Paul: Yeah. I'd like to see her show some of *her* feelings.

Doug: If she showed some of her feelings, would you feel that she cared?

Paul: Yeah.

Doug: So that a woman has to show her feelings—maybe show that she's upset—before you know that she cares, or is concerned about you?

Paul: Well, now, I don't, uh, I don't know about that. If she laughed once in a while that would be all right too.

Anne: Paul, I haven't found anything in here to laugh about. I *am* concerned, or I wouldn't be here. I wonder what I can do to make clear to you that I am concerned and involved, besides getting upset or laughing with you.

Paul: Well, you could pay attention when people talk, and at least look interested—I guess you already do that—you could tell us something about yourself.

Doug: What would you like to know about Anne in relation to you?

Paul: In relation to me?

Doug: Yes—what's really most important for you to know about Anne right here, right now?

Paul (to Anne): Do you like me?

Anne: Yes. There isn't anyone here I dislike.

Doug: It was because Anne is kind of quiet that you thought she didn't like you?

Paul: Yeah.

Doug: I wonder who else in your life, in your past perhaps, was quiet and you thought didn't like you?

This example shows how a cotherapist coming in as moderator can say things which would be more awkward, less effective, and have quite different connotative meanings if they were said by the target of the patient's anger. There is some resolution of the immediate interpersonal situation, in that Paul finds out, rather directly, that Anne is not angry with him as he had assumed. Once that point is reached, Doug can begin the exploration of factors which will, it is hoped, lead to the development of insight on Paul's part.

The interpersonal situation is somewhat similar when sexual feelings rather than anger are being explored. The moderator can facilitate discussion without seeming either offended or seductive. It is more difficult for the target therapist to avoid one of those positions, particularly if there is some countertransference. The permission function of the moderator is somewhat different than when anger is involved. Anger is less easily concealed than sexual desire. The moderator's disclaimer of anger in an angry interchange between cotherapist and patient is therefore more credible than a disclaimer of sexual feelings. The main difference, however, has to do not so much with credibility—that won't be a problem if the trust level in the group is high enough to discuss sexual feelings toward the therapists anyway—as with inclusion of the moderator as recipient of desirable feelings. The moderator's feelings aren't likely to be hurt if he isn't included in the patient's anger; but what about desire? With cotherapists of the same sex, there may be an implicit issue of jealousy or rivalry—at any rate, the patients may be watching for some signs of this. When cotherapists are of opposite sex, the implicit issue may be one of possessiveness, and the moderator's willingness to help explore feelings may be viewed as a kind of permission for the patient to have sexual feelings toward inappropriate sex objects. Since most of us have such feelings at times, discussion of these issues may be particularly helpful to the group.

A cotherapist functioning as buffer and alleviator rather than facilitator is working to blunt or lower the potential intensity of the interaction. This type of team function differs from that of the moderator in that the buffering therapist makes explanatory statements while the moderator invites further interaction. A buffering therapist, then, finds himself making statements of the general form, "What George (the cotherapist) meant by that is . . . ." This buffering role is listed as one in which cotherapists are functioning in a similar style because it requires both therapists to be attending to the same person or stimulus, dimension, to be in agreement about what should be done next, and to be confident enough in the cotherapy relationship to handle what is in effect some corrective action. When it is done well, buffering helps keep the episode on track, helps keep the group focused on the work it is doing. When it is done poorly, buffering saps intensity rather than helping to redirect it.

Complementarity. Therapists may agree before group starts that one will attend primarily to group and the other primarily to the individual. If you don't have much experience, you may not yet know which you prefer or even if you prefer this kind of teamwork (as opposed to similarity or parallelism). In the absence of decision, what tends to happen is that you and your cotherapist will do these interchangeably. That's all right. You may find that you prefer attending more to the individual, or to the group, or to take a complementary stand, depending on what your cotherapist is doing.

The biggest advantage of this type of cotherapist teamwork is that it allows for the range of group experience—the three focal points of group—to be covered while each therapist covers only a part of that range. It is analogous to a zone defense in team sports. If you know that your cotherapist is going to be attending to the rest of the group, you can devote your full attention to working with one patient or one subset of patients.

In this situation, the therapist who is attending to the group probably has the more difficult task. The focus is broader, there are more people to attend to, and there is little or no verbal interchange so you don't know what they're feeling or thinking; the verbal activity is generally limited to the dyadic patient-therapist interaction where the intensity or energy is. This is not to imply or assume that group is or should be a succession of such dyadic interactions, except during the early sessions. When these interactions do occur, it will sometimes be most helpful if you attend to the group rather than zeroing in with your cotherapist on the same patient or stimulus dimension.

There is always the question of how you know when to do which—when to move to a similar or a complimentary or a parallel function. There are three types of answers:

(1) do what your supervisor or your theory tells you;
(2) do what you have agreed with your cotherapist to do;
(3) do what feels right.

It is not unusual for all three of these to lead to the same mode of teamwork. If you are doing a first or second group with your supervisor as senior cotherapist, you're not likely to get into intense one-to-one interactions with patients unless a patient really takes out after you. If that happens, your supervisor/cotherapist can, and probably will, move in as moderator or buffer. If you're doing a group with a colleague and see him getting drawn—or drawing—into an intense one-to-one episode with a patient, you will ideally have discussed beforehand what to do in this situation. However, more typically, you won't have done so, and you're left in a quandary. This is the time to do what feels right. If your instinct is to move to similar functioning, go ahead; if it is to attend to the group, trust your instinct. If your relationship with your cotherapist is not dysfunctional, and you head off in the wrong mode, he'll tell you, and you can adjust accordingly.

So your cotherapist engages intensely with one or two patients, and you think, O.K., there he goes, and you look around at the rest of the group. The problems you face generally start with what to attend to, what to do about what you've attended to, and when to do it (see chapter 6). The problems are compounded by the presence of an actively engaged cotherapist. Then the things to look for which are most likely to be fruitful involve the response—or non-response—of the other patients. Boredom, empathic responses, and efforts or readiness to break into the ongoing interaction are probably the most salient things to look for. If one group member looks bored by what is going on, but the others are attentive, then his boredom should be noted. Boredom almost always involves closing off some aspect of experience; it is seldom that *nothing interesting is going on* (the most frequent rationale for boredom) but rather *I wish to block out what is going on, or my response to it*. This formulation of boredom, which is consistent with the Gestalt conceptualization, is not likely to be verbalized or (at first, anyway) agreed to by the bored group member. When one group member is bored, or two, and the rest are attentive, it may be worthwhile after the episode is over to check with that patient to determine what he was blocking out.

On the other hand, you may find that most or all of the group looks bored except for your coleader and the group member with whom he's working. That may be a good time to say something that will alert your cotherapist to what the rest of the group is doing. If he and the patient he's working with are into some very idiosyncratic material, they may wish to arrange to meet outside of group to pursue the discussion. If they are into an area which is at least potentially threatening to the rest of the group, and the group responds with boredom, you are both at choice point: you may wish to involve the rest of the group and deal with the threat, or complete the episode with the individual patient and then include the group. The point here is to be aware of the choices, and of the roads available but not taken.

Empathic responses on the part of patients who are not in the spotlight will take various forms depending on the content which the patient-therapist dyad is focusing on. These responses are non-verbal and may involve very small interpersonal cues: shifts in posture, in skin tone (blanching or reddening or turning blotchy, with the patient showing no other signs of emotion at all), or in facial expression. Sometimes tears will well up, and then disappear or be wiped away very quickly. The patient who sits silently on the sidelines and allows a tear to trickle down his cheek, making no effort to wipe it, is not offering a subtle cue about what he is feeling; for all that it may be genuine, it is a very strong bid for attention. Whether or not to break in on the spotlight, or to allow the empathic patient to do so, depends on a variety of factors including your assessment of the possible consequences of breaking in, or of waiting until there is some closure and the spotlight is ready to shift.

Parallelism. This term refers to a mode of cotherapist functioning in which the therapists attend to the same stimulus configurations but make very different types of comments. The differences lie in the level of abstraction at which interpretations are made, not in varying interpretations themselves. Some Transactional Analyst cotherapists work in this way, with one therapist engaging with the group, while the other writes on the blackboard or flipchart. The therapist functioning on the more abstract plane relates what is happening, or has just happened, in group to the body of theory within which the cotherapists are working or (less commonly) to broader issues of society outside the group.

Cotherapy teamwork: concluding comment. It is possible to negotiate with your cotherapist on only a very small part of what will happen in group. If you are both inexperienced, then what you will be able to anticipate is of course less than if either or both of you have been there before, and there will be less that you can agree on beforehand. In some groups, the structure of the group, or of the cotherapy relationship, will more or less dictate which teamwork style you'll follow most frequently. In other groups, particularly those that you do with an equally inexperienced colleague, learning how to function as a team is like learning how to do a dance that neither of you have done before and for which you get instruction only between performances. There is no reason why the interpersonal skill with which you seek to understand and influence patients should not be applied also to the cotherapy relationship, so that you come to sense almost intuitively where the other person is, where he is going, and how best to join your efforts so that the team functions with the ease, grace, and elegance of an art form.

Chapter 8

Problems

In this chapter we will describe some of the problems the novice might reasonably expect to encounter during the process of learning how to do groups. The chapter is organized around each of the necessary components for doing a group: a room, a cotherapist, a supervisor, and patients. It is of course possible to omit the cotherapist and even the supervisor. Omission of the cotherapist deprives you (and the group) of the potential benefits of a second therapist's presence; that, as we have seen, may be a mixed blessing. Omission of the supervisor, however, raises serious ethical and, in some instances, legal issues and, for the novice therapist, is wrong.

Rooms

Unless you are in an unusual clinical setting, you are not likely to have a great deal of choice about rooms. Some rooms will be available for group, and they will be more or less desirable. A good room is one which is large enough, comfortable, carpeted, and quiet. The less institutional the room, the easier it will be for people to relax in it. Ideally, the furniture should be arranged, and the carpet thick enough, so that people can sit either in chairs or on the floor. The best rooms for groups are probably to be found in clinics which are located in houses.

A good room facilitates the establishment of the atmosphere of warmth and supportiveness in which intimate self-disclosure can occur. A poor room slows the process. In rooms which are cold and institutional and uncomfortable, people are slower to become at ease with one another and with the group. If you have a choice of rooms, you won't have a problem; you will have a problem when there is no choice: then you either will have to do group in a room which is marginally suitable, or not do group at all. If the room is poor, you will have to allow for the fact that the room will indeed make a difference.

Cotherapist Problems

In chapter 7, we discussed the cotherapist relationship. Here, we will consider dysfunctional cotherapist relationships and some things it might be possible to do about them. A dysfunctional relationship is, first of all, a poor relationship between two people. People define "poor relationship" in different ways. If you feel that the relationship is poor, then it is. It is not necessary to *justify* the feeling. It may be necessary to do something about it. A poor relationship between cotherapists inevitably affects the group. The first action to take then is to attempt to define the problem ideally in such a way that it can be resolved.

For purposes of the present discussion, we will define cotherapist problems as falling predominantly into either an affective or a cognitive realm. The affective realm centers on feelings of like-dislike, approve-disapprove, and similar feelings.

The cognitive realm centers on assessment of competence—the assessment you make of your cotherapist's competence, and your hunches about the assessment he's making of yours. Most problems, of course, contain both affective and cognitive components.

Problems in the affective realm: negative feelings. Perhaps the most difficult problem to resolve is the one in which you have no specific complaints, but have come simply to dislike your cotherapist. The cotherapy relationship is in many respects analogous to a marital relationship, even when both therapists are of the same sex. The analogue stems from the necessity of spending many hours of intensely emotional experience with your cotherapist and (to a lesser extent) from the tendency of groups to assign sex-role stereotypes to the cotherapists. Coming to dislike your cotherapist, then, is rather similar to coming to dislike your spouse.

The analogue can, however, be carried too far. The cotherapy relationship is not a marriage. The personal commitment to one's cotherapist is different from, and less than, the personal commitment to one's spouse. Within some limits, it is possible to work effectively with a cotherapist whom you dislike. (For some people, like or dislike is irrelevant to working well with another.) In cotherapy, as in marriage, difficulties occur when affective variables are more important to one member of the pair than to the other. Cotherapists who share a cognitive, task-oriented approach may not even consider whether they like each other. If they are dissimilar, however, they encounter difficulties similar to those of a marital couple where one spouse seeks verbal reassurance of affection while the other prefers to offer behavioral but not verbal reassurances. "George, do you love me?" asks Agnes after twenty years of marriage. "Hell, I married you, didn't I?" replies George. The analogue in cotherapy is, "George, do

you like me?'' and his task-oriented reply, ''Well, you're a
good therapist.''

One of the elements which makes this problem so difficult to
resolve is the reluctance of cotherapists and supervisor to
discuss or, at times, even to perceive the problem as a valid
interpersonal one. If affective components of professional
relationships are important to you, you're not likely to be very
willing to confront your cotherapist, much less your supervisor, with the statement that you dislike him. Such statements
will also seem out of place in a business relationship, and it is
always difficult to justify feelings.

But even unjustifiable feelings should be taken seriously. If
you have a need to like your cotherapist (and be liked by him)
in order to function effectively, that need should be respected
by both cotherapist and supervisor, even if neither have that
particular need. *Ad hominem* solutions, attacking the
legitimacy of the need, serve only to deepen the problem.

Therefore, if you need to like your cotherapist and you don't
like him, it will generally work out better to dissolve the relationship—or, if necessary, the group—unless the group will be
ending within a tolerably brief period. Limping along indefinitely with a cotherapist you dislike may help you to learn how
to tolerate frustration, impatience, and many other negative
feelings. That learning does not take long. The benefits of
adversity are small, however, and are frequently overrated.

The most common problem between cotherapists is disagreement strong enough to cause anger. The question is whether to
resolve the disagreement and the anger in the group's presence
or in private. The rationale for resolving it in group is that seeing the therapists resolve their differences and their anger provides a role model for the patients. The patients, however, did
not come to group to see their therapists argue or resolve their
differences. Arguments between cotherapists are generally

disruptive of group, and they are not sufficiently productive to justify either the group's time or its energy.

The question, then, is what to do when you get really angry with your cotherapist during group. When your anger has become so obvious to the group that the group cannot really continue until some note is taken of the anger, or when the resolution of the anger is likely to be rapid and satisfactory, then it is better to move openly toward confrontation and resolution. If the anger is not obvious to the group, then save your anger until later. If your anger is obvious but rapid resolution is not possible, then deal with it minimally, and work on the resolution elsewhere.

Some people, including therapists, handle anger more openly than others. If you become angry with your cotherapist during or after group, it may not be difficult for you to confront him with your anger and to resolve it. But if angry confrontation is not your style, then you are likely to have any of several rationalizations as to why you should not be confrontive. Generally, these rationalizations include the fear that the relationship will break up (usually it won't); that you wish to avoid hurting your cotherapist's feelings; that you fear retaliation; and so on. Whatever the rationalizations, you (or your friends or supervisor) may raise the question of whether or not confrontation is desirable even though it is not your usual style, for after all, a therapy group is involved, and there is some obligation to the patients, and failure to confront your cotherapist with your anger might adversely affect the group. While there are always exceptions, in general it is better *not* to try something which is not your style. If being confrontive is not your style, then it is not likely that you will do it very well; furthermore, you will risk increasing rather than decreasing the difficulties. People who are confronters do well at confronting; people who aren't, generally don't. Successful resolution need not usually involve confrontation. Finally, if you don't have a workable way of resolving your anger, you may consider withdrawing from the group. Staying on in group, and staying angry with your cotherapist, and trying to keep these feelings hidden for the good of the group may, on the contrary, adversely affect the group.

The general principle, then, is to do what works for you, has worked for you in the past, in dealing with your anger. If no way of dealing with your anger has really worked for you in the past, then withdrawing from the situation is probably the most responsible course, followed either by avoiding similar situations in the future, or by learning to deal with your anger. The latter might involve seeking therapy for yourself.

Problems in the affective realm: positive feelings. Sometimes cotherapists fall in love. Maintaining professional objectivity (indeed, rationality) about someone with whom you are falling in love is at best difficult; consequently, your assessment of any group interactions in which your loved one is involved may be clouded. In an episode, for example, in which a group member is exploring his sexual feelings toward your cotherapist and you know that she finds him attractive, it will be difficult for you to assess your responses as correctly as if you were not falling in love. Most often (though not inevitably) such uncertainty leads to defensiveness in the supervisory session, and it is usually impossible to learn anything while one is being defensive.

Avoiding such falling in love with your cotherapist may require restricting your choice of cotherapist to someone with whom you are unlikely to fall in love—for most of us, a member of the same sex; or to agree beforehand that positive feelings toward each other are an important part of the cotherapy relationship and will be discussed with your supervisor. Alas, such an agreement is likely to be honored only until the strength of mutual attraction begins to transcend the group-therapy situation and comes to involve your private life—that is, to the point where such an agreement begins to have importance. Another agreement, and one which is sometimes made only tacitly, is not to act on one's feelings of attraction toward one's cotherapist until after the group is terminated. That solution is difficult, but it is not unworkable.

In general, solutions which prohibit, devalue, or condemn falling in love with one's cotherapist are unworkable; solutions which may work, however, involve acknowledging that these things happen, that one's judgment is sometimes impaired by one's feelings, and that one can nonetheless continue to function adequately. For example, the group member who begins to explore his sexual feelings toward the cotherapist with whom you are falling in love is most likely to have some oedipal concerns, and if he does not inquire about your feelings toward your cotherapist, you should probably volunteer them. It's generally best, in this situation, to give the patient permission to continue to explore his feelings, to let him know that you like her too ("I can certainly understand why you would feel sexually attracted to her" is not altogether a cop-out), and that you will not attack or reject him for having such feelings. The situation can be handled like any other in which the patient generates strong feelings in you: you report the feelings but don't act on them. Regardless of your emotions at this point, you know that the patient is not going to act on his feelings, and it may be helpful to him to know that you aren't going to act on yours either, at least at this time.

A related problem involves sexual attraction to your cotherapist (the distinction is between seeking after a sexual companion and a life companion). Feelings of sexual attraction between cotherapists of opposite sex are not uncommon. Feelings and plans involving making one's cotherapist one's life

companion are more rare; however, cotherapists do occasionally marry.

Feelings of sexual attraction become problems in cotherapy
relationships if they give rise to seductive behavior in group.
The conventional wisdom is that sexual affairs should await
termination of the cotherapy relationship. Failure to follow the
conventional wisdom need not lead to disaster, but it generally
adds a challenge to the already complex and difficult task of
conducting a therapy group.

Problems in the cognitive realm. Problems in this domain
generally involve, or are related to, the assessment of competence. This includes the ability to conceptualize what is going
on in a manner which is fairly similar to your own, and the
application of the particular technique being learned. There
may be also a rather global assessment of the cotherapist's
competence as a person.

If your assessment of what is going on in group differs from
that of your cotherapist, it will be difficult to agree on what to
attend to, when to attend to it, and how to attend to it. Consider the following example:

Mildred (breaking a short silence): John doesn't bother me.
Diane (one therapist): Who are you talking to?
Mildred: To you, I guess.
Diane: Why not talk to John?
Mildred: He doesn't bother me.
Diane: Tell that to John.
Mildred: He heard me.
John: What?
Mildred: Nothing.
Diane: Mildred, why did you suddenly announce that John
   doesn't bother you?
Mildred: He doesn't.

John: Doesn't what?
Diane: We seem to be not getting anywhere.
Dan (other therapist): Mildred, you really like John, don't you?

Post-group discussion revealed that Dan had assessed Mildred's opening statement as one of liking or affection, while Diane had perceived it as Mildred's attempt to deny hostile feelings for John. Which cotherapist is "right" is not the point here. There is so much discrepancy in the way each cotherapist had assessed the situation that there is little probability of them functioning as a team, or agreeing on much of what happened in group after that point. Other examples might include differences in the assessment of interactions as being angry or friendly, warm or cool, sexual or social.

This example illustrates also a group interaction which isn't going anywhere—perhaps because of the therapist intervention, or because of the low interest or intensity, or because the group is virtually paralyzed by the tension between Diane, Mildred, and John. When your cotherapist comes in from left field just as you feel that you are getting somewhere, the effect is more marked:

Carolyn: It's really hard for me to talk seriously about important things. I smile and make jokes about them.
Diane (one therapist): Is that something you'd like to change?
Carolyn: Yes.
Diane: What would you like to do about it?
Carolyn: Practice saying things that are serious and looking serious when I say them and not laugh about it.
Diane: Would you like to practice that in here?
Carolyn: Yes.
Dan (other therapist): Did your parents laugh and joke about serious things?

Carolyn: My father did, and still does. I never know when he's
    serious.
Dan: Tell us what he's like.

Dan has turned the focus from a potential here-and-now interaction into one of the past—a reminiscence of Carolyn about
her father. In the post-group discussion, Diane reported feeling
that she was wrenched out of her frame of reference and into
Dan's, while Dan reported that he felt he had prevented the
group from getting into a highly artificial and frivolous kind of
interaction.

Such differences of perception may indicate either your
cotherapist's inability or his refusal to enter into your frame of
reference. A tug of war in group is not likely to be fruitful. If
you can figure out his frame of reference and try to facilitate
what he's doing, fine; if not, it might be better to back off and
wait until after group to get things clarified. But if such differences happen often, you will probably come to feel that your
cotherapist is incompetent, insensitive, or both, and you may
want to terminate the relationship.

Here the cotherapists were in disagreement about what is
going on. But cotherapists may agree about what is going on
and disagree about what to do about it. The latter usually involves a disagreement about focusing, that is, what to follow
up on.

Disagreements about focusing occur most often when one
therapist wants to focus on here-and-now interactions, and the
other wants to focus on the patient's discussion of a person not
present or of an event to which the rest of the group was not
privy. Generally, focusing on there-and-then interactions tends
to decrease intensity and to lessen the degree to which other
group members engage in the interactions. There are times
when increase in intensity should be avoided, as when dealing
with emotionally labile patients seeking to develop greater

cognitive control. And there are times when focusing on there-and-then interactions leads to moments of great emotional intensity involving the entire group followed by behavior change in the patient. Indeed, some of the most dramatic moments you will ever experience in group may come from focusing on there-and-then with indivdiual patients rather than here-and-now with group. Thus, it may turn out that what you thought was an error by your cotherapist in terms of focus, ends up very well indeed. This is the criterion for resolving such disagreements: did it work? If so, it was a success. If not, you have something to talk about in the post-group review or in the supervisory session.

In general, problems about what to follow up on are not as difficult to resolve as problems having to do with your assessment of what is going on. Disagreements about focusing tend to get ideological and may boil down to the belief that "My technique is better than yours," or that "I can apply our technique better than you can." Disagreements about what is going on in group involve your assessment of reality, and disagreement about such an assessment tends to be quite threatening, for your sanity, ultimately, is being questioned.

If you find that you and your cotherapist are in constant disagreement about what to attend to, you will probably find it difficult to avoid assessing his competence. Repeated disagreement about procedure has a cumulative effect. For many people, respect for competence is a necessary component of respect for the person and may be a prerequisite for liking him. Sooner or later, if you continue to work with a cotherapist whose competence you do not respect, you may begin to feel contempt.

Confronting your cotherapist, in this instance, is quite unlikely to be fruitful. If he is really incompetent, there is not much that he can do about it. If you are convinced of his incompetence, there is not likely to be anything that he can say, in a confrontation, which will alter your judgment. Complaining to your supervisor about your cotherapist's ineptitude is similarly unlikely to be fruitful. If your supervisor does not share your assessment, you may find yourself defending your own competence, and against a more formidable foe than your cotherapist. If the supervisor does share your assessment, it is his job to do something about it.

There is, then, considerable risk in either direct confrontation, or in complaining to your supervisor about your cotherapist's competence. You risk that the issue of competence will be turned against you, or that you will be perceived as a malcontent, or as one who is manifesting emotional disturbance. In the late 1970s, the issue of competence in psychotherapy is only beginning to be raised, and students who raise that issue may suddenly find themselves embroiled in that political battle rather than in a struggle to develop competence in group therapy.

Therefore, when a question of competence is raised—or a question of whether or not your cotherapist will *ever* be able to develop a minimally adequate level of competence—it is better to terminate the group if that is a viable option, or to withdraw. Hanging on until the group ends may look like the easiest course, but unless you are facing a very few meetings, like three or four, you may find that hanging on is considerably more difficult than you had anticipated.

There are of course other sources of disagreement between cotherapists about what to do with what is attended to. We have discussed focusing, and alluded to level of intensity of emotional interaction. If your cotherapist consistently seeks to move the group onto a level of intensity either higher or lower than what you are comfortable with, his emotional stability rather than his technical competence is more likely to be called into question, since intensity is an affective rather than a cognitive variable.

The present discussion is following a general outline of problems in what is going on, what to attend to, and what to do with what is attended to. There remains a consideration of disagreement about when to attend to it. The issue of timing is a technical one with which your supervisor should be of help. While you may disagree with your cotherapist about the timing of interventions and of interpretations, such disagreements are usually readily resolved in post-group or supervisory sessions; people are more readily willing to talk about timing than about other areas of disagreement.

Timing gets to be a problem because people's response or reaction times differ. (Reaction time is the interval between perception and response—between your perception of a red light and the time your foot hits the brakes.) Some people have naturally shorter reaction times to interpersonal stimuli than others. If yours is shorter than your cotherapist's, you'll find yourself getting there first; if it's longer, you'll find your cotherapist taking the words right out of your mouth.

What is at issue here is not competence nor particularly the ability to think fast, but rather differences in personal *tempo*.[13] If you and your cotherapist perceive the same things happening in group and are in agreement about what to do about them, and what to say, but one of you responds faster than the other, that may be because of tempo. If you're slower, you may ask your cotherapist to wait for a moment before beginning to respond. If you're faster, you may need to deal with your feelings of impatience—not only with your cotherapist but with slower-paced patients as well. Differences in tempo, once they are identified, can usually be settled through negotiation in the

13. The author is indebted to Richard P. Comerford for calling his attention to the role this variable plays in psychotherapy.

post-group discussion or in supervision. If such differences are not identified, and especially if they are not resolved, they may turn once again into an issue of competence. The quicker therapist tends to be seen—and to accept that evaluation—as the more competent. But the rose of quickness carries with it the thorn of impatience. Compassion is more important than speed. Ultimately, response time is an important part of learning not only how to live with one's cotherapist, but also how to work effectively in group—and in individual—therapy.

Cotherapist problems: concluding comment. After reading this section, you may wonder why we recommend a cotherapist model. The answer is, by and large, that it increases the range, type, and style of expertise available to the group. In addition, it offers the advantages for training which are described in chapter 7. Developing a good cotherapy relationship may be in some ways as difficult as evolving a good marriage, and the rewards are to some extent analogous. However, the bonds between cotherapists are not as firm or strong as marital bonds, nor should they be. Withdrawing from a difficult cotherapy situation, which is frequently recommended, need not have the same negative connotations as divorce. However, you may find yourself in a situation where withdrawing from cotherapy, or resigning from the group, would have such serious consequences as to be unavailable remedies. Soemtimes such withdrawal may be construed as evidence of your emotional instability; sometimes the virtue of persevering and learning through adversity—a virtue we think little of, as we said above, but which is sometimes extolled—may be presented as sufficient reason for you to stay in a cotherapy relationship which is intolerable.

The most probable outcome of sticking, for a semester or a school year, with a poor cotherapist relationship is that neither of you will learn what you might have learned; that you will probably have had (or nearly had) some ugly confrontations; and that your patients will probably not have benefited as much as they would have had the cotherapist pairing been more compatible. We think that withdrawing or resigning from a poor cotherapist relationship should not be a solution of first resort, nor of last resort, unless the consequences include a threat to your pursuit of further training for your chosen profession.

Problems with the Supervisor

The supervisor relationship is one in which the potential for injustice is considerable, because of the actual or perceived power differential between supervisor and student. A supervisor can, with relative impunity, make you feel quite miserable, sap your self-confidence, and challenge the strength of your grasp on reality. In addition, a poor report from a supervisor to a director of clinical training may have a significant effect on your career, while a poor rating of the supervisor by you is seldom of major consequence to the supervisor. This power differential permeates the supervisory relationship, severely limiting the choices available to the student responding to problem behavior by the supervisor.

Most problems in the supervisory relationship involve one or more of the following:

1. The supervisor does not provide satisfactory or adequate information to you about how to do groups;

2. The supervisor is judgmental, rigid, insensitive, and harsh (as you experience him);

3. The supervisor interprets error in the application of technique as symptoms of your emotional turmoil and seeks to turn the supervisory session into a therapy session.

There are of course other types of problems in supervisory relationships. As with cotherapy relationships, good, effective responses may be infinite, but as what is wrong is easier to specify, the supervisory relationship often becomes one in which the supervisor emphasizes faults and then helps to correct them, rather than finding and praising you for your virtues.

Often, also, student and supervisor conceptualize the supervisory task differently. Students generally want quite specific information—how do you do this, what should I say when this happens, what are the consequences of this intervention, how do you make these decisions, and the like. Supervisors are usually therapists who have been asked to assume supervisory responsibilities by virtue of their experience with groups (or with individual therapy, or, sometimes, by virtue of the fact that they are available and no one else is). Supervisors sometimes approach supervision in the same way that they approach therapy; they help, that is, the student to find his own answers and they prefer not to be explicit in the manner, say, of a classroom teacher. The supervisor thus attempts to teach by the Socratic method—and the student in this perceives evasiveness, indecisiveness, and a withholding of information. (There is at the time of this writing virtually no formal training in supervision skills and techniques.)

The Socratic method, or any method which emphasizes that you find your own solutions and answers, is certainly valid and effective, but it takes an inordinate amount of time—more than is generally available in clinical settings—and it also presupposes that the student has enough knowledge, experience, or theory to put the answers together himself. Reading Yalom (1975), or Foulkes and Anthony (1965), or even the massive works edited by Kaplan and Sadock (1971), and Sager and Kaplan (1972), or the present volume, may still not provide the student with enough theory and technique to benefit from a Socratic method, especially within the available supervision time.

Ideally, then, and especially at first, the supervisor should be willing to be quite directive, providing information, solutions, and answers. Gradually, as the student shapes his own tools, the supervisor can be less active and more probing. However, since supervisors are primarily therapists, or have had considerable training in therapy, they may regard an informative, didactic, directive approach to group therapy as just as inappropriate as it would be in individual therapy, and student requests for more specificity and less ambiguity as inappropriate efforts to reduce anxiety.

Once again, the best way to handle this problem is, as far as possible, to avoid it. Just as it is best to do your first group with a cotherapist whom you already know and like, so it is best to seek supervision from a clinician you already know or about whom you can find out. (This solution holds true for the other supervisory problems as well.) But sometimes it is difficult to find out before the supervisory relationship begins whether a supervisor's style meets your needs. If you have not yet done a group, you may not know what to ask or what to look for, and if you are new to individual therapy as well, you will have little experience in what kind of supervision is best for you. If, on top of all this, you are new to the clinical setting in which you're working, you may not yet know whose judgment about competence to trust. In that case, all that you have to rely on is the reputation of the training program and your own assessment that the program as a whole can meet your training needs.

A somewhat different problem is presented by that supervisor who espouses a theoretical model in which you have no interest or confidence, who guides you toward events which you regard as unimportant or trivial or dull, and toward therapist interventions which you would feel foolish uttering. (We touched on this point in chapters 3 and 5.) Sooner or later in this situation, both your sanity and your aptitude are likely to be called into question either by yourself, if you tend to be intropunitive, or by your supervisor.

While there are other possible problems posed by insufficient or unsatisfactory information from the supervisor, we will briefly consider just one more—and one which it will be easier for you to resolve. People's communicative styles differ, and your supervisor may simply be more parsimonious with words than you wish him to be. The source of your dissatisfaction, that is, may be a style or personality difference. When you find yourself dissatisfied with a supervisor who has been highly recommended, you may find that such a style difference accounts for at least some of the difficulty. Frequently, forbearance accompanies awareness, and with that the problem diminishes.

If the problem of inadequate or unsatisfactory information from the supervisor stems from his using a non-directive, non-committal model, one which might be appropriate for individual psychotherapy but is, given your small basis of knowledge, theory, and technique of group, especially frustrating to you, you may attempt to convince your supervisor that a more directive approach would be more beneficial. Trying to say that your point of view is right and his wrong won't, of course, get you anywhere but into trouble. But in this most ambiguous of the healing arts, there is room for more than one correct interpretation, intervention, comment, point of view—or approach. If you supervisor will allow for your point of view, he may be willing to be more directive. But even with such a supervisor, this will involve confrontation, which is, because of the power differential between you, a rather risky business. When your supervisor begins to interpret, rather than respond to, your requests for greater specificity, it is time to consider survival tactics.

Cruel supervision. Sometimes a supervisor will be hypercritical, not only tearing down your every comment, but also subjecting it to ridicule. This may be more common in academic settings, where work must be found for tenured faculty, and is relatively rare in clinics. It may appear that the supervisor is satisfying his own self-esteem needs by derogating his students. But there is also a tradition, though more in academia than in the clinic, of being cruel to graduate students and postdoctoral fellows. There are of course many academic traditions, including that of the humanistic teacher. Ritualized cruelty has survived from earlier times in such institutions as the doctoral oral examinations as practiced at some universities or by some professors, and this on occasion finds its way into supervisor relationships. It is as though the supervisor had forgotten how it feels to be a student and on the receiving end of derogatory criticism. Such people sometimes justify their cruelty on the grounds that they endured it while they were students, and now it is their turn to dish it out. Thus does the tradition survive.

People who promulgate the tradition of cruelty would be unable to do so without victims. The number of willing victims is probably even smaller than the number of supervisors who seek them. The clinical settings in which such supervisors lurk may tend to funnel students toward them. You may find yourself required by the clinic to receive supervision from a supervisor who is sadistic, and who will interpret your efforts to escape him as an unwillingness on your part to learn through adversity.

One solution is to call for help. If help is not available within the clinic, then go to your training director. There are, in some schools, grievance committees, but these you should consider as a last resort short of changing schools. Factors which tend to inhibit calling for help include fear of reprisal, fear that calling for help will be to no avail, and fear—amounting at times to a positive article of faith—that no one else has ever been in a similar situation or could possibly believe how bad it is for you. The cruel supervisor, and to some extent the system which harbors him, may tend to emphasize the utter uniqueness of the situation, implying or stating explicitly that you are the only one with whom he has had any trouble. Yet, once the complaint is made, you may well find that yours is only the latest in a series of such complaints, that something can be done— perhaps too slowly to be of help to you, but still something— and that there is ample protection from reprisal. On the other hand, sometimes the good guys lose.

Another solution, not necessarily an alternative to that proposed above, is to go public: to let as many people as possible know what is going on in the supervisory sessions. Publicity tends to inhibit cruelty, and if the sadistic supervisor knows that what he is trying to do to you will be talked about, that knowledge may have an inhibiting effect.

Most students tend to underestimate their own power relative to their supervisors. The power of the supervisor is rarely as great as it is perceived. The supervisor may or may not be answerable to the training director. The training director, or *someone* at the clinic, has a vested interest in maintaining good relationships with your school. The leverage which the school has, in this situation, is the threat of withdrawing its trainees, including you, from the clinic, or advising its students not to seek or accept appointments there, or, ultimately, complaining to the accrediting agency sanctioning the clinic. All of these are fairly powerful levers. There is, therefore, clear motivation in most clinical settings which have students maintain good relationships with the schools which provide clinical trainees. Somewhere along the line, then, there is likely to be someone who has the responsibility for protecting you from the cruel supervisor and who is willing to exercise that responsibility. It might take a while to find him. If you find yourself needing to make such a search, it is reasonable to assume that (a) you are not emotionally defective, and (b) you are not alone; the victims of the past and those of the future send you greeting.

Supervision as therapy. This is a problem only when one member of the supervisory dyad (usually, although not always, the student) objects to personal therapy being done during, and as part of, the supervisory session. It is not a problem if both parties agree, preferably at the time of contracting for supervision, that personal therapy is a legitimate part of the supervisory relationship.

It is sometimes difficult to know how to draw the line between supervision and therapy. Both are concerned with behavior change in the therapist as he does therapy. That behavior change is called (and represents) learning. Therapy is concerned with behavior change in areas other than the application of technique or the development of a point of view from which effective therapeutic interventions can be made.

So it's legitimate for your supervisor to observe that you tend to get angry easily when, for example, attempting to deal with cold, impassive, hostile females. But it's not legitimate for him to wonder (aloud) *why* that is so, unless you have a therapy contract with him. Conversely, it's also legitimate for him to refuse to engage in such speculation with you if he believes, as does your author, that therapy and supervision are incompatible endeavors.

If you object to your supervisor doing therapy on you, you may get caught in the Catch-22 of the mental health professions: your rejection of therapy is proof that you really need it and that you lack even the minimal insight or awareness that you do. If you deny, to such a supervisor, that you have major emotional problems, you are clearly utilizing the ego defense mechanism of denial. The stronger your denial, the stronger your defense must be; and the stronger your defense, then clearly the stronger the turmoil which is being defended against and thus the stronger your need for therapy. The possibility that your rejection of personal therapy is valid may not be considered.

This can be an anguishing problem because your grasp of reality is being challenged by someone who ought to know about such things. Even if you know cognitively, or intuitively, that you are basically in good shape, a supervisor's insistence that you need therapy can generate acrid doubts.

Therefore it is advisable to establish clearly in the contract you make with the supervisor the role that personal therapy is to play in the relationship. The recommendation offered here is that it should play no role at all. Your supervisor will have to make a report of some sort, an evaluation, to those responsible for deciding whether or not you can or should continue to receive training and the blessings of whatever training system you are in. If a therapy contract is included in supervision, that report may contain or be influenced by your supervisor's opinion on how well you bared your soul during supervision and on the extent to which you are guilty of unresolved emotional turmoil. The reason that this is so is that your supervisor, in addition to being of service to you in the learning of the techniques of group psychotherapy, is an agent of the clinic, of the training institution, and ultimately of the profession which you are seeking to join. His divided loyalties may incline him to report for the benefit of others. Your therapist is, however, *your* agent, and cannot ethically serve the interests of others as a result of his knowledge of you.

Problems with the supervisor: concluding comment. We have touched here on a few problems and a few solutions in the supervisory relationship. There are, of course, other problems, and they can be more severe than those discussed above. For example, your supervisor may conclude that you are incompetent, when you know damn well that you're not—or think that you are not. Or maybe he's a little bit right. . . . It is difficult to imagine a problem in the supervisory relationship which is not serious or potentially grave. Problems in these relationships can drive you out of the clinical setting—out of the training institution or school or degree program that you're in, and ultimately out of the mental health professions. If you have grossly misjudged the clinical setting in which you are seeking training—and that's not hard for a student to do—you may find little support from the system or from your colleagues for your position and for what you believe in. In such a situation, the available alternatives may be to conform, or to leave the field. It is possible that many talented and potentially skilled therapists choose to withdraw because they are confronted with situations where to conform would be a violation not only of belief but of personal style. This issue is in urgent need of research.

If you are considering leaving the mental health professions because the supervision or the clinical setting is intolerable for you, consider also that each clinic is as unique as each patient who walks through its doors, and that although there are barren, dry wastelands in the interpersonal world, so are there fertile fields and green hills. Even for you.

Problem Patients

Problem patients are those who, after the group starts, you wish you'd turned down during the screening interview. They are problems because they are disruptive of group, or because they require an inordinate and disproportionate amount of your energy. Problem patients may have difficulty with the structure or arrangement of the group, with functioning within the group, or with both.

Your supervisor will help you learn how to deal with problem patients. In the present volume, therefore, we will discuss only briefly the types of problem behavior which you might encounter in the first few sessions of a group. The most common problem with the structure of a group early in its life is the patient who comes late or intermittently. The most common problem of functioning within the group is premature self-disclosure. The patient who is most likely to have difficulties with both structure and with the group, and is most likely to keep you wondering what to do next, is one who monopolizes the spotlight. We will discuss each of these in turn, and in the concluding comment of this section take a look at the factors which might make some patients especially difficult for you to understand and help because of personality variables.

Late or intermittent attendance. Coming late is disruptive at two points in a group session: initially, when no one knows whether or not to start; and midway, when, as it happens, the patient may come in. Inevitably there is a disturbance in the flow of experience of the group. If the patient does not come at all, there is only one disruption; the group will have wasted some time waiting in the hope or expectation that he would show up.

Consistent lateness and intermittent absence can be interpreted as symptoms of insufficient commitment to group. The remedy proposed by a number of group therapists (see, e.g., Yalom 1975) is, in effect, to take the patient to task and to threaten him with expulsion from the group. Such a patient may discover that he is not truly interested in group, and withdraw. Sometimes a discussion—outside the group—will help to clarify the reasons for his lateness for him, and a change in the patient's behavior may result. Discussions during group about latecoming need to be handled quite carefully because of the potential for scapegoating, especially if you're angry at the patient too.

How much of an issue to make of latecoming depends mainly on three factors: how much it bothers you and your co-leader; how much it bothers the group; and how much it bothers your supervisor. If you feel it important for patients to be prompt, and especially if you are an invariably prompt person yourself, it is worth making an issue of. However, if you ask patients to be on time because their being late annoys you, it is probably better to tell them about your annoyance than to cloak it in therapeutic concern for the patient's, or the group's, well-being.

But if there is an agreement about someone's coming late, groups can usually be quite tolerant of latecomers. If group starts at 3:30 and one patient can't get there before 3:50, it is possible to ask the group to accept that fact. Generally (although not always) they will. The first point of disruption—the waiting for the latecomer—does not then occur, and the second point of disruption—in the unexpected arrival—is minimized because the lateness is expected, and the latecomer will slip in as unobtrusively as possible. If a group refuses a latecomer, you may have to find another group for him. You may wish to accept a patient who will have to be late for group only contingent upon that latecoming being accepted by the other group members. Sometimes therapists are more inflexible than patients about such arrangements.

The intermittent attender is a somewhat more difficult problem. He is the patient who misses half the sessions in the first month of group, and consistently misses one meeting a month for, say, three months. If you don't take a stand, the group will, sooner or later, as it forms and becomes cohesive. The group will attack an intermittent attender who contributes when he is there sooner than it will attack someone who comes on occasion, says little, and misses the next two weeks.

The extent to which you seek to contact the intermittent attender outside of group and review with him the magnitude of his commitment to group, or his priorities, should depend on what you are comfortable with and what your supervisor suggests. A patient who is motivated to change behavior and who finds group facilitative of such change will come, on time, every time, barring natural disaster. If he's coming late, or intermittently, he's either not as motivated as you thought, or he doesn't find group as helpful as he had expected, or he's having some difficulty beyond his control in getting there. Contacting the patient outside of group to find out what is going on may be helpful (to you; the patient most likely already knows what is going on). Whether or not such seeking out of recalcitrant patients is fruitful is a matter between you and your supervisor.

Groups are generally less tolerant of intermittent attenders who know they're going to miss, than of patients who know they have to be late. The intermittent attender may not ever be included in the group, and after a time becomes neither fish nor fowl, neither one of "us," nor a new group member, nor yet a stranger. It becomes quite difficult for group members immersed in cohesiveness and inclusiveness to relate to such a patient except with hostility.

Other disruptions. Two other types of disruption which you may encounter early in the life of a group are the patient who gets up, in the midst of a delicate or tense or dramatic moment, to go to the toilet; and the patient who dramatically gets up and dashes out in tears.

When patients go to the toilet during group, it can be suggested to them that they go before group starts. However, their going may be a protective device, enabling them to withdraw temporarily from group, to pull themselves together, and to re-enter without ever admitting that they could not tolerate staying. Little should be made of this at first. If the pattern continues, it would seem desirable to ask the patient to sit near the door, and to leave and return as unobtrusively as possible.

Asking the patient not to leave during group may reflect your good intentions to minimize disruption, but may also put considerable strain on what is after all a rather primitive defense mechanism.[14] When the group is cohesive, when there is some interpersonal safety and intimate self-disclosure has begun to occur, than it may be possible to get the patient to look at this particular behavioral pattern. Focusing on it before the group is cohesive and safe may simply embarrass—or threaten—the patient to the point where he will feel unable to return to group.

The patient who gets up, tearful, and runs out of the room, usually causes a major disruption of group. Group may try to go on as if nothing had happened (though rarely), and you may have to get the group to acknowledge what has just happened. This is one of those times when your own sense of reality has little to buttress it in terms of the behavior of the others in the room (see chapter 3), and that can be a very creepy feeling.

More often, the patient's exit will stop the group. People will look at you, wanting to know what to do, and what you are going to do. They may feel guilty and responsible for having driven the patient from the room. Some action needs to be taken.

When a patient leaves the room in this manner, it may look as though he were headed for Patagonia on a jet plane. However, only quite rarely does he leave the clinic building. Most patients head only for as quiet or private a place as they can find, and that is usually the restroom. For this reason, the cotherapist of the same sex should go looking for the fleeing patient. Walk, don't run. If he's not in the restroom, check other areas that are unoccupied and open. If he's in none of the likely places, he really doesn't want to be found, and you

14. It is generally sound practice to ask your patients to have their health checked, so that a physiological problem (as, in the present instance, a possible bladder infection) be not wrongly and wastefully interpreted as a psychological one.

should stop looking for him and return to group. If you do find him, you're in a one-to-one interview with a patient who's upset. The patient should be encouraged to return to group, but the therapist should not insist; if he won't come back this time, try for the next time. Don't press, unless there is, in your judgment, incipient psychosis or incipient suicidal behavior. If he doesn't wish to return, try to get from him some indication of what he would like for you to tell the group when you return.

What the group members need to know is that the patient is all right or is being taken care of, and that they did not force him out, but that he chose to leave. The feeling of guilt is almost always present, especially when the patient who fled has first generated a good bit of hostility toward himself. You may have to help the group deal with its guilt, collectively and individually, before it can turn to other matters.

You may also have to attend, to some extent, to your own feelings of guilt and incompetence at having allowed matters to get so far out of hand that a patient would get up and leave group in tears. Replaying the tapes—if you are taping— it is sometimes possible to spot the point at which you said this thing rather than that, which caused him then to rush out of the room. Closer examination, perhaps with your supervisor, may reveal that the patient came to group halfway—or more— expecting to leave at some point. At times, however, the patient's leaving may seem to you rather clearly a result of your handling the situation less than optimally because of your lack of experience. Then it may be helpful to remember that withdrawing from group, whether it be by coming late, or intermittently, or going to the toilet, or storming out, is a protective mechanism which serves to keep you or the group from inflicting damage on the patient. It may be that later on, when you have more experience, you will be able to see warning signs. Or it may be that even then patients will find it necessary to storm out, and all the skill and wisdom and experience in the world, on your part, could not prevent them from doing so. And there's no way to avoid feeling sad when this happens.

Premature self-disclosure. Self-disclosure is premature when it involves a greater degree of intimacy or openness than the group—or the patient—is ready for at this time. Premature self-disclosure usually consists of telling people who are still strangers facts about one's past, facts which one would ordinarily share only with close friends, or families, or one's therapist. If it is going to occur, premature self-disclosure occurs in the first or second—rarely, in the third—session of a group.

It tends to happen fast, and it is almost by definition unexpected. It may begin as you are surveying, at the beginning of the first or second session, how people are feeling; or it may come during a lull or pause, as between episodes. Suddenly, the person you would least expect it from says, "I'd like to say something. I'm here because I need to learn how to get along with people. I ain't never been able to get along with people. Never had a date, never had sex—I'm still a virgin at 32—and besides that, I have bad thoughts about sex with my cousin. My doctor, the one who told me I needed group, told me I should talk about these things and I want to get well, so here I am . . . ."

This example is relatively mild. Others can include disclosures about recent hospitalizations, including diagnostic information; sexual deviations; or grossly deviant behavior on the part of parent or spouse or sibling which the patient links to a behavioral deficit of his own.

Such premature self-disclosure, especially about so great a deviance, is quite frightening to a group which does not yet have sufficient cohesiveness to offer comfort to its members.

Usually premature self-disclosure has two results. One is that the discloser does not return to group more than once after he has dumped his "deep dark secrets." The other is that, in that group, intimate self-disclosure by other patients will take somewhat longer to reach than in groups where such a disclosure has not occurred.

It is very difficult to know whether or not to interrupt someone who is engaging in premature self-disclosure. If you try to stop the patient, you may be cutting off something that is not only valuable but also interesting to hear; and you may be establishing a norm, for that group, that people should not talk about the ways in which they are deviant. But usually, by the time you decide that the patient needs to be stopped, it is too late. On rare occasions you may be able to perceive what is happening and get the patient to postpone his self-disclosure until the group is more able to handle it. Such a perception and such a postponement comprise a manifestation of rare skill and talent. The rest of us are usually going to lose a patient— the discloser—and will have a slower starting group.

The place to look for the premature self-discloser is in the screening interview. Such people usually fail to meet several of the criteria for the selection of patients outlined in chapter 1. Look especially for diagnoses denoting psychosis or pre-psychotic personality disturbance, such as schizoid personality; talkativeness; or recent hospitalization which included group therapy. If all three of these factors are present, it may be worthwhile to talk with the patient about self-disclosure during the screening interview. One of your tasks may be to help the patient shift his own focus from the type of group he was in as an inpatient, to the type of group he is about to enter. If patients carrying diagnoses of one of the schizophrenic disorders know what is expected of them, what the unwritten rules are, they can sometimes come through quite appropriately.

The monopolist. This is the patient who keeps the group's energy, and usually its attention, focused on him. If he is not in the spotlight, he manages to keep you aware of that fact, and to keep you wondering what he is going to do next. In the early stages of group, the monopolizer is most likely to be verbally active and aggressive. Later on, he may use other means of controlling the group interaction.

The monopolizer typically takes a great deal of time to say relatively little, builds up slowly to a statement that is of genuine poignancy, and then says, "But I've taken up too much of the group's time. Go on to someone else." The monopolizer also typically responds empathically to what other group members say, but turns the response into something about himself: "That's really neat. That must have been difficult for you to talk about, especially since you don't know any of us all that well yet. That's helped me to get to know you, and I want you to know that I appreciate it. I used to . . .," and he's off.

One of the things which makes the monopolizer difficult to deal with is that at the same time he's keeping the group's attention focused on himself, he manages to give the impression that he's fragile. Deep down there is some considerable anguish; by dint of virtually superhuman effort he's managing to hold himself together as he tries diligently to enter the group, doing good in order to get the good which the group will have to offer. Put more roughly, the message is, *don't interrupt.*

Whether or not you heed that message will depend on your own preferences (and *chutzpah*) and on your supervisor's advice. There are some tactical advantages to letting one patient monopolize the early sessions of group, and some theories consider it wrong to turn off a patient who monopolizes the group's energies and yours.

The position taken here is that the effect of monopolizing conversations is probably a major factor in what brought the patient to group in the first place, and that it must be dealt with. Allowing the patient to engage in, and continue, that behavioral pattern is likely to produce, in group, the same reaction it would outside the group: anger, attack, and/or rejection. For the patient to experience this sequence yet again in the very place he came to for help in escaping it is not particularly therapeutic. Group can offer an interpersonal context in which the patient can experience what happens when he does not follow the familiar pattern and sequence.

That involves turning him off. One way of doing so is to label the behavior, or agree with the patient when he says he talks too much. Allow that he must have some need to do so, and that it may be frightening or difficult to him to do something different, and get him to agree to be verbally active for a specified amoung of time—such as one sixth of the time in a six-member group.

Your supervisor will have more specific suggestions. When you first encounter the monopolizer, during the first session or second or—rarely—third of group, it is probably best to let him go on, for that one session, and then to discuss him with your supervisor. The patient is not likely to generate much of an attack from the others that early in group, and waiting to talk with your supervisor may be preferable to taking on someone whose interpersonal message is *don't interrupt,* and who knows how to make you feel awful if you try, because he lives there, and you don't.

Concluding comment: personality variables. We have discussed, in this section, patient behavior which tends to be disruptive to group and is therefore a problem. What we have not given is any kind of formal description of diagnostic categories, of patient attributes, independent of group or therapist. The last reference to such attributes, aside from a fleeting one in this section, was clear back in chapter 1 on the selection of patients. There are some patients who are going to be problems for you because you can't understand them or empathize with them, or because they make you so angry so fast that it's difficult for you to be therapeutic with them (see also the next chapter).

What type of patient will be most difficult for you to work with (or easiest—but this is a chapter on problems, not joys) depends on a rather complex interplay of patient characteristics and symptomatology, and your own personality. If you're a beginning therapist, you may have no idea of what type of patient you work best or poorest with. You may already be aware of the fact that some patients are easier for you to work with than others, and that the type of patient who is easiest for you is not necessarily easiest for others. You may assume that, as your experience grows, and your skill, you will be able to work with a broader range of patients, indeed perhaps with anyone who comes through your door. However, there is considerable evidence that this is not the case, and that you won't be able to work equally well with everyone (Berzins, Friedman, and Ross 1974).

The fact that you have one or two (or more) people in your group whom you really can't figure out and don't like working with is not a further reflection on your lack of competence, although that is how it may feel; rather, it is evidence that you cannot be all things to all men. If you have chosen your cotherapist with skill and luck, then perhaps he can attend to these patients, just as you can attend to others. Sometimes the problem is not the patient, and not you, and not the technique, but lies in that mysterious chemistry of interpersonal attraction of which a therapy group is but a small, if special, part.

Chapter 9

Inpatient Group Therapy

Inpatient group therapy is in many respects different from outpatient group therapy. Indeed, the difference is so great that inpatient group therapy—or rather therapies, for here, too, there are many techniques—may be regarded as a different kettle of fish altogether. The major difference is, of course, the inpatient status itself. That status signifies a major disruption in the life of each patient in the group. Admission to inpatient status constitutes a nadir in the lives of many people, as Goffman (1959) has most eloquently argued. Differences between outpatient and inpatient groups involve then the severity of disturbance of each patient, the purpose and function of groups, the role required of the group leaders, and other differences which depend in part upon the type of inpatient facility in which the group is offered.

Training in inpatient group therapy in the United States is obtainable in four types of settings: psychiatric wards of general hospitals (including university teaching hospitals); state hospitals; private psychiatric facilities; and Veterans Administration neuropsychiatric facilities. In these settings, group therapy is made available to the widest variety of patients, ranging from the acutely and floridly psychotic to those who have been hospitalized for decades with what is labelled "chronic illness."

Despite the ranges of psychopathologies, the plethora of techniques, and the gamut of purposes of groups, inpatient groups can generally be classified a) as to the probable length of hospitalization—short or long term, acute or chronic, crisis or continued care; and b) as to the level of functioning of the patients: high, intermediate, and low.

In some hospitals, and particularly on admissions services, groups may be highly heterogeneous, comprised of acutely and of chronically ill patients who have little in common other than their presence in the room. In other settings, especially off the admissions service, groups may tend toward a dismaying homogeneity of silent, passive, withdrawn patients whose apathy and despair can cast a pall on the aspirations of even the most determined young therapist. In this chapter, we will consider the short-term inpatient group characteristic of admissions wards in state hospitals and of the psychiatric wards in general hospitals. In the following chapter, we will discuss the long-term groups comprised of chronic patients in state hospital units—units which used to be known as back wards, but which may now carry such euphemistic titles as "Continued-Care Facility."

The Purpose of Admissions Service Groups

The purpose of group will depend in large part upon the purpose of the clinical unit in which it is housed. Generally, the purpose of any inpatient group ought to be to facilitate the patient's return to the community. A lesser, but by no means uncommon, goal might be to facilitate the patient's adjustment to the hospital. Sometimes that is the most that can be done, but such a goal increases the probability of permanent hospitalization and should therefore be regarded in the same light as the administration of morphine or heroin to the terminally ill.

In inpatient groups, the most important question is, "What has to change before the patient can return to the community and make a successful adaptation to it?" In short-term hospital settings, and sometimes in others as well, the answer frequently includes change in the patient's living arrangements outside the hospital: in marital status, in job, in geographic location, and the like. In this instance, the purpose of group is to help the patient to define what needs changing, and to render initiation of change less difficult and therefore more probable.

Usually the patient's own coping mechanisms need to change as well. Such changes usually require considerably more time than changes in behavior resulting from administration of medicines, and are not likely to occur as as result of participation in a short-term admissions-service group. (This is difficult to accomplish even in longer-term groups.)

Short-term admissions service groups, then, may serve a number of purposes, but the facilitation of change in behavior is not usually one of them. Why then do such groups exist at all, and of what benefit might they be to a patient who will be on the ward for a week or two or three and attend no more than six or nine sessions?

The answer is that group does different things for different people, depending in large part upon their needs and interests. For most people, admission to a state hospital is an extremely frightening and disruptive experience. Group may serve a supportive function—an opportunity for patients to complain about ward policies and procedures, ask about what is happening to them, and the like: an informational function. For the disoriented patient, group may provide an opportunity to begin his reorientation. The hallucinating or delusional patient may find that although others do not share his disturbed perception, neither do they turn away in fear or disgust, nor snicker nervously. The confused patient may find, in the group room, relative quiet, a respite from the rapid influx of chaotic stimuli on the ward and outside the hospital.

All of this boils down to two functions, or purposes, for admissions-services groups. One is to facilitate the disposition process: to help the patient decide where to go next—whether to another ward in the hospital, or back out into the world. The other purpose, more limited, pertains to what the therapist can do for patients who are floridly psychotic. It involves touch, contact not necessarily physical, but interpersonal. If for one minute out of an hour's group session you can be in contact with, in human touch with, a person in the depths of madness, then you have not solved the world's ills, but you will have done a great thing.

The Selection of Patients

On admissions wards where a group therapy program is already established, the student therapist is not likely to be consulted about the selection of patients for group. On wards where there is no, or hardly any, established group program, the student may be given carte blanche—and may find that supervision is minimal or quite difficult to arrange.

In either case, there are some selection principles; or, to be more precise, the student should know what selection principles are being used—or are available—since selection procedures and criteria strongly influence what happens in group. Of critical importance is the principle that the group leaders are the final arbiters of admission to the group. On some wards, the group members are allowed to determine who is invited to come to the group; on others, the physician assigns group in the same way that he prescribes drugs, and the group leader lacks veto power. The student would do well to avoid the latter situation, since it allows for the possibility of patients being in the group whom the group leader does not want there and who may be quite disruptive or even combative.

Group patients on admission wards will tend to vary widely in age, intelligence, race, and diagnosis; a desirable homogeneity of background is not likely; adhering to strict selection criteria would result in small groups even on large (50 + bed) wards.

It is desirable, then, as well as practical, to select patients on the basis of inclusiveness rather than exclusiveness, omitting only those with manifest, severe behavioral disturbances. Patients who are floridly psychotic are not likely to benefit from group, and their presence usually impairs the ability of the group leaders and of the group to function effectively. Some group leaders allow acutely disturbed patients to attend group, in the belief that the less disturbed patients will have a calming effect upon them, but a less severely disturbed patient, placed in the same group as one who is more or less literally climbing the walls, will more frequently become upset, and the agitated patient will not become calmer. In the psychoses, interpersonal influences are at best minimal.

Homogeneity of the severity (but not type) of pathology is then what should be sought after. Patients who are quite agitated should not be referred for, or accepted in, group. Patients who are so extremely withdrawn as to be nonresponsive to environmental stimuli should also be excluded— whether such behavior is attributed to the apathy of depression or that of schizophrenia.

In addition to patients who are quite agitated or quite withdrawn, patients with impaired consciousness should also be excluded; they also are not likely to benefit from group. Whether the impairment results from some intrinsic process, such as injury or disease, or is a side effect of tranquillizing medications, does not matter. However, patients who are disoriented as to time, place, and person, but are fully conscious can be considered as possible candidates for group unless they are so agitated that they would probably disrupt group, or unless their disturbance is associated with impaired consciousness.

A second criterion for exclusion involves the willingness or ability of the therapists to handle or tolerate behavior which they find upsetting or disturbing. Some psychiatric inpatients are not merely unpleasant, but intolerably so; in some cases that might be why they are inpatients. Such patients may be skilled in getting others to respond to them with anger, hostility, and rejection, and it is not always possible for therapists to avoid responding to them in the same way.

The rationale for admitting such a patient to group is that group offers the patient an opportunity to work out some of his problems and to explore alternative ways of relating, ways which do not generate so much hostility. However, change in behavior is seldom a viable goal for short-term admissions service groups. What tends to happen is that the group interaction intensifies both the maladaptive behavior and its reciprocal: the patient succeeds even more in getting people angry, and if scapegoating does not occur, the other group members tend toward silent and passive observation of the battle between the offensive member and the therapists. Good seldom comes of this on an admissions service.

There are, no doubt, other contraindications. The general principle in this setting is to include all patients, except those who will be more disruptive of the group than the group leaders, and the other patients, can tolerate.

Pre-group screening. Relatively few admissions services are so amply staffed that there is time for exhaustive pre-group screening. Indeed, the kind of careful screening procedure which is so important in outpatient groups is usually unnecessary and perhaps undesirable on an admissions service. Some screening is desirable; a patient should not automatically be referred for group upon admission to the ward.

When a patient is first admitted to the ward, a process of assessment, both formal and informal, begins. The formal assessment will consist, at a minimum, of the admitting physician's physical and mental status examinations. These examinations must be performed within twenty-four hours of admission at all accredited hospitals. Formal assessment may include additional psychodiagnostic testing, and other procedures. Informal assessment is the subjective judgment of staff and patients about the magnitude of disturbance of the newcomer; although it is based on first (and frequently superficial) impressions, it strongly influences how others on the ward begin to relate to the new patient.

In the screening process, the group leader should, if possible, avail himself of both the formal and informal assessments of the patient. The most important question to ask is probably some variant of the general form, "Is this patient too disturbed (or disturbing) to be in group?" Whether the patient can benefit from group is frequently more difficult to ascertain from the formal assessment process. The informal process, perhaps codified as "clinical judgment" by mental health professionals, may provide more useful information. First impressions are important because they guide the initiation of interaction. But first impressions are seldom codified in admission assessment procedures.

The screening interview itself should be as brief and succinct as possible. It need not be held in an interview room; an informal brief conference in the day room (or wherever the patient is to be found) has much to commend it. The patient is in a situation where he has very little freedom or autonomy. He is summoned hither and thence. Things are done to him about which he may be informed but is seldom asked. Coming to the patient, rather than *summoning* him to yet another conference with strangers, is at least courteous and perhaps less frightening, and allows the patient rather more autonomy—it is easier to refuse and walk away in a day room than in an interview room—and may, however slightly, enhance his feeling of being in control of something.

In general, this interview with the patient is merely an orientation to let him know who you are, what you want of him, and when and how you expect it to happen. The interview with the patient should not be initiated until you are reasonably sure that you will accept him in group. An interview might go something like this: "Hello, Mrs. Jones, I'm Dr. Horn and this is Dr. Phelps. We're group therapists. We'd like for you to come to group therapy this afternoon. Will you do that?" If the patient asks questions (about half won't), the questions should be answered *briefly,* and any questions calling for a discursive response should be referred to the group session itself.

In general, group should be presented as a place (or means) for patients to get some help. If you suggest that group is a place to talk about your problems, you'll have difficulty with the patient who feels that he has no problems. The patient who says that he doesn't need help can be asked why he is in the hospital, and that can lead to a brief discussion of what group might be able to offer.

The question may arise of how much coercion to use to get a recalcitrant patient into group. A therapist on a locked admissions ward is perceived by the patient who has no key as quite powerful; anything the therapist does, including the issue of such a relatively mild invitation as "We'd like for you to come to group" may be experienced as a coercive demand because of the power differential between the therapist and the patient. That may be undesirable, but it is also unavoidable. What is avoidable is linking attendance to ward privileges, pass cards, and the like by the person who has the authority to give or withhold such privileges. This kind of coercion is seldom fruitful on an admissions service and frequently signifies negative countertransference. Patients should have the right to refuse group. If moderately strenuous efforts at verbal persuasion are not successful, more vigorous efforts may produce the patient's presence but not his participation in group.

Contracts with the patient about what to work on in group should not be made during the pre-group screening interview. There are two reasons for this. One is that the patient is likely to be too anxious to conceptualize, let alone make a commitment to, working on some aspect of interpersonal behavior. The second is the heterogeneous nature of the group itself, which is likely to change from session to session. The emotional atmosphere may make it difficult for the patient to plan to work on anything specific. Contracts to work on specific issues should be made during each group session, not in pregroup screening.

Technique: Some General Considerations

The three tactical goals of the group therapist are:

(1) to reduce anxiety;

(2) to initiate, facilitate, and encourage communication; and

(3) to support, reinforce, and consensually validate those aspects of a patient's experience which are not psychotic.

These tactical goals hold good for each group session, and through the series of sessions, across the life of a group. In an inpatient admissions group, what you are frequently faced with is, in effect, a series of initial group sessions. This is due primarily to the relatively rapid turnover in group membership: in a group which meets three times weekly, a membership which is stable across all three meetings is likely to be rare. It may be possible, on occasion, to facilitate communication among the patients and even to seek some validation by the group of the healthy aspects of a patient's experiences, but for the most part you will be dealing with the reduction of anxiety.

The magnitude of anxiety of an inpatient group differs from that of outpatient groups: it is the difference betweeen the Himalayas and the Allegheny mountains. In both inpatient and outpatient groups, some of the anxiety of the initial group session is situation-specific: the anxiety stemming from being in a new situation, with strangers, not knowing what is expected or what to do or what will happen, fearful of being judged and of other people—these are not uncommon anxieties about group. In addition to the anxiety generated by the situation, there are the anxieties which each patient brings with him: anxieties which stem from the patient's assessment of the world and of his ability to survive in it. In inpatient groups, that assessment is frequently so overwhelmingly negative as to be intolerable.

There are many ways of categorizing, conceptualizing, and accounting for deviant—psychotic—behavior; for instance, as primarily of biochemical etiology, as learning deficits, or as environmental deprivation. Each view is fruitful in some context. For group therapy, which is above all interpersonal, the most fruitful way of conceptualizing psychosis is as a disturbance in interpersonal behavior, an impairment of the desire or ability to relate with other people. From this point of view, death and madness are solitary experiences; joy can never be attained in isolation; interaction is both healthy (or health-producing) and potentially joyful. This argument has been most cogently advanced by Pesso (1973).

It follows that the task of the group therapist is to facilitate interaction among patients. The first barrier to interaction is anxiety. The anxiety of the psychotic patient frequently (although certainly not always) stems from his assessment of the world as an unsafe place, and of his ability to function in it as not equal to the task. It is as though the patient says to himself, there is no safety in this world, only danger, and I am not strong enough to resist the danger. Therefore I will be, am being, have been, overwhelmed by my enemies, or by evil. . . .

This is an intolerable way to live. Some psychotic behavior may be understood as the patient's effort to seek a safe place within his self or within his own fantastic re-creation of reality. Thus some psychotic patients relate to themselves rather than to other people, and lose the consensual validation of reality which keeps us sane.

Before healing can occur, the patient must have a safe place to experience himself. To provide such a place is sometimes a difficult and challenging task for the group leader in what is, after all, a madhouse. Yet anxiety will generally diminish in proportion to the degree that group is seen as a safe place.

A number of factors will facilitate establishment of the group as a safe place. One is the environment. The group session should, if possible, be held in a quiet place, away from patients who are screaming or pounding. The group members need to be sure, especially if there is or has been physical violence on the ward, that there is little or no danger of such violence during the group session. The group room must be protected from intrusion, either by aides summoning patients to other activities (a frequent type of intrusion) or by patients wandering in. Locking the door to the group room, however, is not a good solution, since it makes prisoners of all those group members who lack keys.

The careful selection of patients is a second factor which facilitates establishment of the group as a safe place. The range and severity of pathology observable in the day-room at any time is quite wide, and disoriented or loudly hallucinating patients are often in the same room with, or quite near, patientsfor whom such behavior is very frightening. Exclusion from group of patients with such marked degrees of agitation may be reassuring on several counts to the group members—including some evidence that the staff does not, after all, regard all as equally crazy.

But the group leader is the most important factor in establishing and maintaining the group as a safe place. The group leader should, ideally, be perceived as powerful, benevolent, fair, and just: powerful, to banish the patient's internal demons and to vanquish those external demons which make of virtually any admissions service in a large psychiatric hospital such a frightening place; benevolent, to meet the patient's need (at least his need for survival) without rending him asunder; and fair and just, and not vindictive.

The group leader, then, must act the role of a powerful and benevolent quasi-parent, the role of one who, in terms of the leadership styles described in chapter 2, is active rather than passive, cue-emitting rather than cue-suppressing, and authoritarian rather than collegial—an active, controlling, at times quite directive and assertive leader. The danger of being over-assertive is, in this context, less of an error than being under-assertive. Novice group therapists tend not to function in those styles, even when suited by personality to do so. Their reticence stems at first from uncertainty and lack of confidence. Admissions-service groups, therefore, are not good places for novice co-therapist pairs to begin doing groups; the student doing his first group should, if possible, seek a more experienced therapist as coleader.

The model for therapist behavior in this situation is set forth in chapter 4. In conducting an inpatient group, the therapist will find the dynamics described in that chapter particularly helpful. Those dynamics may be considerably enhanced if the therapist is in reality the giver of permissions and approvals: if he in fact can grant privileges, such as canteen visits, pass cards, and the like, and can in fact grant ultimate approval in the form of discharge from the hospital or at least release from the locked ward. But such privileges, we repeat, should not be contingent on group attendance.

Even when the therapist does not have such direct administrative responsibility for the patient, he is more closely allied with those who do than with the patient. The group therapist should not be without influence over the giver of passes and privileges; to renounce such influence is to make group irrelevant. Group therapists on inpatient locked wards tend to be perceived as powerful because they *are* powerful relative to the patients. That power, or perceived power, should be used as openly as possible to make of group a safe place for the patient to be.

One other general consideration should be mentioned before we look at some specific techniques. That is the issue of confidentiality. A patient may ask, on occasion, that something he says in group remain confidential; or he may ask whether what he says will be reported back to the doctors or to the ward personnel. Patients should be told the truth. The truth, in this instance, is that what patients say in group may in fact be reported back in some detail. There can be no confidentiality on an inpatient psychiatric service. (You would not, of course, discuss the patient with another patient or outside of professional circles.)

This means that there are some things that patients might want to talk about, in confidence, that they are not going to discuss for fear that you will report the fact or content of the discussion to others. That is a real and necessary limitation of inpatient group psychotherapy—and, for that matter, of individual psychotherapy as well. Sometimes it is possible to negotiate with the patient about the kind and amount of information that will be reported to others. Such negotiation is most easily accomplished in individual psychotherapy. It is more difficult in an outpatient group, and virtually impossible to accomplish in an inpatient group. The patient may choose to remain silent, and it is important for the therapists, and the rest of the group, to respect that silence. If the patient chooses to proceed without a guarantee of confidentiality, the type of material which is most likely to emerge tends to pertain to the relationship between the patient and his doctor or the staff. Sometimes, however, what emerges is highly personal and idiosyncratic.

The issue becomes particularly critical if you suspect that a patient would talk about contemplated suicide (or homicide) if granted a guarantee of confidentiality. There may be some valuable information which you will have to forego. You need not hear from the patient's own lips that he contemplates suicide before you take appropriate action.

Technique: Starting the Group

Even if you have yourself done all of the screening, it will still usually be helpful to re-introduce yourself and make some brief statement of what the group is about. An exception is if you are the physician in charge of all of the patients in the group, so that your name and face have some salience for them beyond what is involved in the group.

There is no particular formula for describing what the group is about. You'll have to find words that suit you, given the purpose of group and the emphasis on interpersonal issues suggested above. One example of this type of introduction is this:

I'm Dr. Egglesworth. This is a group therapy session. This is an opportunity to talk about what's on your mind: what brought you here, what your fears are, what your hopes are, what you'd like. Group is a place, a time, when we can help each other.

A more succinct introduction is, "Group therapy is where you talk about your problems. We're here to talk about your problems. Who wants to start?" Such an introduction has the advantage of being brief. However, it is likely to be followed by silence. An invitation to talk about one's problems in a group full of strangers—and insane strangers at that—is not likely to be accepted. In addition, many patients do not perceive *talking about* as particularly fruitful, nor do they necessarily conceptualize what is happening to them as *their* problem. The invitation "to talk about what's on your mind" seems less threatening. Frequently, what is on someone's mind is whether they can get a pass card, or key, or some privilege, such as visiting the canteen, or calling home—and such a request is frequently the beginning in many inpatient groups. These requests should be referred to some time outside of group. A specified time—"I'll talk with you about that right after group [or at 4 o'clock, etc.]," is better than "I'll talk with you about that later on." The more specific you can be, the better.

Another way that inpatient groups sometimes start is that the patients begin to complain about conditions on the ward, or about the incompetence of their doctors, or about the side effects of their medicines. Such complaints should be listened to attentively (the first time or two), and if the complaints about the ward, for example, have some validity, they should be acknowledged. Acceptance and understanding, however, are probably more important than expressing a willingness to do something about these conditions.

Sometimes, after a patient has complained bitterly about conditions on the ward, or the noise, or the food, etc., it is possible to ask, "How would you like for us, here, to help? What would you like for us to do?" If the situation is one in which the patient has primary responsibility, it may be more appropriate to ask, "What are you going to do about that?"

Of course, another way that inpatient groups start off is with silence. Whether they start off with silence, requests, complaints, or in some other way, it is usually desirable, within the first few minutes, to ask each patient to say her or his name, especially on large wards where the patients may not know each other; in small highly staffed situations where patients and staff know each other already, this is less important.

The amount of verbal activity in an inpatient group will probably vary considerably from one session to the next, as will the amount of interaction. In general, the interactions are one-to one: patient-therapist, patient-therapist. Sometimes it is as though there were no others in the room but you and the patient; no one listens or attends to what is going on except you and the patient who is speaking (or has your attention) at the moment. That is the interpersonal isolation mentioned above.

Inexperienced therapists sometimes invite patients to address each other, in the belief that such instruction will facilitate interpersonal interaction. "Mrs. Fischer, how does Miss Sikes look to you today? Tell her, now, look at her, and tell her." Mrs. Fischer may indeed comply, but the interaction is most likely to be farcical or wooden. Patients aren't going to give a damn about each other's opinions until they are ready to; they are not going to be ready to until group is a safe place. One way to begin making group a safe place, in this context, is to facilitate the type of interaction that most readily presents itself: one-to-one.

This is a tactical suggestion. Since all that you are likely to get anyway with such an inpatient group is a series of one-to-one interactions, patient to therapist, you may as well go ahead and engage the patients, one-to-one, as fully as possible or appropriate. If you can get a patient to interact with you, that is probably better than the patient remaining silent and withdrawn into himself. Further, if you engage with the patient, and the engagement is both meaningful and satisfactory to him, the chances that he might be willing to engage with another patient are enhanced.

Engagement, here, requires that you take a stand. The impersonal approach favored by some physicians and some psychotherapists is not likely to be fruitful: there is no safety with someone who is impersonal, and such a stance is not likely to reduce anxiety *in this context.* (In other types of interaction, such as physical examinations of the patient, and perhaps at times during individual psychotherapy, an impersonal approach might be anxiety-reducing.) Taking a stand involves allowing your opinions to be known; that is, it involves therapist self-disclosure. Such self-disclosure should be limited to opinions and/or feelings which (a) have direct relevance within the patient's frame of reference and (b) pertain to here-and-now interactions in the room with people who are physically present. The following examples illustrate this point:

Patient: Tell me, doctor, do you believe in ESP?
Doctor: No, I don't. Some people believe in it. I don't share their beliefs, and that is OK.
Patient: Well, I believe in ESP. There is something about you, an aura, that I knew, I knew at once that you would not knowingly do me harm.
Doctor: I think that what you are saying is that you feel you can trust me.
Patient: Yes.
Doctor: I'm glad you feel that way.

In this example, the first thing to note is that the therapist gave a direct answer to the question. His answer was as clear and unequivocal as he could get it. He also said something about himself, about his beliefs, and about how he will handle differences of opinion. The patient's next comment does not make much literal sense. The therapist took it symbolically, and translated[15] the comment into language which is less idiosyncratic and closer to consensual meaning. He then again took a stand ("I think that . . .") in the process of checking whether or not his translation was correct. His final statement is again a personal one, ("I'm glad . . .") but still limited to that particular patient at that time. Another example:

Patient: Doctor, do you believe in ESP?
Doctor: You want to know if I believe in ESP.
Patient: Yes, I do.
Doctor: Why is it important for you to know that?
Patient: Because, I just wanted to—I thought that—
Doctor: I wonder if anyone else here believes in ESP?

In this example, the therapist first repeats the patient's question, although he heard and understood it quite well. His repetition is simply a device to buy time while he tries to think of what to say next—and then he dodges the question by responding to it with another. Answering a question with a question is generally poor technique, obstructive rather than facilitative; it doesn't help the patient get where he's trying to go. Finally, the therapist diverts the question clear away from himself and onto the group, so that the thrust of the patient's

15. Translation refers to saying the same thing in different words, taking care to leave the meaning intact. Interpretation, in contrast, involves placing a different meaning on what the patient is saying or doing. An interpretive comment, in the above example, would take note of the patient's reaching out, or perhaps of the significance of the aura.

effort to engage him one-on-one is thwarted and diffused. It is as though the patient reached out and found only a phantom.

The patient's questions at times will raise real questions for the therapist. It is still important to answer the patient first, and directly, before posing questions of his own. In the second example, both of the therapist's questions could have been asked after an interaction such as the first example took place.

In short, if a patient asks a question, answer it; if you don't know the answer, say so. Your answers should be brief. That the best therapist intervention is a short one is particularly true when anxiety is high, as it is in an admissions-service inpatient group. Cognitive complexity and anxiety appear to be negatively correlated: the higher the anxiety level, the simpler the cognitive functioning of the patient. Patients are not likely to be able to follow long, involved, complex statements, delivered in compound sentences, intended to provide complete and structured responses in the belief that such full responses will be anxiety reducing. Short, declarative sentences are most likely to be understood. Your comments should be brief, simple, concise, concrete, referring to observable behavior, and containing as little ambiguity or indefiniteness as possible. (To be able to follow these constraints and still say something is reminiscent of the old joke: put your shoulder to the wheel and your nose to the grindstone—and try to work in that position.) The simplicity referred to here is *grammatical,* not intellectual. A succession of grammatically simple sentences may refer cumulatively to rather complex conceptualizations.

To start a group, then, engage the patients one at a time. Which patient to engage first is as difficult a decision as in an outpatient group. The principles which apply there do not necessarily apply in inpatient groups. The patient who, in an inpatient group, looks most eager to talk may be manic, hypomanic, or so tenuously in contact with reality that engaging

with him at the very start of the group will make things more
rather than less difficult. The patient who looks most frozen,
frightened, or most apathetic may well be most in need of being
reached out to. The best procedure to follow is to use your
common sense, and to attempt to engage the patient who looks
both in need of being reached out to and most likely to
respond. If you're not sure of who that might be, start with the
patient with whom you have the best eye contact. If you don't
have particularly good eye contact with anyone (not an unusual
circumstance), start with the person sitting next to you.

Once again we have reached the moment, at the start of a
group, when it is up to you to *do* something. You are the
therapist, and you feel, more or less strongly, that all depends
on you, and that you are supposed to know what to do. But
nothing in the books is quite like the situation you are now facing, and you don't know what to do. You turn to the patient
sitting next to you and you see the eyes that are dim or blank or
vacant; the bent shoulders and the gnarled nicotine-stained
hands. You think, "Oh Lord, how can I reach this person?
What will I say?" and you have only the vaguest roadmap:
reduce anxiety; make of the group a safe place; facilitate interaction. You hear a voice—it is yours, but it sounds remarkably
like your supervisor's—saying, "Mr. Lang, what would you
like to tell us today?" Miraculously, the blank, dim eyes look
up, and for a moment, just a moment, there is a glimmer in
them, of fear, uncertainty, of—shrewdness.

"I'd like to go home," says Mr. Lang, and the group is
started.

Time structuring. At some point a patient is likely to indicate
that he is not quite ready to respond at just that moment, or
that, having gotten this far, he's not quite ready to go further.
It is as important for the therapist to know when (and how) to
disengage, as to engage with patients. When a patient is saying

not yet, it is important to let him know that (a) you will get back to him and (b) you will do so in some specified time. "We'll come back to you in five minutes" is generally a useful and helpful comment because it lets the patient know that you are giving him time to gather his thoughts, but a finite time, and that you will give him an opportunity to continue. Patients sometimes indicate that while they are not ready to talk today they may be ready next time. Then it is easier (and, in a sense, mandatory) to start next time by inviting those patients to begin.

Structuring, in general, tends to reduce anxiety because it makes the immediate future more predictable. The more predictable the future, the less anxious the patients. Group leaders not uncommonly determine who in group wants to "work," and then divide the available time so that each patient will know the amount of time he has to work. Transactional Analysts put a great deal of emphasis on time structuring in this way. Usually, both the anxiety level and the level of sophistication of the patients will preclude attempting to time-structure admissions-service groups. The statement that "we'll come back to you in five minutes"—or perhaps in ten—offers probably a small enough chunk of time to have some meaning in the conceptual world of a highly anxious patient.

Verbal and nonverbal communication. A major problem for the therapist of a state hospital is that most patients are neither practiced nor skilled in talking about affect or relationship between affect and behavior, while psychotherapies are by definition primarily verbal. The therapist who inquires, "How did you feel about that?" is likely to get a reply like "Fine," or "All right," rather than a verbal report of affect. Similarly, patients learn (but are seldom taught) that the term *sick* in a mental hospital refers to behavior rather than to physical illness. Until they learn this difference, patients may respond with confusion to this novel use of the term. Although these differences between patients and therapists in communicative styles is probably most marked in state hospitals, they may be characteristic of other inpatient settings as well.

One major contributor to this divergence in style is the social class difference between patient and therapist first emphasized by Hollingshead and Redlich (1958). Relatively old, this study is a classic whose findings have stood the test of time and of various changes in our culture. Psychotherapists still tend to come from Classes II and III, middle and upper-middle, and state hospital patients from Classes IV and V, lower-middle and lower. The tendencies which Hollingshead and Redlich ascribe to psychiatrists to offer psychotherapy to Class II and III patients, and medication and hospitalization to Class IV and V patients, can still be seen on most admissions services of large mental hospitals. These attitudes are less likely to be manifest on inpatient units serving primarily middle-and upper-class patients.

A second contributor to the handling and divergence in style of communicating affect may be embedded more in personality than in cultural factors. Whitehorn and Betz (1954) identified a personality dimension which is characterized at one end by (among other things) verbal articulateness, and, at the other, by a modal masculine "strong, silent" stereotype. Berzins, Friedman, and Seidman (1969) suggest a relationship between the latter (type B) and schizoid behavioral patterns where symptomatic behaviors appear.

These factors—social class and personality—weigh against most patients in an inpatient admissions-service therapy group being able to talk much about their feelings. These factors point in the same direction regarding the expression of affect: feelings lead to action, not talk.

Since most of the psychotherapies, including group psychotherapy, facilitate talk rather than action, the patient is being asked to involve and commit himself in an arena in which he may have little investment and little skill, and for which he may have little esteem. The therapist must realize the limitations inherent in his treatment modality, and must refrain from setting technical goals which are not likely to be either attainable or fruitful. The attempt to get inpatients to talk about feelings is frequently an inappropriate technical goal.

Nonetheless, patients do experience affect, and they do communicate affect, if not verbally then nonverbally. The cues are different, perhaps more ambiguous, perhaps muted; but they are usually there. In chapter 6, we saw that the therapist attends to a host of small details about the patient and how the latter interacts with the group. In inpatient groups, the nonverbal presentation of self may be of considerably greater importance than the verbal interaction. To the extent that nonverbal presentation is form, and verbal interaction is substance, *there may be no meaning in the substance,* and form may be the entirety of the communication. Thus, the patient who babbles incoherently may be trying to reach out, to make contact. The response to such a patient—"I'm sorry, I can't understand you"—takes form for granted and assumes that there must be some meaning in the substance.

How do you determine what might be an appropriate response here? By looking at the patient rather than by listening to him. He may want reassurance and direction—"It's all right. Sit down now. It's all right."—with a smile and a nod to where he is to sit. He may want comforting in some way; or perhaps the babbling is intended to provoke rejection. The point is that the essence of the patient's affect may be conveyed in nonverbal performances, and to the extent that you can respond along these lines, your chances of reaching him are enhanced.

The babbling patient is more likely to be encountered on wards other than the admissions service. In admissions-service groups, silence, monosyllabic replies, and confused looks are common responses to therapist attempts to get patients to talk about their feelings. It is then more difficult to find out how to reach them on an affective level.

The question is whether the therapist should even try to deal with patients' feelings in this type of group. The answer is yes. While you are not aiming for the development of insight or significant behavior change, you are aiming for the reduction of anxiety, the facilitation of communication (not necessarily verbal), and the reinforcement of nonpsychotic behavior. One of the first steps in the reduction of anxiety may involve the perception, by the patient, that he is understood, and that the understanding does not provoke hostility. A nonverbal communication with the patient may be quite reassuring.

Nonverbal communication need not involve physical touch, nor is what is being suggested here the ritualized but silent behavior popular in encounter groups. In inpatient admissions-service groups, nonverbal communication should probably be visual rather than tactile or motoric. For the frightened paranoid patient, for example, the smallest smile of acknowledgment may suffice to reassure him that his fear has been seen and understood, and that it will be responded to gently. For the depressed patient, perhaps a look of kind concern and a shift in body posture, attentive and receptive, may be meaningful and effective: it is impossible to prescribe what will work with which patient, or within which type of patient.

How, then, is the novice therapist to learn? Ideally, by watching a more experienced therapist, and by talking with him afterward. And by realizing that what is said, especially in this type of group, is less important than what is done and felt: by attending more to nonverbal than to verbal interactions; by attempting to convey, nonverbally, the attitudes of acceptance and understanding, of recognition without revulsion, and of his confidence in his abilities to combat the demons of madness.

Ending the group session. As with outpatient groups, there is no specific formula for ending the group, but there are some general guidelines. If there is no clock visible, you should notify patients about ten minutes in advance of the time group is to end; that is, it may be desirable, or perhaps necessary, for you to assume the kind of time monitoring, and of pacing, that you would expect outpatients to be able to handle themselves. Some, if not most, of the members of an inpatient group may have difficulty monitoring time and pacing themselves, and wristwatches and other time-orienting mechanisms of the outside world may be more or less absent in the rather special world of the admissions ward.

A general principle is to make sure that each person who wishes to speak (or to have the attention of the group) either has some oportunity to do so, or has some reassurance that he will be attended to next time. This is generally not difficult. If time elapses before a patient has finished, or a group episode is completed, it is good practice to say something like, "We'll have to stop now. We can start in again at this point next time. See you on Tuesday." Usually, there won't be that much interaction to interrupt.

Another way of ending group is to offer contracts to begin group next time. The patient who is not yet ready to interact, or who wishes to go just one step and no further, today, can be offered, or promised, the opportunity to go first, or can be assured (at the least) that he will be attended to next time. For example:

Therapist: Mrs. Jones, you look pretty anxious just now.
Mrs. Jones: What?
Therapist: You look anxious. Nervous.
Mrs. Jones: I feel fine.
Therapist: Your hands are shaking.

Mrs. Jones: That's all right.
Therapist: Is it?
Mrs. Jones: Is it what?
Therapist: Why are your hands shaking?
Mrs. Jones: Nerves, I guess.
Therapist: You mean bad feelings inside?
Mrs. Jones: Well, I guess.
Therapist: I'd like to know more about that.
Mrs. Jones: Not now.
Therapist: Next time?
Mrs. Jones: Maybe.
Therapist: OK, Mrs. Jones, I'll ask you about your nerves when group meets again on Thursday at 11.

In this example, the therapist, who is marvelously patient, has some difficulty engaging Mrs. Jones. That difficulty is a clue to go slowly with her, and to let her "off the hook," as it were, when she says, "Not now." After having knocked at her door six times, his invitation to her to postpone further inter-action until next time is clearly appropriate, and does not necessarily represent his letting her be evasive. It is, of course, quite important for the therapist to initiate interaction with Mrs. Jones early in the next session, and, if need be, to knock on her door six times more.

There are several advantages to the "we'll come back to you next time" approach. In addition to its function of reassurance— the sentence should *not* be used if it could be mistaken for a threat—it helps both patients and therapist to begin to struc-ture the time of the next session: to know at least a little of what's going to happen. That can be a factor in reducing anxi-ety: the anxiety of the patient who lives in a most uncertain and unpredictable world, and of the therapist who comes into group with his own uncertainties as to how to proceed.

Sometimes a summary of what's happened during group will be helpful; more often, it won't. If the session has been a series of one-to-one interactions, patient to therapist, and anxiety levels have been high, there will be little point in summarizing because all you'll have to work on is a series of fragments. If there has been some genuine group interaction, a summary might be helpful. If you feel it important to make some kind of summary statement of a session characterized by serial dyadic interactions, some general comment as to the intensity level might be appropriate.

You may find that stopping the group takes more than your statement, "It's time to stop for today," or "We have to stop now"—or some such statement which would, in an outpatient group, result in the group members bestirring themselves, getting up, and leaving the room. What it really takes, sometimes, to get the group stopped is your standing up. That is a signal, always to the patients, and sometimes to your cotherapist as well, that the group is really over. It is another instance of the general rule that, with inpatients, what you do is more important than what you say.

Chapter 10

Group Psychotherapy with Chronic Schizophrenic Patients

This chapter is addressed to the novice who finds himself with treatment responsibilities for chronically hospitalized patients in large residential treatment centers. If there is no demonstrable organic brain impairment, and no more than mild impairment of intellectual functioning, such patients are most likely to be labeled schizophrenic.

A large proportion, although usually not a majority, of patients at state hospitals and Veterans Administration neuropsychiatric hospitals may carry diagnoses denoting organic brain dysfunction, including geriatric disorders. In addition, a proportion of the patients will manifest functional mental retardation, although this condition may not be reflected in the diagnostic label. Differential diagnosis of mental retardation and simple schizophrenia is frequently quite difficult, and the conditions are not mutually exclusive. The specific group psychotherapeutic techniques which are most appropriate for retarded patients are not discussed in the present volume.

A chronically hospitalized schizophrenic patient is one who has no demonstrable organic or major intellectual impairment, who has been hospitalized for some time, and whose prospects for release are minimal. A student walking on to a ward, or continued-care facility housing such patients might be surprised at how ordinary they look. They may be sitting quietly, watching television or chatting with friends or with aides, or perhaps looking off into the distance, as if momentarily lost in thought. At times, one or two individuals may become agitated or tearful, but this tends to be the exception rather than the rule.

The student may then ask himself why many of these people are hospitalized, and why the doors are locked (if they are). An attempt to answer such questions might lead him to peruse the patients' charts. The case histories contained in the charts frequently seem to be chronicles of failure and tragedy and defeat. Many patients will have had multiple admissions to the hospital: administration of one of the phenothiazines is followed by improvement and discharge; the patient, once in the community, fails to take the medicine and readmission occurs. It is as though the patient does not want to "get well."

It is difficult to imagine patients on a medical ward refusing medication to ease pain or cure disease. Some mental patients, however, will refuse medication prescribed for them known to produce changes in their behavior. Chronically hospitalized patients not uncommonly will also more or less actively resist psychotherapeutic efforts, group or individual, to facilitate those changes in their behavior which might lead to discharge from the hospital. The student may be surprised and puzzled on first encountering the vehemence with which deviance is embraced by the chronic patient. The student's confusion not infrequently is followed by anger, and then despair, and then a fervent desire to leave the hospital and work in an outpatient clinic, preferably in suburbia. Students with a medical background and experience on inpatient medical wards where patients are cooperative rather than antagonistic toward efforts at healing them may have even stronger adverse reactions. But students from other disciplines, and entry-level mental health workers without advanced training, such as nurses' aides, may also be unprepared for patients who seem to be embracing the disease and more or less actively resisting efforts by doctors, nurses, social workers, and others to cure them.

Why is this so? Why does the chronically hospitalized patient so often fail to appear interested in "getting well" and seeking discharge from the hospital? The answer to these questions may depend in large part upon how one conceptualizes schizophrenia. There is, or at any rate, there ought to be, some relationship between one's conceptualization of schizophrenia and the therapeutic interventions. If schizophrenia is regarded as a disease process, based on some neural or biochemical deficit, then somatic therapies (including medication) will probably be seen as most appropriate. If it is regarded as a social or familial process, then therapy would involve modifying the social or familial systems within which the patient functions, or at least the interface between the patient and these systems. And if schizophrenia is conceptualized as a set of learned responses or behavioral deficits, then therapy would include experiential and perhaps didactic learning experiences. From each of these conceptualizations it is possible to account for the antagonism or indifference of the chronically hospitalized patient toward efforts at cure.

Yet none of these conceptualizations of schizophrenia is particularly helpful to the group therapist. A way of thinking about schizophrenia is needed which will have some relevance for group therapy, will help the therapist make some sense out of schizophrenic behavior, and will offer or suggest some fairly specific tactics and techniques in the application of group therapy to this type of chronic patient population.

Schizophrenia applies to a wide and somewhat disparate range of phenomena, including the realm of the interpersonal. Group therapy is an interpersonal phenomenon. We will view schizophrenia from a social psychological standpoint—which, as we saw in chapter 4, is the standpoint from which Freud undertook to explain group phenomena—and we shall focus on the interpersonal aspects of schizophrenia. We will start with the hypothesis that *schizophrenia is an adaptive response* by the patient to his life situation.

In this chapter, then, we will discuss schizophrenia as an adaptive set of responses. We will discuss some techniques which may help to make sense out of what appears to be aimless or disordered behavior to the student who is beginning to attempt group psychotherapy with chronically hospitalized schizophrenic patients. We will conclude with a discussion of some of the problems the student may encounter in the clinical setting—what might be termed the politics of group therapy on an inpatient ward—and with a brief look at the effect on the therapist of working with patients for whom the probability of recovery is so slim.

Schizophrenia as an Adaptive Response

Our task here is twofold: first, to begin to understand the behavior, and perhaps to some extent, the world, of the schizophrenic patient, as that understanding is relevant to group therapy; and second, to use that understanding to devise therapeutic interventions in group. The role of theory is discussed more fully in chapter 3.

We begin with a set of assumptions. The first assumption is that behavior is purposive. The interpersonal behavior of an individual is intended to produce or evoke some effect or state of affairs which is usually, but not always, more satisfying to him than various other possible alternative outcomes.

If behavior is purposive, and interpersonal behavior is intended to produce some particular interpersonal effect, then it follows that the effect, or end-point, of behavior *is that which was intended.* Our second assumption, then, is that people are generally successful establishing or maintaining the interpersonal state of affairs that they seek. Individuals who prefer an interpersonal atmosphere characterized by high emotional intensity will generate that intensity or find settings where it exists. Individuals who prefer an interpersonal atmosphere characterized by hostility and distrust are literally expert at generating hostility and distrust. If they are quite expert at it, such individuals may be labeled as having paranoid characteristics. Individuals who prefer to avoid significant interpersonal contacts are skilled at generating rejection, and if they are skilled enough, they may be labeled schizophrenic.

These are generalizations. There are of course exceptions, some of which are quite significant. We are concerned here with adults, and perhaps with adolescents, who have no demonstrable organic impairment, and no major intellectual deficit. We are applying the two assumptions presented above—that behavior is purposive, and that adults are skilled at achieving their interpersonal purposes—to chronically hospitalized schizophrenic patients.

It would seem to follow that these long-term or permanent hospitalizations are sought and chosen. In some instances, the choice may indeed be both conscious and rational, as Laing has suggested (Laing and Esterson 1971). But for most patients, hospitalization either appears to be the only viable option, or it is an incidental side effect accompanying other choices which are more central to them.

Let us clarify the latter point with an example, for it is central to our thesis of schizophrenia as an adaptive response. This is a fictionalized account of a real patient:

A woman lived for many years with her domineering mother. She married in order to escape the parental home, but shortly afterward her father died and her mother came to live with the newlyweds. The marriage ended, and this woman, whom we shall call Mary, lived with her mother and tended to her for the next fifteen years. Her effort at independence had met with failure. Her mother kept Mary dependent; Mary never learned a marketable skill, nor how to drive, nor manage a checking account, nor choose her clothes. Mother took care of that. And mother taught Mary that Mary's anger at her, and Mary's occasional striving toward independence and a separate existence, was *evil*. So if Mary was very angry, it meant she was very evil. Expressing anger was a sure path to hell. And the mother taught Mary that the world, outside their house, was tremendously complex, harsh, and fearsome. What she did, in sum, was to succeed in maintaining a mother-child relationship with her daughter for thirty years after it should have ended.

When her mother died, Mary was consumed with guilt and with fear. She did not know much about the world and was afraid to try to find out, on her own, as herself. When she did venture out, she acted the way she had seen her mother act. She tried to re-create her mother in herself, to *become* her mother, and in this way to assuage her own guilt. In addition, what Mary chose to adopt and to mimic was not her mother's style in general, but rather the way her mother acted when drunk. The mother had apparently been an alcoholic.

Mary solved a number of problems by acting as though she were her drunken mother. Principally, she assuaged the guilt by denying the potency of her own wish that her mother would die: she lived on in Mary. She also solved the problem of how to live in the world by acting as her mother had when her mother had needed taking care of (was drunk). And there were other problems which were resolved by Mary's acting in this way.

In effect, Mary chose hospitalization. But she did not set out to get herself into the hospital, or on to a ward of chronic schizophrenic patients. She set out to try to live with herself, in the face of overwhelming guilt, and to live in the world, in the face of overwhelming fear. Hospitalization was a side effect.

It is not difficult to imagine the diagnostic problem that Mary posed upon admission to the hospital. She looked and acted drunk. It was only when her behavior persisted past any possible aftereffect of alcohol or other drug intoxication that a diagnosis of schizophrenic reaction began to be considered.

Therapy with Mary would be difficult in part because she has little, if anything, to gain from adopting less deviant behavioral patterns and returning to the world. The hospital is a predictable and relatively safe environment. Her physical needs are met, she is allowed a modicum of independence (she has a grounds pass), and the complexity of her world is not greater than she can handle. Return to the community involves entering an unpredictable environment where she cannot be certain that her physical needs will be met and which is characterized, according to her mother, by complexity beyond Mary's capacity to manage.

In this example, schizophrenia is an adaptive response of an individual choosing madness because other options were not apparent to her. The approach to the understanding of schizophrenic behavior presented here is similar to that of Laing and Esterson (1971).

A behavioral pattern more typical of chronically hospitalized patients is perhaps one which involves interpersonal avoidance. The chronically hospitalized patient is often difficult to understand and hard to hear; words are slurred or mumbled, the sounds which he makes are sometimes not words at all, and the patient seems more to be talking to himself in your presence than engaging with you.

So it seems that chronic patients either avoid interpersonal contact or, if they do reach out, do so in ways that are inappropriate, difficult to respond to, and deviant.

Peter is a 35-year-old man who has been hospitalized for 15 years. He can usually be found standing just outside the entrance to the building in which he is housed. He is tall and chubby the way many patients are who eat nothing but the starchy institutional food. He wears a faded blue shirt and overalls that are two sizes too large for him. His hair is cut quite short and is unkempt; his teeth are brown and jagged.

As you approach the entrance to Peter's building, he sidles up to you, eyes fixed firmly on the ground, wearing an orgiastic smile. When he is about four feet away from you, he darts a quick glance in your general direction, says "Hullo," and moves quickly away from you with the quite distinctive gait that young children have when they are walking just in front of a parent from whom they are expecting a swat on the bottom.

It is more or less clear that Peter has attempted to reach out to you. If you respond with a hello and a friendly smile, he will stop about twenty feet away from you, still wearing his orgiastic grin, and begin studying the corner of the building intently; if you take no notice of him, he does not go quite so far away. Since he does this each time you come to the building, it becomes easy, after a while, to ignore him, or to mumble a "hello" back to him rather absently: something is happening between you, but not much, and not much energy is invested in the interchange.

The end result of Peter's interaction is quite similar to the typical interpersonal stance of patients who are more withdrawn. His effort to engage with you, if that is what it was, has resulted in failure: you ignore him on your way into the building. This end result may be regarded as either desired and intentional on Peter's part, or a result which he does not know how to avoid. If it is desired and intentional, then we may hypothesize (a) that Peter has learned that he is safer, his chances for survival greater, if he is ignored by people; (b) that he has learned that he is more likely to be ignored, in the long run, if he engages in some minimal interaction which is repeated, invariant, until people "get used to it;" (c) that he has at least a little ambivalence about interpersonal interaction; otherwise, we may hypothesize, he would have adopted the more withdrawn stance which produces the same interpersonal end result.

Thus, this rather deviant behavioral pattern can be seen to have adaptive value for Peter, *since it produces the result which he intends.*

It is not always possible to discern, during the course of an interaction with a chronically hospitalized patient, what the intent or purpose or function of the deviant behavior pattern might be. The interpersonal situation at the conclusion of the interaction provides the best clue. A reasonable and potentially fruitful therapeutic ploy is to assume that the state of affairs which prevails at the end of an interaction is, in fact, what was intended. The most common endpoint of interactions with, and among, chronically hospitalized patients, is the maintenance or increase of interpersonal distance and interpersonal isolation.

An undesirable and unhappy state of affairs for many people (and especially group therapists!) seems thus at times a more satisfying, or less unsatisfying, state of affairs for the chronically hospitalized patient. If, as we suggest, deviant behavior is adaptive and, at least to some extent, intentional, we may hypothesize (a) that the deviant pattern represents the best effort at adaptation which the patient is capable of making, given his sociocultural background, prior learning, genetic makeup, and the choices he perceives as available to him; and (b) that the behavior meets some need, or represents an effort to meet some need. Usually, with chronically hospitalized patients, safety needs are paramount.

The concept that the patient's present (or pre-therapy) behavior represents his best effort at adaptation may, at times, be difficult for the therapist to hold on to. Chronically hospitalized patients are typically characterized by a lack of motivation for change, for interaction with others, for improving upon what seems to us the barren and sparse existence of a state hospital ward. When such a patient refuses even to try a new behavior, and seems indifferent to the feelings of others, including the therapist, it is tempting to ascribe the patient's miserable state and his lack of motivation for change to either the severity of the illness or to some characterological flaw. Some mental health workers may virtually abandon rehabilitative efforts with this type of patient. Recalling that the patient may be doing the best he can, given the choices that were available, and that there may now be other choices, may help the therapist avoid this type of nihilism.

The concept that the patient's behavior meets some need might at first seem both so trite and so obvious as not to need mentioning. However, grossly deviant behaivor is more often interpreted in mental hospitals as resulting from some deficit or impairment (see Johnson 1963), than as an effort at adaptation, a coping mechanism. This view has clearly proven fruitful in the treatment of the mentally ill and its merit is not at issue here. However, for the group therapist seeking to understand and to influence interpersonal behavior, it is not as fruitful a viewpoint as it is for the psychiatrist treating "ego psychopathology" (Johnson's phrase, 1963), or prescribing medicines. If the patient's behavior is conceptualized—and understood—in terms of meeting some need, the group therapist may more easily retain his focus on interpersonal rather than on intrapsychic events.

Behavior, then, is purposive; it may be regarded as intended to meet some need; behavior, that is, is defined here as goal-oriented. The task of the therapist is to determine, sometimes in a process of discovery shared by the patient, what the goals of various behavioral patterns are. Assuming the legitimacy of the goals themselves, the therapist and the group can provide alternative choices—or, put more precisely, can help the patient to discover, explore, and experience alternative ways of reaching those goals and meeting those needs. The emphasis is on present and future, rather than on the past, on what the patient is trying to do, rather than on what he has done. And the emphasis is on interpersonal rather than intrapsychic events.

One way that the therapist can (sometimes) determine what the patient's goals are—not life goals, but what the patient is trying to do in the present, ongoing interpersonal situation—is to assume that *whatever* the end-point of the situation is constitutes the patient's goal. Deviant and even bizarre behavior is, from this point of view, no less orderly, purposive, understandable, and *effective in producing a desired outcome,* than behavior which is less rare or offensive.

Starting from our concept of schizophrenia as an adaptive response, we have suggested that deviant and apparently dysfunctional behavior patterns can be understood as goal-oriented attempts at survival and adaptation. For the rather special circumstances of a therapy group, we will assume that *all* observable behavior during the group session pertains in some way to the group, its members, or the therapists; and that deviant, bizarre, and disruptive behavior represents the patient's effort to cope with the group. That is, we assume that all of a patient's behavior during a group session, including unresponsive behavior, is purposive and addressed, at least in part, to the present interpersonal situation. With these assumptions, which represent a rather special way of conceptualizing schizophrenia, we can begin to formulate some intervention strategies for which group therapy is uniquely suited.

Technique: Some General Considerations

In the admissions-service group, as we have seen, the first task of the therapist is to reduce anxiety. With chronically hospitalized patients, the first task is to establish contact with, or between, patients. Contact, in the sense we are using the term here, involves a personal interaction here and now between two individuals who accept personal responsibility for their share of the interaction. The tendency of those patients who are willing to talk will be to talk about events and people who are removed in time and space from here and now, and to be vague and inferential ("Some people don't like it when people say certain things."). The task of the therapist is to reduce the vagueness, and to focus as much as possible on what is happening here, in this room, at this moment, among these people.

Establishing interpersonal contact with people who have a life-long investment in avoiding such contact is a difficult art.

It is probably more of an intuitive than a cognitive process. If an interaction feels right, it probably is; if it doesn't, it probably is not. The learning process for the student therapist may involve building confidence in his perception of his own internal processes. Confidence in your own internal processes can be built through interaction with your cotherapist and with your supervisor, and, most importantly, through interaction with patients as they begin responding *to,* rather than *at,* or against, you. It is difficult to learn from a book how to attend to and build confidence in your perception and interpretation of your own internal processes. That is because book learning involves reaction and response but not interaction: there's no one there to check things out with.

The level of anxiety in this type of group may be quite low or difficult to determine; it may not offer the therapist a guide to initiating interaction, a function which anxiety level can serve in other types of therapy groups. The absence of anxiety is sometimes regarded as a poor prognostic sign. The student may encounter an occasional supervisor who embraces the converse proposition that the presence of anxiety is a good prognostic sign, and who may regard efforts to create anxiety in one's patients as therapeutic (Armstrong and Rouslin 1963). But for some people, madness is a defense against anxiety, and efforts to defeat those defenses may only drive the patient farther and farther away from interpersonal contact. The reduction of anxiety remains an important responsibility of the therapist even in groups of chronically hospitalized patients.

The term *schizophrenia* does not refer to the absence of affect, but rather to the splitting off of affect from cognitive functioning, so that the feelings which we would expect to accompany some verbal statements are simply not in evidence (Bleuler 1950). The group member who tells you confidently and calmly that he is a good man surrounded by evil, for example, wants to create the impression that he is not afraid; he does it so well that you may miss the import of his words. If you were surrounded by evil, you'd be quite frightened and would show it. Or perhaps you would put on a show of bravado, a whistling in the dark. In the patient the anxiety, or the terror, may also be there, but it is hidden, hidden so deeply that neither confrontation nor reassurance can touch it. It is not necessarily wrong to respect the patient's wish that his terror remain secret. Nor is it wrong for you to hope that such a wish can be modified.

Other general technical considerations include those described in chapter 9. The group should be a safe place for the patient to be and, perhaps, to grow. The therapist's role in establishing and maintaining that safety is paramount. Patients are not likely to be skilled at talking about their feelings, or to particularly value such an activity. What is happening in group is probably more important than what is being said. The main problems for the group leader with these patients are most likely to be establishing contact and handling disordered behavior should it occur during the group session.

Technique: Intervention Strategies

The context in which therapeutic intervention takes place necessarily determines much of the form of the intervention. The goals or purposes of group give form and validation to the strategies the therapists may adopt. In what follows, the context is a group of chronically hospitalized patients who are functioning relatively well within the hospital, requiring little or no custodial or nursing care, and minimal supervision. The purposes of group include meeting the hospital's obligation to provide treatment for its patients and training for its students, and also to help patients attain a maximal level of independence either inside or outside its walls. We are concerned here with a group of patients whose functional level is high and whose participation in group is voluntary. Groups of inter-mediate and low functioning patients tend to be less voluntary and more structured; intervention strategies in such groups are of course different.

One way of beginning to establish interpersonal contact is to assume that everything that the patient says or does has some relevance to, and is intended to produce some effect in, the present here-and-now group situation. A corollary assumption is that the effect which is produced is the effect which was intended. Neither of these assumptions may be true, but both may be fruitful.

In short, the strategy here is to assume that all activity during the group session is interpersonal, that all activity by any one patient is related to, or aimed at, another specific person in the room—sometimes it takes a lot of work to get to that point—and that his activity is intended to produce a specific response in the recipient. The strategic goal (as distinct from the tactical goal, which is the establishment of interpersonal contact) in-volves the formation of a group consensus which the patient can accept and about which he cares. The end point is the reduction or abandonment of the interpersonal isolation to which the patient fled when he embraced madness as a means of survival.

It may not be possible, however, to define all activity during the group session as interpersonal. Nor can even the most skilled therapist invariably succeed in getting the patient to be concrete and specific rather than vague, general, and symbolic. Some patients who start out by referring to "everyone" or "people" or (most ominously) "they" will simply refuse to designate any one individual, inside or outside the present room. And sometimes it will be impossible to determine what specific response the activity is intended to produce. More will be going on, during the session, than the therapist can, or should, respond to. Some of the time you won't respond because it isn't necessary or appropriate to do so; some of the time, because you don't know what on earth to do. As with outpatient groups, it may be important to acknowledge to yourself that you cannot make every possible interpretation or intervention—an acknowledgment which may help you to choose those interventions which are most likely to get you where you want to go. With chronically hospitalized patients, where you want to go involves engaging the patient, trying to figure out what he's after (interpersonally), and making available some alternative and hopefully less deviant ways for him to get it.

One of the purposes the group serves, then, is to function as a reservoir of interpersonal resources from which the patient can draw without being overwhelmed or devastated. We have touched, more or less in passing, on a number of differences between inpatient and outpatient groups, and, within the former, on differences between admissions-service groups and those comprised of chronically hospitalized patients. Yet one way in which all three types of group are *similar* is in the willingness of patients to be of help to one another. Schizophrenic patients, whose motivation for improvement as defined by others appears to be zero, will facilitate change in others as long as they themselves do not feel threatened. The first step toward facilitation of change is for the patient to find or discover that he can meet some of his needs more satisfactorily in an interpersonal context than in solitude, or through fantasy, or magical thinking. Generally, if the group members know what those needs are, they will move to meet them as effectively as they can.

Determination of what a patient's interpersonal needs or interests are is a task fraught with ambiguity. The patient himself may give few cues as to what he wants or expects from the group, and no indication other than his voluntary presence that he has any interest at all in being there. He may respond inconsistently and unpredictably to efforts to get him to interact with the therapist. It is not unusual for a patient to give the impression that (a) he wants and needs some interaction, perhaps some relationship with you, and (b) he cannot tolerate that which he seeks. It is an ambivalent message, perhaps reflecting the patient's own ambivalence about interpersonal relationships, which may be summed up as though the patient were saying, "Go away closer." One response to this message might be, "We won't come too close, but we won't go away either." The response may be offered by members of the group verbally or non-verbally, as well as by the therapist. One interpretation of this kind of interaction is that some ambiguity about interpersonal distance within the group has been reduced. Patient comments in chronically ill groups (as well as, incidentally, in outpatient groups, though to a different degree) are frequently characterized by ambiguity and inconsistency, as well as by vagueness and abstractness. In addition the disturbance in formal thought processes characteristic of schizophrenia—as, for instance, the looseness of associations, or the formation of neologisms—may further obscure the meaning of the verbal message. The group members, as well as the therapist, can help the patient reduce the ambiguity and clarify the meaning of the message. For example:

Therapist: George, what would you like to do today?
George: Yes. Well, almost exactly. I'm not entirely, uh, well, could you, uh, precision, of course, become—I mean get, uh, what I'm saying is that I don't, uh, nothing in particular, to be more exact, do you mean me? No, huh. Yes. Nothing. I think so, Yes. OK, you know?
Therapist: No. I'm not sure what you mean.
George: Tough shit. That was clear.

Therapist: Not to me. I wonder if it was clear to other people in the group?

Madeline: George doesn't have anything in particular that he wants to do today, do you George, and can I bum a cigarette?

George: Yeah. Go ahead with someone else. (Offers Madeline a cigarette.)

Another function of group is to provide the patient with information. The types of information which can perhaps more effectively be communicated by other patients rather than the therapist, and are relatively easy to elicit from group members, may be classified as follows:

(a) Information about the patient's communication with others. If the therapist says that he does not understand what the patient is saying, the patient may interpret the therapist's response as a ploy or maneuver, or as rejection or condemnation. If other group members also seek clarification, the patient may be less likely to assume that he is in fact being understood. The comment, "that's crazy talk" has a very different impact if it is made by the therapist or by another group member.

(b) Information about the consequences of some behaviors. For example, "When you scream at the nurses, they will get your medication increased until you're sleepy. That's why you sleep all the time." This comment, coming from the therapist, may sound critical. Coming from other patients, it doesn't. The consequences associated with actions may be quite clear, quite obvious to the therapist. It may even be reasonable to expect that such consequences—like getting more medication, or being put in seclusion for screaming at nurses—should be clear to the patients as well. But reasonable expectations frequently do not hold with chronically hospitalized patients. Drawing the group into offering information about the consequences of behavior requires skill and patience. It is especially worth the effort when group members offer information which the therapist assumed too obvious to mention.

(c) Information about the accuracy of the patient's reality testing. This is the consensual validation function of the group. Grossly deviant distortions of reality are best handled by the therapist: "My uncle owns this hospital" is not the kind of comment that is taken seriously by other group members. On the other hand, "Social workers get upset when you tell them you don't like your doctor" may more easily be handled by the group—after the therapist has helped the patient to go from the general statement to the specific, e.g., "My social worker yelled at me yesterday when I told her I didn't like Doctor Zwiesalniecks."

There are probably other purposes which the group may fill in the service of the patient. All of these purposes may fall under the general heading of offering interaction without rejection and without devastation.

The preceding discussion has focused on the verbal rather than the nonverbal aspects of interaction. Yet, particularly in this type of group, the nonverbal domain may be of equal, or even of greater, importance. Some of the usual interpersonal nonverbal cues may be absent: chronically hospitalized patients are frequently cue-suppressors, with blank, impassive facial expressions, little variability in tone of voice, and few or none of the small movements of fingers or limbs which connote nervousness. That the patient is present in the room at all, where he sits and who he chooses to sit next to, and the amount of eye contact, may be the only indications that something is going on, that the patient is committed to the group and to the interaction. A moment's eye contact and the faintest glimmer of a smile may be as much interpersonal engagement as some patients can handle during the first several months of group.

Intervention strategies: concluding comment. The preceding discussion centered, for the most part, on what might happen during a group session. Indeed, it was suggested that the therapist concentrate on what is manifestly happening during the group session, to the exclusion of all else. There was no discussion of how to get the patient to the point of looking at what needs to change before he can leave the hospital. That has to come later, if at all. The abyss of madness is not a canyon but a crevice; the phenomenal world of the schizophrenic patient seems at times as narrow as that of a child and as complex as that of any adult. The task of therapy is to broaden that world without increasing its complexity. It is not an easy task. The first step upward is to reduce interpersonal isolation, and it is a difficult step to take.

A patient who is ready to look at the world beyond the consulting room, beyond the hospital, may be ready to leave the ranks of the chronically hospitalized and join those for whom there is some chance of recovery, when recovery is defined as discharge from the hospital. But the likelihood that chronically hospitalized patients can be brought to this point is slim. A group of chronically hospitalized patients may not be ready to look at what needs to change before they can be discharged until after a year or more of weekly group meetings. Even then, as they begin to look at what it would take for them to "make it" on the "outside," they may hesitate. To help patients to get better so that they can leave the hospital and enter the job market, and then, because of keen competition in the marketplace for jobs, go on welfare because no one will hire them, may do the patients a disservice.

In sum, it is difficult to avoid being pessimistic about engagement and involvement with groups of chronically hospitalized patients. What the student may bring to such groups is enthusiasm, a healthy distrust of "The System," and a conviction that he can succeed where others have failed because those others didn't know what they were talking about. That formulation is true just often enough to make it worthwhile to espouse if the student is so inclined. The probabilities, however, are that the student will engage in a great deal of effort and experience rather minimal return in terms of feeling competent and effective.

The Politics of Inpatient Group Therapy

Group therapy is a social enterprise which depends upon the active collaboration of a large number of people for its successful management. Successful management includes the assignment of a room suitable for the conduct of group therapy, and the getting or bringing of both patients and therapists to that room at approximately the appointed time. The social context of an inpatient group is a hospital ward, and the success of the group is related to the organizational and functional structure of the ward, to morale among staff and patients, and to how smoothly the system is running.

The student coming on to the ward to lead a group enters a social system with a structure and history which may extend back over decades. The student may find it difficult to gain entry into that system. Entry problems almost invariably result in problems in the management of group, that is, of getting patients and therapists together in the right room at the right time. The politics of most wards are such that students have high status and low power. Students are, therefore, vulnerable to power and status conflicts with the staff. (Psychiatric residents may be an exception; they sometimes have moderate to low status and high power.) In addition, conflicts among staff occasionally may affect the student. Because of the student's relatively high status, ward personnel are not likely to openly refuse to collaborate with the educational effort. Acquiescence and agreement are more typical—"Of course we'll bring these patients to the group room at ten. No, it's not too inconvenient. Yes, we'll keep them from going to the canteen or on a shopping trip. Why, yes, indeed." And then comes ten o'clock on the appointed day, one patient shows up, two are in the canteen, two are on a shopping trip, and one is simply unaccounted for—on a locked ward. The student, attempting to find out how this happened, will quickly discover that no one is at fault; there simply were a series of misunderstandings, unusual coincidences, which resulted in patients being scattered rather than coming to group. The first time or two this happens, it will seem quite credible and plausible. After the third or fourth time, the student may begin to feel paranoid.

There are many reasons why ward personnel may sabotage student-led groups. (Ward personnel include physicians who have a tendency to decide to transfer or discharge patients just as they begin to contribute to and benefit from group therapy.) Resentment of the student's high status and bright future may be one reason. More work for the ward personnel caused by the presence of students is frequently another. If the hospital's orientation is primarily, or heavily, toward service rather than training, purely training activities may be resented by service-oriented staff. The ward may function as a closed society which regards transient students as intruders; this tendency may be especially pronounced in therapeutic community programs where staff cohesiveness is central to the functioning of the treatment unit. And there is a plethora of other possible reasons.

A student usually can't do very much about the discrepancy between what the treatment unit says it will do, and what it actually does. Persistence in the face of passive-aggressive opposition may lead to increased hostility, while the student's reticence may allow ward routine to remain undisturbed. If the group therapy program is not an integral part of the ward routine, but is viewed as grafted on for administrative or training purposes, the student may have to carry the burden of the task of reducing the "irrelevance" of group therapy. If the training program is already an integral part of the ward routine, but the student experiences difficulty either in obtaining referrals or in getting the patients to the group room rather than to occupational or recreational therapy (for example), the task of establishing group therapy as an integral part of the ward routine may be the reconciliation of training and service needs.

Students, confronted by such a situation, may feel frustration or despair. They come to the hospital to learn about group therapy, and they spend their time and energies trying to get people into the group room. But a group session is rather like the flight of an airplane: a great deal of preparation must go into it, both before and after the actual flight. Since group is a social enterprise, the group leaders may at times have to exert as much time and energy dealing with the interpersonal context within which group occurs as with the group itself. Learning how to establish and maintain relationships with the people who are responsible for getting patients into group is at least as important a part of learning how to do groups as is the development of technical competence. The student who is more or less handed a group, upon coming to the hospital, will gain valuable experience with inpatient groups, but may have some rather painful learning to do once out in the "real world" when groups fail to materialize.

There is, of course, a limit to the virtue of having to learn hospital-ward politics in order to be able to convene a therapy group. At some point the politics stops being a learning experience and becomes a bore, or a battle. Then the educational institution is most likely to be the student's ally and advocate in trying to insure that training in group therapy is provided by the hospital. This is not always the case; but, in general, the university has accepted the obligation to provide or arrange for training, while the hospital's concern is for its patients—or, its staff.

Sometimes—perhaps even most of the time—things go smoothly: a good room is provided for group, and the ward personnel collaborate cheerfully in the process of getting patients there at the right time. The question for the student is how to distinguish in advance between such a situation and one in which he will have to spend much of his time and energy fighting the system in order to have group. Two criteria frequently provide clues. One is the sanctioning that the group program has; the other is the extent to which group is intrinsic to the tasks defined by the ward as its reasons for existence. If the group program is really supported by the hospital administration, units clear down the line tend to be supportive. On some wards there may be a discrepancy between the ostensible and actual wielders of power. A successful group program requires the compliance of both. Group is more likely to happen if it is perceived as being generated by ward personnel rather than as required, for more or less capricious reasons, by some distant central office. The student who is assigned to a ward where these criteria are not met may be able to do little more than brace himself for a difficult time—and to return to these pages in mid-semester for some reassurance that his situation is neither unique nor necessarily a reflection of his deficiencies as a student, a therapist, or a politician. It is difficult to alter a social system from a position of high status, low power, and transient duration.

The Problem of Therapist Morale

Chronic patients are by definition those who do not recover or show major improvement. Success and the experience of effectiveness or competence by the therapist is, therefore, improbable. The student who arrives full of enthusiasm may leave embittered at year's end. Indeed, in general, the longer that therapists work with schizophrenic patients, the more pessimistic they become about prognosis. The most significant therapeutic advances with these patients have been in pharmacotherapy, not psychotherapy. If patients would only take their pills, the number of inpatients would decline still further than it already has.

Group psychotherapy with chronically hospitalized patients, then, is most likely to be a futile experience. Discharge from the hospital is most likely to depend on factors having relatively little to do with the effectiveness of therapy, and not much more with the magnitude of deviance demonstrated by the patient. The availability of bed space, the existence of aftercare resources in the community, and above all the willingness of the patient's relatives or spouse to take him in and tolerate his deviant behavior probably influence the discharge rate more than the amount of individual or group therapy the patient received. There is in fact some debate as to whether psychotherapy should be carried on at all (see Eysenck 1966).

The most probable outcome of working very hard with a group of chronically hospitalized schizophrenic patients over the period of a school year . . . or two, or three . . . is failure. Change in patient behavior is improbable, regardless of the skill with which technique is applied, with which the patient is engaged, and his interpersonal needs met—and it is improbable regardless of the definition of success used by the therapist and his supervisor.

The student therapist whose morale is *not* affected by this set of probabilities may well have made an inappropriate vocational choice. Low morale is endemic and ubiquitous in state hospital staffs. The magnitude of the crash from hope to despair is probably related to the strength of therapist expectations of success: the stronger the expectation, the harder the crash. If the crash is too hard, the student may abandon psychotherapy as a vocational choice. Yet, to go into a period of training in group psychotherapy with the expectation of failure also seems futile.

One resolution of this problem is to define success very carefully, keeping in mind the magnitude of the task and the high probability of failure. Success, with chronically hospitalized patients, may be defined as making a difference in the patient's life, so that he is less miserable when you leave than he was when you first met him. That is a quite limited goal, but is one which is at least susceptible of attainment in this most intractable of patient populations. And, however limited a goal it may be, it involves the reduction of suffering, which is what a therapist is, or ought to be, all about.

References

Armstrong, Shirley W., and Rouselin, Sheila (1963). *Group Psychotherapy in Nursing Practice.* New York: Macmillan.

Bach, George R. (1954). *Intensive Group Psychotherapy.* New York: Ronald Press.

Barnes, Graham (1974). Personal Communication.

Bednar, R. L., and Lawlis, G. F. (1971). Empirical research in group psychotherapy. In *Handbook of Psychotherapy and Behavior Change,* ed. S. L. Garfield and A. E. Bergin. New York: John Wiley.

Berne, Eric (1964). *Games People Play.* New York: Grove Press.

_____(1966). *Principles of Group Treatment.* New York: Grove Press.

Berzins, J. I., Friedman, W. H., and Seidman, E. (1969). Relationship of the A-B variable to patient symptomatology, and psychotherapy expectancies. *Journal of Abnormal Psychology* 74: 119–125.

Berzins, J. I., Friedman, W. H., and Ross, W. (1974). *Toward Patient-Therapist Matching.* Unpublished manuscript.

Bion, W. R. (1961). *Experiences in Groups.* New York: Basic Books.

Bleuler, Eugen (1950). *Dementia Praecox, or the Group of Schizophrenias.* New York: International Universities Press.

Davis, F., and Lohr, N. (1971). Special problems with the use of co-therapists in group psychotherapy. *International Journal of Group Psychotherapy* 21: 143-158.

Eysenck, Hans (1966). *The Effects of Psychotherapy.* New York: International Science Press.

Ezriel, Henry (1973). Psychoanalytic group therapy. In *Group Therapy,* ed. L. R. Wolberg and E. K. Schwarz. New York: Intercontinental Medical Book Corporation.

Feinstein, Barbara, and Cavanaugh, Catherine (1974). Treatment of long-term hospitalized mental patients through the use of volunteers as group leaders. *International Journal of Group Psychotherapy* 24: 439-451.

Foulkes, S. H., and Anthony, E. J. (1965). *Group Psychotherapy: The Psychoanalytic Approach.* 2nd ed. Harmondsworth, England: Penguin.

Freud, S. (1922). *Group Psychology and The Analysis of The Ego.* New York: Hogarth.

Goffman, Ervin (1959). *Presentation of Self in Everyday Life.* Garden City, N.Y.: Doubleday Anchor.

Golembiewski, Robert, and Blumberg, Arthur, eds. (1970). *Sensitivity Training and the Laboratory Approach.* Itasca, Ill.: Peacock Publishers.

Gootnick, Irwin (1975). Transference in psychotherapy with schizophrenic patients. *International Journal of Group Psychotherapy* 25: 379-388.

Grotjahn, Martin (1977). An attempt to analyze the therapeutic process in groups. *Group: The Journal of the Eastern Group Psychotherapy Society* 1: 3-9.

Hall, Calvin, and Lindzey, Gardner (1970). *Theories of Personality.* 2nd ed. New York: John Wiley.

Hilberman, Elaine (1973). Are Women Human? Paper presented to North Carolina Neuropsychiatric Association, Raleigh, North Carolina, October 19.

Hollingshead, A. B. and Redlich, F. C. (1958). *Social Class and Mental Illness.* New York: John Wiley.

Horwitz, Leonard (1970). Transference in training groups and therapy groups. In *Sensitivity Training and the Laboratory Approach,* ed. R. Golumbiewski and A. Blumberb, 167–178. Itasca, Ill.: Peacock Publishers.

_____(1977). A group-centered approach to group psychotherapy. *International Journal of Group Psychotherapy* 27: 423–440.

Jackson, D. D., ed. (1960). *The Etiology of Schizophrenia.* New York: Basic Books.

Johnson, James (1963). *Group Therapy, A Practical Approach.* New York: McGraw-Hill.

Kaplan, Harold, and Sadock, Benjamin (1971). *Comprehensive Group Psychotherapy.* Baltimore: Williams and Wilkins.

Kopp, Sheldon (1977). *This Side of Tragedy: Psychotherapy as Theater.* Palo Alto, Calif.: Science and Behavior Books.

Laing, R. D. (1968). *The Politics of Experience.* New York: Ballantine Books.

Laing, R. D., and Esterson, A. (1971). *Sanity, Madness, and the Family.* 2nd ed. New York: Basic Books.

Lakin, Martin (1972). *Interpersonal Encounter: Theory and Practice in Sensitivity Training.* New York: McGraw-Hill.

Lazarus, Arnold A. (1968). Behavior therapy in groups. In *Basic Approaches to Group Psychotherapy and Group Counseling,* ed. G. H. Gazda. Springfield, Ill.: Charles C Thomas.

_____(1971). *Behavior Therapy and Beyond.* New York: McGraw-Hill.

Lieberman, M., Yalom, I., and Miles, M. (1973). *Encounter Groups: First Facts.* New York: Basic Books.

MacLennan, Beryce (1965). Co-therapy. *International Journal of Group Psychotherapy* 15: 154–166.

Mullan, Hugh, and Rosenbaum, Max (1963). *Group Psychotherapy.* New York: Free Press of Glencoe.

Paulson, I., Burroughs, J. C., and Gelb, C. B. (1976). Co-therapy: What is the crux of the relationship? *International Journal of Group Psychotherapy* 26: 213–224.

Peres, H. (1947). An investigation of non-directive group therapy. *Journal of Consulting Psychology* 11: 159–172.

Perls, F., Hefferline, R., and Goodman, P. (1951). *Gestalt Therapy: Excitement and Growth in the Human Personality.* New York: Dell.

Perls, F. (1969). *Gestalt Therapy Verbatim.* Lafayette, Cal.: Real People Press.

Pesso, Albert (1973). *Experience in Action.* New York: New York University Press.

Polster, Erving, and Polster, Miriam (1973). *Gestalt Therapy Integrated.* New York: Brunner-Mazel.

Powdermaker, Florence, and Frank, Jerome D. (1953). *Group Psychotherapy: Studies in Methodology of Research and Therapy.* Cambridge: Harvard University Press.

Rogers, C., Roback, H., McKee, E., and Calhoun, D. (1976). Group psychotherapy with homosexuals: a review. *International Journal of Group Psychotherapy* 26: 3–28.

Rose, Sheldon (1977). *Group Therapy: a Behavioral Approach.* Englewood Cliffs, N.J.: Prentice-Hall.

Rosenbaum, Max (1971). Co-therapy. In *Comprehensive Group Therapy,* ed. H. Kaplan and B. Sadock. Baltimore: Williams and Wilkins.

Sager, Clifford, and Kaplan, Helen (1972). *Progress in Group and Family Therapy.* New York: Brunner-Mazel.

Samuels, Arthur S. (1971). The reduction of interracial prejudice and tension through group therapy. In *Comprehensive Group Psychotherapy,* ed. H. Kaplan and B. Sadock, pp. 724–753. Baltimore: Williams and Wilkins.

Shaffer, John, and Galinsky, M. David (1974). *Models of Group Therapy and Sensitivity Training.* Englewood Cliffs, N.J.: Prentice-Hall.

Simkin, Jim (1972). The use of dreams in Gestalt therapy. In *Progress in Group and Family Therapy,* ed. C. Sager and H. Kaplan. New York: Brunner-Mazel.

Sullivan, H.S. (1954). *The Psychiatric Interview.* New York: W. W. Norton.

Wechsler, I. R., Messarik, F., and Tannenbaum, R. (1962). The self in process: a sensitivity training emphasis. In *Issues and Training,* ed. I. R. Wechsler and E. H. Schein. Washington, D.C.: National Education Association, National Training Laboratories.

Whitaker, Dorothy, and Lieberman, Morton (1964). *Psychotherapy Through the Group Process.* New York: Atherton Press.

Whitehorn, J. C., and Betz, B. (1954). A study of psychotherapeutic relationships between physicians and schizophrenic patients. *American Journal of Psychiatry* 3: 321–331.

Wolf, A., and Schwartz, E. K. (1962). *Psychoanalysis in Groups.* New York: Grune and Stratton.

_____(1971). Psychoanalysis in groups. In *Comprehensive Group Psychotherapy,* ed. H. Kaplan and B. Sadock. Baltimore: Williams and Wilkins.

Wolpe, Joseph (1958). *Psychotherapy by Reciprocal Inhibition.* Stanford, Cal.: Stanford University Press.

_____(1969). *The Practice of Psychotherapy.* New York: Pergamon Press.

Yalom, Irvin, D. (1975). *The Theory and Practice of Group Psychotherapy.* 2nd ed. New York: Basic Books.

Zimpfer, David G. (1976). *Group Work in the Helping Pro-professions: A Bibliography.* Washington: Association for Specialists in Group Work.

Zinker, J. (1977). *Creative Process in Gestalt Therapy.* New York: Brunner-Mazel.

Index